5/1/2002

Best of the Best
from
IOWA

Selected Recipes from Iowa's
FAVORITE COOKBOOKS

Con:

Happy Birthday 2002!

From your loving husband

Daret.

One of the covered bridges of Madison County, the Cutler-Donahoe Bridge.

BEST of the BEST from
IOWA

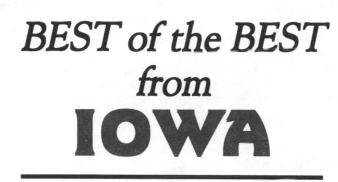

Selected Recipes from Iowa's
FAVORITE COOKBOOKS

EDITED BY
Gwen McKee
AND
Barbara Moseley

Illustrated by Tupper England

QUAIL RIDGE PRESS

Recipe Collection © 1997 Quail Ridge Press, Inc.

Reprinted with permission and all rigths reserved under the name of the cookbooks or organizations or individuals listed below.

Amana Colony Recipes © 1948 Homestead Welfare Club; *The Amazing Little Cranberry Cookbook* © 1994 by Regi Donaldson; *The American Gothic Cookbook* 1996 © Penfield Press; *Cherished Czech Recipes* © 1988 Penfield Press; *A Cook's Tour of Iowa* © 1988 University of Iowa Press; *Cooking Healthy with a Man in Mind* © 1997 Healthy Exchanges, Inc.; *Country Lady, Nibbling and Scribbling* © 1994 Alice Howard; *Dandy Dutch Recipes* © 1991 Penfield Press; *The Des Moines Register Cookbook* © 1995 University of Iowa Press; *The Diabetic's Healthy Exchanges Cookbook* © 1996 Healthy Exchanges, Inc.; *Dutch Touches* © 1996 Penfield Press; *German Heritage Recipes Cookbook* © 1991 American/Schleswig-Holstein Heritage Society; *German Recipes* © 1994 Penfield Press; *License to Cook Iowa Style* 1996 © Penfield Press; *The Lowfat Grill* © 1996 by Donna Rodnitzky; *Madison County Cookbook* © 1994 St. Joseph's Catholic Church; *Neighboring on the Air* © 1991 by University of Iowa Press; *New Tastes of Iowa* © 1993 by Kathryn Designs; *101 Great Lowfat Desserts* © 1995 by Donna Rodnitzky; *Recipes from Iowa with Love* © 1981 New Boundary Concepts, Inc.; *Return Engagement* © 1989 The Junior Board of the Quad City Symphony Orchestra Assn.; *Sharing Traditions from People You Know* © 1996 American Cancer Society/Iowa Division; *Singing in the Kitchen* © 1992 by Mavis Punt; *Spanning the Bridge of Time* © 1996 Diana L. Neff; *Up a Country Lane Cookbook* © 1993 University of Iowa Press; *Välkommen till Swedesburg* © 1996 Swedish Heritage Society; *Wildlife Harvest Game Cookbook* © 1988, Wildlife Harvest Publications, Inc.

Library of Congress Cataloging-in-Publication Data

Best of the Best from Iowa: selected recipes from Iowa's favorite
cookbooks / edited by Gwen McKee and Barbara Moseley.
    p. cm.
  Includes index.
  ISBN 0-937552-82-8
    1. Cookery, American. 2. Cookery--Iowa. I. McKee, Gwen
II. Moseley, Barbara
TX715.B485637372 1997
641.59777--dc21   97-37161
                                                              CIP

QUAIL RIDGE PRESS
P. O. Box 123 • Brandon, MS 39043
1-800-343-1583
Email: Info@QuailRidge.com • www.QuailRidge.com

CONTENTS

Preface 7

List of Contributing Cookbooks 9

Appetizers and Beverages 11

Bread and Breakfast 25

Soups 47

Salads 55

Vegetables 77

Seafood, Pasta, Hot Dishes 99

Poultry 119

Meats 133

Cakes 161

Cookies 187

Pies 215

Catalog of Contributing Cookbooks 251

Index 275

Best of the Best Series 287

Elk Horn's authentic Danish Windmill.

PREFACE

Iowa is known for its farm land—some of the nation's richest. These fertile lands lead the nation in the production of corn, oats, soybeans, hogs, beef cattle, popcorn, poultry, and dairy products. It is no wonder at all that hearty meals and good recipes have always played a significant part in the Hawkeye State.

Having just celebrated its sesquicentennial, Iowa is already moving forward to the next 150 years. Iowans use new and innovative ideas to creative recipes, using what is available, plus searching out different and delicious ways to bring good food to the table. Unforgettable treasured recipes that have been handed down for generations are gathered from the historic Amana Colonies, to the sights of Dutch windmills, to the Bridges of Madison County and beyond. Such delights as Pride of Iowa Cookies, Swedish Meatballs, Stuffed Pork Chops, Dutch Hankerchiefs, and Moon Bars fill these pages. Eighty-nine favorite cookbooks from every nook and cranny of the state have submitted their favorite recipes to make up this outstanding collection.

Many celebrities, including John Wayne, Grant Wood, Mamie Eisenhower, Glenn Miller, and Herbert Hoover have called Iowa home. And there are so many beautiful places in Iowa that there is much to brag about; but the treasure dearest to our hearts is the wonderful food heritage that is ever present. We are delighted to share over 400 of these delectable recipes with you. You'll want to treat your family and friends to Iowa Corn Pancakes, Pink Champagne Salad, Ground Nut Stew, Peaches and Cream Cheesecake Pie, Stormy Weather Chili, Yummy Cherry Bars, Pigout Cake . . . umm, umm, ummmm . . . whether you're preparing a "hot dish" to take along, or inviting guests in to enjoy an evening meal with you, we trust these recipes will bring you much pleasure and many ooh's, and aah's.

The compiling of *Best of the Best from Iowa* involved many people, much work, and many, many hours of phoning, editing, testing, etc. No task of this magnitude could be completed without the help and cooperation of so many wonderful people, including cookbook committees, publishers, food editors, tourism personnel, and countless individuals who were proud to share their knowledge of food and cooking in Iowa. Our special thanks go to our office staff who made this task lighter, and to Tupper England, our "Best" illustrator, who always lends just the right touch. The friendly and helpful people within the city, county and state tourist bureaus provided us with photographs and interesting bits of information that we scattered throughout the book: Did you know that Elk Horn is the site of the largest Danish settlement in the US?; or that Eskimo Pies—the popular ice cream treats— were invented in Onawa in 1920; and isn't it interesting to learn that Buddy Holly, the Big Bopper, gave his last concert at the legendary Surf Ballroom in Clear Lake? We also used photographs for chapter openings to show Iowa's natural and historic beauty, with illustrations that will get you into just the right mood for cooking up some of these wonderful Iowa dishes.

We invite you to enjoy as we do these favorite recipes from 89 selected cookbooks from all over the Hawkeye State.

Gwen McKee and Barbara Moseley

Contributing Cookbooks

Alta United Methodist Church Cookbook
Amana Colony Recipes
The Amazing Little Cranberry Cookbook
The American Gothic Cookbook
Appanoose County Cookbook
Applause Applause
Armstrong Centennial
The Berns Family Cookbook
Blue Willow's "Sweet Treasures"
Celebrating Iowa
Centennial Cookbook
Cherished Czech Recipes
Colesburg Area Cookbook
Community Centennial Cookbook
Cook of the Week Cookbook
A Cook's Tour of Iowa
Cookin' for Miracles
Cookin' for the Crew
Cooking Healthy with a Man in Mind
Country Cupboard Cookbook
Country Lady Nibbling and Scribbling
Dandy Dutch Recipes
The Des Moines Register Cookbook
Diabetic's Healthy Exchanges Cookbook
Dinner for Two
Dutch Touches
Enjoy
Favorite Recipes
Fire Gals' Hot Pans Cookbook
First Christian Church Centennial Cookbook
Fontanelle Good Samaritan Center Commemorative Cookbook
From the Cozy Kitchens of Long Grove
Generations of Good Cooking
German Heritage Recipes Cookbook
German Recipes
The Great Iowa Home Cooking Expedition
Home Cooking with the Cummer Family
I Love You
Iowa Granges Celebrating 125 Years of Cooking
The L.o.V.E. Chocolate Cookbook
Lehigh Public Library Cookbook
License to Cook Iowa Style
The Lowfat Grill
Lutheran Church Women Cookbook

Contributing Cookbooks

The Machine Shed Farm Style Cooking
Madison County Cookbook
Marcus, Iowa Quasiquicentennial Cookbook
Mom's Favorite Recipes
The Nading Family Cookbook
Neighboring on the Air
New Beginnings Cookbook
New Tastes of Iowa
Oma's (Grandma's) Family Secrets
101 Great Lowfat Desserts
125 Years—Walking in Faith
125th Anniversary Celebration Cook Book
The Orient Volunteer Fire Department Cookbook
Our Heritage
Our Savior's Kvindherred Lutheran Church
Quasicentennial / St. Olaf of Bode
Recipes from Iowa with Love
Return Engagement
SEP Junior Women's Club 25th Anniversary Cookbook
Saint Mary Catholic Church Cookbook
Sharing Our Best
Sharing Traditions from People You Know
Singing in the Kitchen
Spanning the Bridge of Time
Special Fare by Sisters II
Special Recipes from Our Hearts
Spitfire Anniversary Cookbook
St. Joseph's Parish Cookbook
St. Paul's Woman's League 50th Anniversary Cook Book
Stirring Up Memories
T.W. and Anna Elliott Family Receipts
A Taste of Grace
The Taste of the World
Teresa's Heavenly Cakes and Treasures
Thompson Family Cookbook
Titonka Centennial Cookbook
Trinity Lutheran Church Centennial Cookbook
Up a Country Lane Cookbook
Välkommen till Swedesburg
Visitation Parish Cookbook
The Walnut Centennial Cookbook
Wildlife Harvest Game Cookbook
Woodbine Public Library
x_____Community Cookbook
Zion Lutheran Church Cookbook

Appetizers
and
Beverages

Iowa farm scene.

Citrus Mint Drink

2½ cups water
2 cups sugar
Juice of 2 oranges
Juice of 6 lemons (or equivalent
  of lemon juice concentrate)

Grated rind of 1 orange
2 handfuls mint leaves
Gingerale

Heat water and sugar to dissolve sugar. Boil 10 minutes. Add fruit juices and grated rind. Pour this hot syrup over washed mint leaves. Cover and let stand at room temperature for at least one hour; strain. This makes a concentrate which may be kept in the refrigerator. To make drink, pour ⅓ cup concentrate over 12-ounce glass of crushed ice and fill with gingerale. Stir to blend. Can adjust amount of concentrate to taste.

From the Cozy Kitchens of Long Grove

Exline Slush Punch

2 packages raspberry
  Kool-Aid
3 quarts water
6 ounces frozen lemonade

6 ounces frozen orange juice
2 cups sugar
1 quart gingerale

Combine all ingredients until thoroughly dissolved. Freeze. Stir occasionally. When ready to serve, add gingerale.

X_____ Community Cookbook

Fruit Slush

3 medium bananas, diced
1 pint frozen strawberries
6 ounces frozen lemonade
6 ounces frozen orange juice
1 large can crushed
  pineapple

1 cup sugar
1 pint bottle 7-Up
1 can mandarin oranges

Mix all ingredients together. Spoon into paper cups and freeze. Remove from freezer 45 minutes before serving.

Centennial Cookbook

Yellow Birds

Perfect for a summer afternoon with friends.

1 (6-ounce) can frozen orange juice	12 ounces white rum
12 ounces canned pineapple juice	6 ounces crème de banana
	18 ounces water

Mix together in a large glass pitcher. Add a generous amount of ice and serve in your most summery glasses. Serves 8.

Recipes from Iowa with Love

Ruby Slipper

1 ounce cranberry liqueur	Splash of Rose's Lime Juice
4 ounces Merlot (or other dry, red wine)	

Pour liqueur into a 6- to 8-ounce wine glass. Add the red wine. Add the lime juice. Stir gently. Serve. Makes one serving.

The Amazing Little Cranberry Cookbook

Blackberry Wine

4 quarts blackberries	Juice of 4 oranges
10 quarts water	1 yeast cake
10 pounds sugar	3 pounds ground raisins
Juice of 3 lemons	10 quarts water

Boil blackberries in 10 quarts water for 15 minutes. Add sugar while the mixture is hot. Cool and add juice from lemons and oranges, then stir in yeast and mix well. Put in a large crock. Stir twice a day for 7 days. Add ground raisins and 10 quarts water. Stir twice a day for 10 days until wine stops working. Strain and bottle with loose caps.

Wildlife Harvest Game Cookbook

Cappuccino Mix

1 cup instant coffee creamer
1 cup instant chocolate drink
  mix
²/₃ cup instant coffee
  crystals

¹/₂ cup sugar
¹/₂ teaspoon ground
  cinnamon
¹/₄ teaspoon ground nutmeg

Mix all ingredients together. Use 3 tablespoons of mix to 6 ounces of hot water.

The L.o.V.E Chocolate Cookbook

Rumtopf

(Rum Pot)

2 cups strawberries
2 cups bing cherries
2 cups red raspberries
2 cups purple plums, pitted
2 cups peaches, peeled and
  sliced
2 cups apricots, sliced

2 cups pears, peeled and
  sliced
2 cups fresh pineapple, sliced
4 cups sugar
5 quarts rum
1 fifth brandy

This recipe requires a large crock with cover. Use only fresh fruit as it comes in season. Start with strawberries in May/early June. Slice and stem fruit; add ¹/₂ cup sugar and ¹/₂ bottle rum. Let sit covered until cherries are ripe. Add cherries, sugar and rum to strawberries, cover and let sit until next ingredient comes in season. Add fruits, sugar and rum through summer. Pineapple will be the final ingredient in October. Let sit 2 weeks, then add ¹/₂ bottle rum. Let sit one week and add bottle of brandy. Start drinking after November 11th. Fruit can be eaten as is or over ice cream. Use 2 cups rumtopf (with fruit) to one bottle white wine and one bottle of champagne for a holiday punch.

From the Cozy Kitchens of Long Grove

Glennis' Taco Dip

1 can refried beans
1 (3-ounce) package cream
  cheese, softened
1 (8-ounce) carton sour
  cream

½ bottle mild taco sauce
Onion, chopped
Lettuce, shredded
Tomato, diced
Cheddar cheese, shredded

In a large plate or 9x13-inch tray, layer as follows: can of refried beans, cream cheese/sour cream mixture, taco sauce, chopped onion, shredded lettuce, diced tomato, and shredded cheese. Dip with Doritos and enjoy!

Variation: May beat 3 avocados into cream cheese/sour cream mixture. Also may use 2 tablespoons hot taco sauce instead of mild.

Country Cupboard Cookbook

Mexican Crock-Pot Dip

1 pound hamburger
1 onion, chopped
1 green pepper, chopped
3 jalapeños, sliced
1 can mushrooms
1 pound Velveeta cheese,
  cubed

1 can mushroom soup
1 can nacho cheese soup
1 can black olives
1 tomato, chopped

Brown hamburger with onions, green pepper, and jalapeños. Add rest of ingredients. Keep in Crock-Pot on low and serve with chips.

125 Years — Walking in Faith

Vegetable Dip

1 cup sour cream
1 cup real mayonnaise
1 tablespoon dry parsley
  (optional)
1 teaspoon dill weed

1 teaspoon Beau Monde Island
  Spice
1 tablespoon dried minced
  onion

Mix together and refrigerate. Good with cauliflower especially. Will keep in refrigerator for 2 weeks.

Lutheran Church Women Cookbook

Very Good Dip

1 (10¾-ounce) can tomato
   soup
1 (3-ounce) package lemon
   Jell-O
1 (8-ounce) package cream
   cheese, softened

1 cup Miracle Whip
2 bunches green onions (tops
   also), sliced
1 green pepper, diced
½ cup celery, diced

Heat together until dissolved, the tomato soup and Jell-O; add cream cheese. Cool; add Miracle Whip. Mix well; add onions, pepper, and diced celery. Keeps well in refrigerator.

Stirring Up Memories

Baked Reuben Dip

1 cup grated Swiss cheese
1 cup drained sauerkraut
½ cup sour cream
2 teaspoons spicy brown
   mustard
1 tablespoon ketchup

2 teaspoons minced onion
1 (8-ounce) package cream
   cheese, cubed
8 ounces corned beef, cut into
   small pieces

Combine all ingredients. Place in glass baking dish. Cover and bake 30 minutes at 350°. Uncover and bake for an additional 5-10 minutes until golden. Serve with crackers. Serves 4-6.

Sharing Traditions from People You Know

Crab Meat Dip

1 (8-ounce) package cream
   cheese
½ cup mayonnaise
1 pound imitation crab meat
½ teaspoon dill weed

Dash of garlic salt
Dash of Worcestershire
   sauce
1 cup sour cream

Mix cream cheese and mayonnaise well; add crab and seasonings; fold in sour cream. May be made the day before serving. Serve in round bread, on crackers or buns.

Visitation Parish Cookbook

Mustard Dip

8 ounces sour cream
8 ounces mayonnaise
8 ounces yellow mustard
¼ cup dry chopped onion

1 package original Hidden Valley
½ cup sugar
3 teaspoons horseradish

Mix all together. Serve with pretzels.

Sharing Our Best

Meatballs in Cranberry-Mustard Sauce

1 (8-ounce) can crushed pineapple with juice
1 tablespoon cornstarch
⅓ cup granulated sugar
1 cup cranberries, chopped
2 tablespoons yellow mustard
1 pound ground pork

2 tablespoons green onion, finely sliced
½ teaspoon salt
2 tablespoons soy sauce
1 tablespoon fresh ginger, grated

Drain the pineapple juice into a small bowl. Set aside. In a 1-quart saucepan, stir together the cornstarch and sugar. Stir in the pineapple juice. Bring mixture to a boil over high heat. Reduce heat to medium-high. Cook 3 minutes. Add cranberries and pineapple. Cook one minute. Remove from heat, and stir in mustard. Set aside.

Mix remaining ingredients in a medium bowl. Shape meat mixture into walnut-size balls. Bring 8 cups of water to a boil in a 3-quart saucepan. Carefully, drop about a third of the meatballs in boiling water, reduce heat to medium-high. Cook 7 minutes. Lift out several meatballs at a time with a slotted spoon, draining as much liquid as possible. Place in a heat-proof bowl. Repeat with remaining meatballs. Pour sauce over meatballs. Keep in warm oven until serving time. Makes 36 meatballs.

The Amazing Little Cranberry Cookbook

Besides Paris, France, Cedar Rapids is the only other city in the world that has its government buildings on an island in the center of the city.

Hot Hors D'Oeuvres

1 pound sausage
1 large hamburger
1 pound sharp Cheddar
  cheese

1 pound Velveeta cheese
2 loaves party rye bread
3 teaspoons Italian seasoning

Brown meats and drain off excess grease. Melt cheeses in double boiler. Mix meats and cheeses together and put on top of bread (sliced in half lengthwise). Top with Italian seasoning. Bake 20 minutes at 300°. Can be frozen before baking. Makes 1½ loaves.

Cook of the Week Cookbook

Shrimp Appetizer Platter

1 package cream cheese,
  softened
½ cup sour cream
¼ cup mayonnaise
2 (4¼-ounce) cans shrimp,
  drained

1 cup seafood sauce
2 cups shredded Mozzarella
  cheese
1 green pepper, chopped
3 green onions, chopped
1 large tomato, diced

Combine cream cheese, sour cream, and mayonnaise. Spread over 12-inch pizza pan or platter, plate, etc. Scatter shrimp over cheese layer, cover with seafood sauce. Then layer on the Mozzarella, green pepper, green onions, and tomatoes. Cover and chill. Serve with crackers.

Cookin' for the Crew

Fried Mozzarella

16 ounces Mozzarella cheese
½ cup all-purpose flour
2 eggs, lightly beaten

Salt and pepper, to taste
1 cup bread crumbs
1 cup olive oil

Cut Mozzarella cheese into small squares, roll in flour, dip in egg seasoned with salt and pepper, roll in bread crumbs, dip in egg again and roll in bread crumbs again. Fry in hot olive oil just long enough for bread crumbs to turn golden brown. Serve hot.

Cookin' for Miracles

Sauerkraut Crisps

1 large can sauerkraut
4 cups flour or more, usually
   more

1 cup sugar or less
1 teaspoon salt
1 cup oil, divided

Preheat oven to 350°. Drain off sauerkraut, saving juice. Mix with flour, sugar and salt, adding juice as needed for pie crust consistency. Oil 2 large cookie sheets. Divide dough in two. Pour oil over top of dough and pat out on the pans like pie crust. Bake at 350°. Cut into bite-size pieces when baked.

Favorite Recipes

Pepper Cheesecake

Must be prepared ahead. Put a big fresh red flower in middle or garnish with black olives and tomatoes.

16 ounces cream cheese,
   softened
8 ounces sharp cheese,
   shredded
1 (1½-ounce) package taco
   seasoning
16 ounces sour cream,
   divided

3 eggs
1 (4-ounce) can diced green
   chiles, drained
½ cup red peppers, diced
½ cup hot salsa sauce
16 ounces guacamole or
   avocado dip

Beat cream cheese, shredded cheese, and taco seasoning until fluffy; stir in one cup sour cream. Beat in eggs one at a time. Fold in chiles and red peppers. Pour in greased springform pan and bake at 350° for 40-45 minutes. Cool for 10 minutes on wire rack. Combine remaining sour cream with salsa and spread on top. Bake for 5 minutes. Refrigerate overnight. To serve, unmold and spread with guacamole or avocado dip. Garnish with fresh tomatoes, olives or cheese. Serve with taco chips. Makes 20-25 servings.

Return Engagement

Pella is the boyhood home of Wyatt Earp. The famous western lawman and gunfighter lived there from age two to sixteen.

Ham Crunch

1 package crescent rolls
2 (8-ounce) packages cream cheese
1 cup mayonnaise
1 package Hidden Valley Dressing (original)

1 pound chopped ham
Vegetables (cauliflower, carrots, green pepper, celery, broccoli, mushrooms tomatoes), cut up
Grated cheese

Flatten crescent rolls on a 10x15-inch jellyroll pan. Bake at 375° for 8-10 minutes. Cool. Mix cream cheese, mayonnaise and dressing. Add chopped ham and spread over cooled crust. Top with vegetables. Sprinkle grated cheese on top. Cut in small squares to serve.

A Taste of Grace

Iowa Antipasto

Iowans traditionally share special treats with friends and neighbors during the holidays. This tasty, low-fat, low-calorie appetizer is a wonderful antidote to all the rich and fattening foods that go with the season. It is good served as a spread on pita crisps.

½ cup olive oil
1 medium cauliflower, cut into bite-sized pieces
1 large green pepper, chopped
½ cup sliced ripe olives
½ cup sliced green olives
1 cup chopped mushrooms, stems and pieces

1 cup Heinz hot catsup
1 cup sweet pickle relish
1 cup dill pickle relish
1½ cups chunk tuna packed in spring water
2 (4½-ounce) cans peeled tiny shrimp
1 cup low-fat Italian salad dressing

Combine the oil, cauliflower, and green pepper in a large saucepan and simmer for 10 minutes, stirring frequently. Add the olives, mushrooms, hot catsup, and pickle relish. Cook and stir for another 10 minutes. Drain the tuna and shrimp in a large colander and rinse with boiling water. Combine with the mixture in the saucepan. Add the salad dressing and mix gently. Divide the mixture into several jars or containers. Freeze what you will not be using within a few days. Yields 6 pints. (1.5 grams of fat per 2 tablespoons.)

New Tastes of Iowa

Parmesan Toast Strips

Try one, you'll want another!

**1½ cups Rice Krispies,
   crushed**
**½ cup grated Parmesan
   cheese**

4 slices toasted bread
½ cup melted butter
½ teaspoon onion salt

Preheat oven to 400°. Combine crushed Rice Krispies and Parmesan cheese. Set aside. Trim crusts off toasted bread. Stack, then cut into 5 narrow strips. Combine melted butter and onion salt. Roll each strip in melted butter mixture and then in the crumbs. Place on baking sheet. Bake 5 minutes at 400°. When you remove them from the oven, they will seem very soggy, but they crisp as they cool.

Note: You can put the slices of bread on a cookie sheet and toast them in a hot oven. Watch, though; they toast quickly.

Singing in the Kitchen

Mini Party Pizzas

**½ pound sausage or
   hamburger**
1 teaspoon oregano
1 clove garlic, minced
1 tube refrigerator biscuits

1 small can tomato paste
1 cup shredded cheese
**¼ cup grated Parmesan
   cheese**

Brown and drain meat. Add oregano and garlic. On greased baking sheet, flatten 10 refrigerator biscuits to 4-inch circles with a rim. Fill with tomato paste and meat. Sprinkle with cheese. Bake at 450° for 10 minutes.

New Beginnings Cookbook

Artichoke Puffs

1 can of 10 buttermilk
  biscuits
1 (18-ounce) can artichoke
  hearts in water

½ cup mayonnaise
½ cup freshly-grated
  Parmesan cheese

Remove biscuits from can; pinch each one in half and re-form into two smaller biscuits to yield 20. Bake according to instructions on can. When done, remove from oven and cool. Slice each in half horizontally to make 40 pieces. Place ¼ artichoke heart on top of each biscuit piece. Mix mayonnaise and cheese together until smooth. Use this mixture to "ice" the top of each artichoke. When ready to serve, broil for 1 - 1½ minutes, until lightly browned. (Watch closely, they brown quickly!)

I Love You

Puppy Chow for People

½ cup chocolate chips
1 stick oleo
½ cup chunky peanut butter

7 cups Crispix cereal
1⅓ cups powdered sugar
⅔ cup powdered milk

Melt the first 3 ingredients together. Pour over the Crispix cereal. Combine the powdered sugar and powdered milk in paper grocery sack and shake to mix. Then dump the coated Crispix into sack. Shake very well to coat cereal.

Cookin' for the Crew

The Devil Made Me Do It Deviled Eggs

12 eggs, hard-cooked and cooled

FILLING:

Mashed yolks
1/4 cup butter, melted
2 teaspoons sweet pickle
   juice
2 tablespoons prepared
   mustard
1 tablespoon Worcestershire
   sauce

1/4 teaspoon dill weed
1/4 cup bacon bits
Salt and pepper, to taste
1/2 cup creamy salad
   dressing
Paprika

Peel eggs, cut in half. Remove yolks; mash with fork. Add all filling ingredients to yolks. Mix until smooth. Refill whites; sprinkle with paprika. Makes 12 servings.

From the Cozy Kitchens of Long Grove

Bacon-Wrapped Water Chestnuts

2-3 cans whole water
   chestnuts
1/4 cup soy sauce
1 tablespoon sugar
1 pound bacon

1 cup Heinz ketchup
1 cup brown sugar
1 tablespoon wine vinegar
1/2 teaspoon Tabasco sauce

Drain chestnuts and marinate in the soy sauce and sugar for about 30 minutes. Cut bacon into thirds. Wrap a piece of bacon around the chestnut and secure with toothpick. Arrange on a baking sheet and bake for about 30 minutes, or until bacon crisps. Drain on a paper towel. While chestnuts are baking, combine ketchup, sugar, vinegar, and Tabasco sauce. Bring to a boil and simmer about 30 minutes. Serve the appetizers in the sauce or with the sauce on the side.

Titonka Centennial Cookbook

Nutty Cereal Snack

1 (12-ounce) package square
bite-size rice cereal (12 cups)
1 (12-ounce) package M&M's
(1½ cups)
2 (2-ounce) packages slivered
almonds
1 (3.75-ounce) package shelled
sunflower seeds

1 cup plus 2 tablespoons
margarine or butter
1½ cups sugar
1½ cups light corn syrup
1½ teaspoons vanilla

In a very large container combine cereal, M&M's, almonds, and sunflower seeds; set aside. In a large saucepan melt margarine. Add sugar and syrup to saucepan and stir to combine. Bring mixture to a boil over medium heat. Boil gently for 3 minutes, stirring frequently. Remove pan from heat and stir in vanilla. Pour syrup over cereal mixture, while stirring, until pieces are coated. Turn out onto waxed paper and let stand, covered with waxed paper for several hours.

Iowa Granges Celebrating 125 Years of Cooking

Peanut Butter Popcorn

½ cup sugar
½ cup light corn syrup

½ cup peanut butter
1 teapoon vanilla

Place 8 cups popped corn in bowl. Heat sugar and syrup until it boils. Remove from heat. Stir in peanut butter and vanilla; mix well. Pour over corn, and coat. Can make into popcorn balls.

New Beginnings Cookbook

Sugared Peanuts

Simple recipe!

2 cups raw peanuts
1 cup sugar

½ cup water

Cook all ingredients over medium heat in a heavy pan until syrup crystalizes. Pour onto a buttered cookie sheet. Bake at 300° for 15 minutes. Salt lightly and stir. Bake 15 minutes more.

First Christian Church Centennial Cookbook

Bread and Breakfast

Historic shops at the Czech Village. Cedar Rapids.

American Gothic Cheese Loaf

Mrs. Nan Wood Graham, sister of Grant Wood and model for the woman in American Gothic, submitted this recipe as a convenient, tasty favorite.

1 long loaf of unsliced French or sourdough bread
1 pound or 2½ cups shredded Cheddar cheese
⅓ cup (or more) mayonnaise
2 tablespoons chopped or dry parsley
2 tablespoons prepared mustard
2 teaspoon finely chopped onion
2 tablespoons lemon juice
⅓ teaspoon salt

Slice the long loaf into thick slices (about 14) on the bias, cutting through just to bottom crust. Mix together all filling ingredients; mix well. Spread thickly between bread slices. Wrap loaf in aluminum foil and place in preheated (400°) oven for 25 minutes, or until piping hot and crusty.

The American Gothic Cookbook

Stuffed French Bread

1 loaf French Bread
1 pound ground beef
1 small onion
Cheddar cheese soup
Salt and pepper, to taste
½ teaspoon chili powder
½ cup Mozzarella cheese

Slice off top of bread and dig out bread, so you have a shell. Break dug-out bread into small pieces. Set aside. Brown meat and onion. Stir in soup, salt and pepper, and chili powder. Heat just until warm. Stir in enough bread to make it thick. Place the loaf on foil, and spoon in mixture. Sprinkle cheese on top. Bake at 375° until cheese is melted. Cut into 1-inch pieces and serve.

Woodbine Public Library

Cheese Bread

8 ounces Monterey Jack cheese	½ teaspoon garlic salt
	½ teaspoon onion salt
1 stick butter (oleo), softened	1 loaf French bread

Mix cheese, butter, and salts with a mixer until smooth. Slit French bread down the middle the long way. Fill with cheese mixture. Wrap in aluminum foil. Bake 15 minutes. Open, stir cheese a little, and bake 10-15 minutes longer. Slice with electric knife.

Alta United Methodist Church Cookbook

Garlic Bubble Bread

Frozen white bread loaf	1 teaspoon garlic powder
¼ cup oleo, melted	¼ teaspoon salt
1 beaten egg	
1 tablespoon dried parsley flakes	

Thaw frozen bread loaf according to package. Cut bread into walnut-sized shapes and dip into the mixture of oleo, egg, parsley flakes, garlic powder, and salt. Place into greased loaf pan, cover, and let rise. Bake at 350° until brown.

Madison County Cookbook

Deb's Maple Bread Ring

DOUGH:

¾ cup warm milk
1 package yeast
3 tablespoons sugar
¼ cup butter, melted

½ teaspoon salt
1 teaspoon maple flavoring
1 egg, beaten
2¾ - 3 cups flour

Mix dough ingredients; let rise about one hour. Grease a 12-inch pizza pan. Divide dough into 3 equal parts. Roll each ball in a circle (12 inches) to cover pan.

FLAVORING MIX:

½ cup sugar
⅓ cup chopped nuts
1 teaspoon cinnamon

1 teaspoon maple flavoring
¼ cup melted butter

Mix together flavoring ingredients. Brush dough with ⅓ of butter and sprinkle with half of Flavoring Mix. Top with second layer of dough, butter, and Flavoring Mix. Top with last dough. Put glass in center and, with scissors, cut from edge to glass, forming 16 pre-shaped wedges.

Twist each 5 times. Let rise about 45 minutes. Brush with egg. Cut out center dough piece. Preheat oven to 350°. Cook for 45 minutes to 1 hour, until golden brown (check often).

ICING:

1 cup powdered sugar
2 tablespoons butter, melted

1-2 tablespoons milk
½ teaspoon maple flavoring

Blue Willow's "Sweet Treasures"

Poppy Seed Bread

3 cups flour
2¼ cups sugar
1½ teaspoons salt
1½ teaspoons baking
  powder
1½ tablespoons poppy seed
1½ cups milk

1⅛ cups vegetable oil
3 eggs
1½ teaspoons vanilla
1½ teaspoons almond
  flavoring
1½ teaspoons butter
  flavoring

Mix all the ingredients together for 1-2 minutes with an electric mixer. Put batter in 2 loaf pans; bake for one hour in a 350° oven. Cool in pans for 5 minutes, then put Glaze on while still in the pans.

GLAZE:

¾ cup sugar
¼ cup orange juice
½ teaspoon vanilla

½ teaspoon almond extract
½ teaspoon butter flavoring

Cookin' for the Crew

Lemon Poppy Seed Bread

1 package lemon cake mix
1 package lemon instant
  pudding
4 eggs

½ cup oil
1 cup hot water
¼ cup poppy seeds

In a bowl, combine all ingredients and beat 4 minutes. Pour into 2 greased bread pans. Bake in 350° oven for 50-60 minutes, or until toothpick inserted in bread comes out clean.

Saint Mary Catholic Church Cookbook

Overnight Sweet Rolls with Cream

3 tablespoons butter or
  margarine
1 cup brown sugar

Chopped pecans (optional)
1 (12-pack) frozen dinner rolls
½ pint whipping cream

Melt butter and brown sugar together. Press mixture into bottom of 9x13-inch pan. Sprinkle with pecans, if desired. Arrange frozen rolls over mixture. Sprinkle with cinnamon, if desired. Pour whipping cream over rolls. Cover and allow to stand at room temperature overnight. Bake at 350° for 30 minutes. Allow to cool for 15 minutes before removing from pan.

SEP Junior Women's Club 25th Anniversary Cookbook

Best Ever Banana Bread

You'll never use another banana bread recipe after tasting this one.

1 cup butter or oleo	2 teaspoons vanilla
3 cups sugar	4-5 bananas, mashed
6 eggs	1 teaspoon salt
3 cups sour cream	5 cups flour
4 teaspoons soda	

Cream together butter, sugar, and eggs. Mix sour cream and soda together in separate bowl, and let stand until foamy. Add the rest of the ingredients to the above mixtures and mix well. Place into 4 greased and floured 9x5-inch bread pans and bake 50 minutes at 350° or until toothpick inserted comes out clean.

Marcus, Iowa, Quasquicentennial Cookbook

Strawberry Banana Bread

½ cup butter or margarine	½ teaspoon soda
¾ cup sugar	1 cup mashed bananas
1 egg	1 teaspoon baking powder
3 tablespoons milk	2 cups flour
1 (3-ounce) package strawberry gelatin	

Cream butter and sugar; add beaten egg. In separate bowl, mix milk, gelatin, and soda. Use high bowl (as this mixture will fizz). Add bananas. Mix together with butter mixture. Sift together dry ingredients and add to the mixture. Pour into a greased loaf pan. Bake at 350° for 40 minutes or until done.

Country Lady Nibbling and Scribbling

Berry Delicious Bread

1 (10-ounce) package frozen
    strawberries, thawed
3/4 cup sugar
2/3 cup oil
2 eggs
1 1/2 cups flour

1 teaspoon soda
1/2 teaspoon salt
1/2 teaspoon cinnamon
3/4 cup chopped nuts
    (optional)

Grease and flour 9x5-inch loaf pan or can be baked in smaller loaf pans. Combine strawberries, sugar, oil, and eggs. Beat on medium speed for 2 minutes. Add remaining dry ingredients. Stir until moistened. Pour into pan. Bake in preheated oven at 350° for 50-60 minutes. Cool in pan for 15 minutes, then remove.

Applause Applause

Ardith's Rolls

2 packages yeast
1/4 cup lukewarm water
2 cups boiling water
1 teaspoon salt

1/2 cup sugar
2 sticks margarine
6 or 7 cups flour

Dissolve yeast in lukewarm water. Pour the boiling water over salt, sugar, and margarine. When lukewarm, add yeast mixture. Add flour gradually. Turn out on lightly floured board and knead until smooth. Let rise in warm place utnil double in bulk (1 1/2 hours). Shape into any type rolls.

For cinnamon rolls, divide in half. Roll each half into rectangle; spread with melted butter and sprinkle with sugar and cinnamon. Roll up and pinch to seal; slice. Place on greased pans. Cover and let rise until doubled (1 hour). Bake at 350° for 15-20 minutes, or until golden brown.

Välkommen till Swedesburg

When Grant Wood was fourteen (1905), his drawing of an oak leaf won a Crayola national contest prize. In 1930, American Gothic was entered in the Annual Exhibition of American Paintings and Sculpture at the Art Institute of Chicago. He won a bronze medal and a $300 purchase award. It was an instant sensation and is still the property of the Art Institute. Wood was born and is buried in Anamosa.

Sticky Maple Bacon Rolls

4 - 4½ cups flour
1 package active dry yeast
1¼ cups water
½ cup butter or margarine
¼ cup sugar
1 teaspoon salt

1 egg, beaten
¾ cup butter
⅔ cup packed brown sugar
1 teaspoon maple flavoring
½ pound bacon, fried crisp,
　drained, and crumbled

In bowl combine 1½ cups flour and the yeast. In saucepan, heat water, ½ cup butter or margarine, ¼ cup sugar, and salt to lukewarm, stirring until butter almost melts. Add to dry ingredients in bowl; add egg. Beat at low speed for ½ minute, then at high speed for 3 minutes. By hand, stir in enough of remaining flour to make moderately stiff dough. Turn dough onto floured surface, knead until smooth and elastic (8-10 minutes). Place in greased bowl, turning once to grease surface. Cover. Let rise until doubled, about 1½ hours.

Meanwhile, combine melted butter, the brown sugar, and maple flavoring. Pour into 2 (9 x 1½-inch) round pans. Punch down dough; divide in half. Cover and let rest 10 minutes. On floured surface, roll each half to an 8x12-inch rectangle. Sprinkle with bacon. Roll up jellyroll fashion beginning with long end. Cut in 1-inch slices. Place, cut-side-down, in round pans 12 slices per pan). Cover; let rise until doubled, about 30 minutes. Bake in 350° oven for 25-30 minutes or until lightly browned. Cool 2-3 minutes in pans, then invert onto rack.

Applause Applause

Christmas Morning Sticky Rolls

2 packages refrigerator
　biscuits
1 (3-ounce) regular
　butterscotch pudding

½ cup oleo
¾ cup brown sugar
¾ teaspoon cinnamon
½ cup nuts

Use regular-size Bundt pan, sprayed with Pam. Cut biscuits in half; roll in balls. Roll in a mixture of cinnamon and sugar. Put in a Bundt pan. Sprinkle butterscotch pudding over biscuits. Cook oleo, brown sugar, and cinnamon until bubbly; pour over biscuits. Cover with plastic wrap and refrigerate overnight if wished or bake immediately at 350° for 25 minutes. When done, invert pan on serving plate. After 5 minutes, remove pan.

Lutheran Church Women Cookbook

Overnight Bread or Rolls

1 teaspoon dry yeast
3 cups warm water
1 cup sugar
2 eggs

½ cup lard
1 tablespoon salt
8 cups flour (or more)

Stir together at 5 p.m. (can use mixer). Knead on floured board and punch down every hour until 10 p.m. Shape into rolls, bread, cinnamon rolls, pecan rolls, or whatever you want. Place apart in greased pans, cover, and let rise on counter overnight. Next morning bake at 350° for 20-25 minutes for rolls, or 30-35 minutes for bread.

German Heritage Recipes Cookbook

Overnight Butterhorn Rolls

1 envelope dry yeast
½ cup warm water
1 stick butter or margarine
¾ cup milk (lukewarm not
  scalded)

1 teaspoon salt
3 eggs
½ cup sugar
4 cups flour

Dissolve yeast in water. Add butter to warm milk; add salt, well beaten eggs and sugar. Combine all and add flour a little at a time. Dough may be a little runny or sticky, so add as much flour as needed without making dough too stiff. Knead well. Put in well-greased bowl with cover. Let stand overnight at room temperature. Knead down in morning. Divide in two; roll out each to ¼-inch circle; cut into 16 pie-shaped pieces. Roll each, starting with large end. Place on greased pan; let rise until very light. Bake at 325° for 20 minutes, or until light brown.

Note: This recipe doubles well and can be used for sweet rolls also. (Do not use quick type yeast.)

SEP Junior Women's Club 25th Anniversary Cookbook

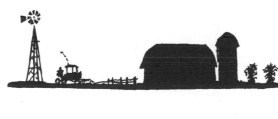

Refrigerator Rolls

¾ cup hot water
½ cup sugar
1 tablespoon salt
3 tablespoons margarine

2 packages dry yeast
1 cup warm water
1 egg, beaten
5¼ cups flour

Mix hot water, sugar, salt, margarine. Cool to lukewarm. Dissolve yeast in warm water. Stir the egg and 3 cups flour in the lukewarm mixture. Beat until smooth. Add rest of flour, mixing well. Place dough in greased bowl; brush top with soft margarine. Cover tightly with wax paper or foil. (I like bowls with lids that fit tightly.) Refrigerate until double or until needed (up to 4 days).

To use, cut off amount of dough required and form into favorite shapes. Cover. Let rise in warm draft-free place until doubled, about one hour. Brush with melted margarine. Bake in 400° oven about 10-15 minutes.

The Great Iowa Home Cooking Expedition

Italian Biscuit Ring

Instead of the same old garlic bread again when you're serving pasta, try this amazingly easy but flavorful alternative. The combo of the two cheeses and the dressing will surprise you—and win you new fans.

1 (7.5 ounce) can refrigerated
   buttermilk biscuits
¼ cup fat-free Italian
   dressing
¼ cup (¾ ounce) grated
   fat-free Parmesan cheese

⅓ cup (1½ ounces) shredded
   reduced fat Mozzarella
   cheese
1 teaspoon dried parsley
   flakes

Preheat oven to 425°. Spray a 9-inch pie plate with olive-oil-flavored cooking spray. Separate biscuits. Cut each into 2 pieces. Dip pieces in Italian dressing, then into Parmesan cheese. Place pieces in prepared pie plate. Sprinkle any remaining Parmesan cheese and Italian dressing evenly over biscuits. Evenly sprinkle Mozzarella cheese and parsley flakes over top. Bake 15-20 minutes. Cool slightly on a wire rack. Cut into 6 wedges.

Each serving equals: Healthy Exchanges: 1¼ bread, ½ protein, 2 optional calories. 118 calories; 2gm fat; 6gm protein; 19gm carbohydrate; 517mg sodium; 2gm fiber. Diabetic: 1 starch; ½ meat.

Cooking Healthy with a Man in Mind

Baking Powder Biscuits

3 cups flour
Dash of salt
3 teaspoons baking powder

1 stick margarine
1 egg, beaten
1 cup milk

Put first 3 ingredients into a bowl and mix. Add margarine. Mix until crumbly like cornmeal. Add beaten egg and milk. Mix together. Put on floured board or counter. Knead. Form in ball and pat into desired thickness. Cut into circles. (Can use glass and flour the rim.) Bake at 375° for 20-30 minutes or until done. The thicker the biscuit, the longer it will have to bake.

Great Iowa Home Cooking Expedition

Cheese-Garlic Biscuits

2 cups buttermilk baking mix
2/3 cup milk
1/2 cup shredded Cheddar
cheese

1/4 cup oleo or butter, melted
1/2 teaspoon garlic powder

Preheat oven to 450°. Combine baking mix, milk, and cheese in mixing bowl, using a wooden spoon, until soft dough forms. Beat vigorously for 30 seconds. Drop by tablespoon onto ungreased cookie sheet. Bake for 8-10 minutes, until golden brown. Combine melted butter and garlic powder; brush over warm biscuits before removing from cookie sheet. Serves 10-12.

Celebrating Iowa

English Muffins

1 package yeast	1 egg, beaten
1/4 cup warm water	1 cup flour
1 1/4 cups scalded milk	3/4 cup cornmeal
3 tablespoons sugar	2 1/2 - 3 cups flour
1 1/2 teaspoons salt	Additional cornmeal
3 tablespoons butter	

Proof the yeast in the warm water. Scald the milk and add the sugar, salt, and butter; let cool. Then add egg, 1 cup flour, yeast mixture, and cornmeal. Beat with a mixer a couple of minutes. Add the rest of the flour and stir thoroughly. Cover with plastic wrap and let rise until double. Stir down and knead 5 or 6 turns. Roll out 3/8-inch thick on floured surface. Cut with 3-inch cutter. Place on cookie sheets sprinkled with cornmeal and let rise until double. Bake on a griddle at 325° for 8 minutes per side. Bake cornmeal side first. To serve, split in 1/2 and put in the toaster until nicely toasted.

Stirring Up Memories

Chive and Black Pepper Corn Bread

3/4 cup yellow cornmeal	1/2 teaspoon salt
3/4 cup flour	1 cup plain yogurt or sour
1 tablespoon sugar	half-and-half
1 1/2 teaspoons cream of	1/4 cup fresh snipped chives
tartar	3 tablespoons unsalted butter,
3/4 teaspoon baking soda	melted
1/2 teaspoon coarsely ground	2 tablespoons milk
black pepper	1 egg, beaten to blend

Preheat oven to 425°. Combine first 7 ingredients in a large bowl. Whisk remaining ingredients in another bowl to blend. Make a well in the center of dry ingredients, add sour cream mixture and stir just until blended. Spoon batter into 8- or 9-inch greased pan. Bake until bread is golden and pulls away from the sides of the pan (approximately 20 minutes). Makes 9 pieces. Can be frozen.

Return Engagement

Corn Fritters

1 egg
¼ cup milk
1 cup pancake mix

1 (12-ounce) can whole kernel
   corn, drained
Vegetable oil
Maple syrup

Blend egg with milk. Stir in the pancake mix until smooth. Fold in the corn. Drop by teaspoonfuls into hot vegetable oil. Cook 4 minutes or until golden brown. Serve with maple syrup.

T.W. and Anna Elliott Family Receipts

Pizza Crust Dough

1 (4-ounce) package dry
   yeast
1 cup warm water

1 teaspoon oil
½ teaspoon salt
2 cups flour

Dissolve yeast in water. Add oil, salt, and flour. Mix until soft dough forms; knead about 5 minutes. Place in a greased bowl; cover and let rise 2 hours, or until double in size. Punch down. Form in pizza pan. Brush dough with a little oil. Make favorite pizza. Bake 20 minutes in 400° oven.

Our Heritage

Super-Easy Ham and Cheese Muffins

Great for breakfast, or with a bowl of soup.

2 cups self-rising flour
½ teaspoon baking soda
1 cup milk
½ cup mayonnaise

½ cup chopped cooked ham
½ cup shredded Cheddar
   cheese

In a large bowl, combine flour and baking soda. Combine remaining ingredients; stir into dry ingredients just until moistened. Fill paper-lined muffin cups ⅔-full. Bake at 425° for 16-18 minutes, or until golden brown on top.

Woodbine Public Library

Pumpkin Apple Streusel Muffins

2½ cups all-purpose flour
2 cups sugar
1 tablespoon pumpkin pie
  spice
1 teaspoon baking soda
½ teapsoon salt

2 eggs, lightly beaten
1 cup canned pumpkin
½ cup vegetable oil
2 cups peeled, finely chopped
  apples
Streusel Topping

In large mixer bowl, combine flour, sugar, pumpkin pie spice, baking soda, and salt; set aside. In medium bowl, combine eggs, pumpkin, and oil. Add liquid ingredients to dry ingredients. Stir just until moistened. Stir in apples. Spoon batter into greased or paper-lined muffin cups, filling ¾ full. Sprinkle Streusel Topping over batter. Bake in preheated 350° oven for 35-40 minutes or until toothpick comes out clean. Makes 18 muffins.

STREUSEL TOPPING:

2 tablespoons flour
¼ cup sugar
½ teaspoon ground
  cinnamon

4 teaspoons butter

In small bowl, combine flour, sugar, and cinnamon. Cut in butter until mixture is crumbly.

Quasquicentennial / St. Olaf of Bode

Cocoa Banana Muffins

High fiber.

1 cup flour	1½ cups All-Bran cereal
2 teaspoons baking powder	¾ cup skim milk
½ teaspoon salt	2 egg whites
2 tablespoons Hershey's cocoa (dry)	¼ cup vegetable oil
½ cup sugar	1 cup sliced ripe bananas (about 1 medium)

Stir together flour, baking powder, salt, cocoa, and sugar; set aside. In a large mixing bowl, combine All-Bran cereal and milk; let stand 5 minutes or until cereal is softened. Add egg whites and oil; beat well. Stir in bananas. Add flour mixture, stirring until only combined. Grease muffin tins or use paper liners; fill ⅔ full. Bake at 400° for 25 minutes or until lightly browned. Makes 12 muffins. Serve warm.

From the Cozy Kitchens of Long Grove

Pineapple Muffins

Crushed pineapple and pineapple juice add the perfect touch of sweetness to these delicious muffins.

1 (20-ounce) can unsweetened crushed pineapple	1 tablespoon baking powder
⅔ cup reserved pineapple juice	¼ teaspoon salt
3 cups unbleached flour	1 cup skim milk
1 cup sugar	3 egg whites
	1 teaspoon vanilla

Preheat oven to 400°. Place pineapple in a strainer over a bowl. Reserve ⅔ cup pineapple juice and the pineapple. Combine flour, sugar, baking powder, and salt in a large mixing bowl.

Combine pineapple, reserved pineapple juice, milk, egg whites, and vanilla in a medium-size bowl and blend well. Add pineapple mixture to dry ingredients and mix with a fork until just blended. Spoon batter just to the tops of muffin cups that have been coated with vegetable spray. Bake for 20 minutes, or until golden. Immediately remove muffins from pan. When muffins are cool, store in an airtight container. The muffins taste best when allowed to sit for 24 hours. Makes 20 muffins.

Nutritional analysis per muffin: 139 Cal; 1% Cal from Fat; 3g Prot; 31g Carbo; 0g Fat; 1g Fiber; 88mg Sod; 9mg Chol.

101 Great Lowfat Desserts

Kringles

1½ cups sugar
1 cup sour cream
1 teaspoon vanilla
3½ cups flour (may very
  according to richness of cream)

1 teaspoon soda
2 teaspoons baking powder
1 teaspoon salt

Mix all together and chill. Heat oven to 450°. Roll out a small portion of the dough with the flat of both hands until it is the length and thickness of a lead pencil. Bring two ends together. Give them one twist and lay across center so it looks somewhat like the letter "B" with ends in the center. Bake on greased cookie sheet or Teflon pan at 450° for 10 minutes or until slightly brown. Using pastry brush, brush each one with butter when taken from oven before placing on rack to cool. Makes 4 dozen.

Note: It is easier to roll them if dough is kept cool, so take out enough dough for one panful at a time and place on a floured board.

Our Savior's Kvindherred Lutheran Church

Georgia's Apple Coffee Cake

The fusion of spices and thinly sliced apples produces a deliciously moist cake.

2 cups unbleached flour
1 cup granulated sugar
1 cup firmly packed dark
  brown sugar
2 teaspoons baking powder
1 teaspoon each cinnamon
  and nutmeg
½ teaspoon baking soda

¼ teaspoon salt
1 (6-ounce) jar applesauce baby
  food
1 cup buttermilk
2 egg whites
4 Red Delicious apples, peeled,
  cored, and thinly sliced

Preheat oven to 350°. Combine flour, sugars, baking powder, cinnamon, nutmeg, baking soda, and salt in a large mixing bowl. Combine applesauce, buttermilk, and egg whites in a small mixing bowl and blend until smooth. Add applesauce mixture to dry ingredients and mix with a fork until blended. Spoon batter into a 9x13-inch baking pan that has been coated with vegetable spray. Gently press sliced apples into top of batter and bake for 45 minutes, or until cake tester inserted into center of cake comes out clean. Makes 18 servings.

Nutritional analysis per serving: 162 Cal; 2% Cal from Fat; 2g Prot; 38g Carbo; 0g Fat; 1g Fiber; 109mg Sod; 1mg Chol.

101 Great Lowfat Desserts

Peach Pudding Coffee Cake

This is a great Sunday morning brunch treat, served warm.

2 cups sliced peaches	**1 cup flour**
Lemon juice	**1/2 teaspoon salt**
Cinnamon	**4 tablespoons butter**
3/4 cup sugar	**1/2 cup milk**
1 teaspoon baking powder	

In an 8-inch square pan, slice 2 cups fresh peaches. Sprinkle with lemon juice and cinnamon. Combine sugar, baking powder, flour, and salt in mixing bowl. Blend in butter and add milk. Spread this batter on top of peaches. Sprinkle the batter with Topping.

TOPPING:

3/4 cup sugar	**1 cup boiling water**
1 tablespoon cornstarch	

Sprinkle sugar and cornstarch over batter. Add one cup boiling water over top. Do not stir. Bake at 350° for 45 minutes.

Blue Willow's "Sweet Treasures"

Swedish Pancakes

2 cups milk	**2 teaspoons sugar**
3/4 cup flour	**Dash of salt**
3 eggs	**1 tablespoon oil**

Put ingredients in order given in blender. Turn blender on and off 3 or 4 times. Let stand 10 minutes or even overnight. Zap again, and pour onto hot griddle in 4-inch circles. (Butter on blender lip keeps it from dripping.) Do not peek under pancake as that breaks seal in baking cake. Turn when golden brown (2 or 3 minutes on each side). Zap blender each time you pour batter onto griddle; don't let batter get foamy. Put butter, syrup, or fruit (lingonberries, raspberries, etc.) on each cake; sprinkle with powdered sugar.

Välkommen till Swedesburg

The "Field of Dreams" movie site is a baseball diamond carved from a corn field where the Academy Award-nominated movie was filmed in the summer of 1988. The "field" is located on two farms three miles northeast of Dyersville.

German Apple Pancakes

¾ cup flour
¾ cup milk
½ teaspoon salt
4 eggs

¼ cup oleo
2 apples, thinly sliced
¼ cup sugar
¼ teaspoon cinnamon

Heat oven to 400°. Place 2 pie pans in oven. Beat flour, milk, salt, and eggs for one minute. Remove pans from oven. Place 2 tablespoons oleo in each pan. Rotate pan until oleo melts and coats sides. Arrange half the apples in each pan. Divide batter between the 2 pans. Mix sugar and cinnamon. Sprinkle 2 tablespoons over batter in each pan. Bake until puffed and golden brown, 20-25 minutes.

The Great Iowa Home Cooking Expedition

Iowa Corn Pancakes

Try them. You will like them!

1½ cups sifted enriched
   flour
2 tablespoons sugar
1 teaspoon soda
1 teaspoon salt
1 teaspoon baking powder
   (optional)

½ cup yellow cornmeal
2 slightly beaten eggs
2 cups buttermilk,
   approximately
2 tablespoons melted butter or
   bacon fat

Mix all the dry ingredients together well. Beat the eggs lightly with a fork and then mix the eggs well with one cup buttermilk. Mix the dry mixture with the egg/buttermilk mixture. Mix well with a hand beater, not a machine mixer. Add melted butter to the mixture and mix. Add buttermilk to the mixture until it is the proper thickness for cooking.

Fry in a Teflon-lined skillet heated between medium-high and high. The skillet is ready for frying when drops of water bounce around and quickly evaporate.

Spanning the Bridge of Time

Apple-Cranberry Pancake Puff

It's yummy and pretty.

½ cup water	½ cup pancake-waffle mix
¼ cup butter or margarine	2 eggs
½ cup buttermilk	

Preheat oven to 400°. Generously grease 9-inch glass pie plate. Bring water and butter to boil in medium saucepan. Stir buttermilk into pancake mix and add to water; beat vigorously until mixture leaves side of pan and forms ball. Remove from heat. Add eggs, one at a time, beating well after each addition. Spread batter evenly onto bottom and sides of pie plate. Bake 17-19 minutes or until golden brown. Fill immediately with fruit filling and cut into wedges to serve.

FILLING:

2 tart cooking apples, cut in thin wedges	⅓ cup coarsely chopped pecans
2 tablespoons butter or margarine	½ teaspoon cinnamon
½ cup pancake syrup	⅛ teaspoon ground nutmeg
½ cup fresh cranberries or ¼ cup raisins	

In 10-inch skillet, cook apples in butter over medium heat 4 minutes or until almost tender, occasionally turning gently. Add remaining ingredients; cook 3-4 minutes or just until cranberries begin to pop. Makes 4 servings.

The Des Moines Register Cookbook

Raised Doughnuts

1 cup milk	2 eggs
1 package yeast	2 teaspoons vanilla
1 cup lukewarm water	1 teaspoon salt
½ cup shortening	7 cups flour
⅔ cup sugar	

Scald milk and cool to lukewarm. Soften yeast in water; add milk. Cream shortening and sugar; add eggs and beat. Add vanilla and salt. Add milk and yeast mixture alternately with flour. Stir until smooth. Let rise until double in bulk; roll and cut. Let rise until double in bulk. Fry and dip in glaze. Yields 50.

Centennial Cookbook

Stuffed French Bread Strata

1 (1-pound) loaf French
  bread
1 (8-ounce) package cream
  cheese, cubed
8 eggs
2½ cups milk or
  half-and-half
6 tablespoons margarine,
  melted
¼ cup maple syrup

Cut French bread into small cubes (12 cups). Grease a 9x13-inch glass pan. Layer 6 cups bread cubes, top with cream cheese cubes, then remaining bread cubes. In a blender, blend eggs, milk, melted margarine, and maple syrup. Pour over bread and cream cheese cubes. Using a spatula, press layers down to moisten. Cover and refrigerate 2-24 hours. Bake uncovered in a 325° oven for 40 minutes. Let stand 10 minutes. Cut into squares and serve with Apple Cider Syrup. Serves 6-8.

APPLE CIDER SYRUP:
½ cup sugar
4 teaspoons cornstarch
½ teaspoon ground cinnamon
1 cup apple cider
1 tablespoon lemon juice
2 tablespoons butter

In a 1-quart saucepan, stir sugar, cornstarch, and cinnamon. Add cider and lemon juice. Cook over medium heat until thick and bubbly. Continue to cook for 2 minutes. Remove from heat and add butter; stir until melted.

Sharing Traditions from People You Know

Elegant Brunch Eggs

2 (3-ounce) packages dried
  beef, torn into pieces
1 cup flour
½ cup butter
1 pound bacon, cooked,
  drained and crumbled
1 quart milk
16 eggs, beaten
Salt to taste
Pepper to taste
1 (13½-ounce) can evaporated
  milk

Place dried beef, flour, butter, bacon, and milk in large skillet. Cook and stir over low heat until thickened. Place eggs in another skillet that has been oiled and heated. Add salt, pepper, and evaporated milk. Cook and scramble gently. In an ungreased 11x14-inch deep casserole, layer half the sauce, then all of the eggs, then remaining sauce. Refrigerate overnight. Bake in a 325° oven for one hour. Serves 16-20.

Special Fare by Sisters II

Breakfast Pizza

1 package crescent rolls
1 pound bulk pork sausage,
  browned
1 cup frozen hash browns,
  thawed
1 cup shredded Cheddar
  cheese

5 eggs, slightly beaten
1/4 cup milk
1/2 teaspoon salt
1/8 teaspoon pepper
2 tablespoons Parmesan
  cheese

Separate the rolls in 8 triangles. Place on an ungreased 12-inch round pizza pan with points to the center. Press sides of each triangle to the next one to seal and up the sides. Spoon on the browned sausage, potatoes and top with the cheese. Mix together the eggs, milk, salt and pepper. Pour slowly over the crust. Sprinkle with Parmesan cheese. Bake at 375° for 25-30 minutes.

Note: You can get ingredients ready a day ahead and then it's a snap in the morning.

Cook of the Week Cookbook

Breakfast Pizza

(For One)

Butter
2 eggs
1 slice bacon (fried and
  crumbled)
1/2 teaspoon Parmesan
  cheese

1 teaspoon water
1 English muffin (split and
  toasted)
2 tablespoons pizza sauce

Use enough butter to grease skillet. Heat until hot enough to sizzle when drop of water is placed on it. Break and slip eggs into skillet. Sprinkle on bacon and cheese. Cook over low heat until eggs turn white on edges, about one minute. Add water; cover skillet tightly to hold in steam which bastes eggs. While eggs are cooking to desired degree of doneness, spread muffin halves with pizza sauce. Top with fried eggs. Makes one serving.

Country Cupboard Cookbook

Pigs-in-a-Blanket
(Saucijzebroodjes)

Pigs-in-a-Blanket are a traditional pastry for Dutch coffee time, mid-morning or mid-afternoon.

DOUGH:

2 cups flour	½ cup shortening
½ teaspoon salt	1 egg, beaten
2 teaspoons baking powder	½ cup milk

Sift dry ingredients together. Cut shortening into flour mixture. Mix beaten egg with milk. (Mixture should total ¾ cup liquid.) Add to first mixture. Blend and knead 8-10 times on floured board. Divide dough into 2 parts. Roll each half of dough to a thickness of ¼-inch. Make 15 rounds of dough from each half using medium-sized cookie cutter.

FILLING:

1 pound lean pork sausage	2 tablespoons cream
½ pound hamburger	Salt and pepper
2 Dutch rusks, crushed, or ¼ cup dry bread crumbs	

Blend filling ingredients. Form 30 small rolls, shaped like link sausages. Place on pastry round and seal edges.

Place filled pastries on a baking sheet with raised edges and bake at 350° for 40 minutes. Serve hot.

Note: Pigs-in-a-Blanket can be refrigerated or frozen after baking, and reheated for serving.

Dutch Touches

Soups

Canoeing on the Mississipppi.

Joe's Onion Soup

½ cup butter or margarine
3 pounds sliced yellow onions
4 tablespoons flour
1 cup white wine
8-10 cups beef broth (or bouillon)

½ teaspoon cayenne pepper
1 teaspoon garlic powder
½ teaspoon paprika
French bread
Mozzarella cheese
Parmesan cheese

In a large pot, melt butter. Add onions and cook until transparent. Add flour and cook for 5 minutes. While stirring, add wine, broth, cayenne pepper, garlic powder, and paprika. Simmer for 1½ - 2 hours. When ready to serve, toast ¾-inch-thick slices of French bread and put into soup bowls. Add onion soup to within 1 inch of top of bowl. Sprinkle with 2 tablespoons grated Mozzarella cheese, and 1 teaspoon Parmesan cheese. Put under broiler until cheese is bubbly.

Titonka Centennial Cookbook

Homemade Potato Soup

6 potatoes, peeled, cut-up bite-size	2 tablespoons butter
2 onions, chopped	White pepper, to taste
1 carrot, pared and sliced	1 teaspoon cornstarch
1 stalk celery	1 teaspoon flour
1½ teaspoons salt	1 (13-ounce) can milk or half-and-half

Put all ingredients except milk, cornstarch, and flour in crockpot. Cover and cook on low 10-12 hours or on high 3-4 hours. Mix cornstarch and flour with milk (stir to be sure it doesn't lump) and add to pot during last hour. May be served with chopped chives on top.

Appanoose County Cookbook

Hearty Potato Sauerkraut Soup in a Crockpot

1 tall can chicken broth (at least 5-6 cups)	¾ pound smoked sausage, cubed (can use Polish sausage)
1 can cream of mushroom soup	1 cup chicken, cut up
1 (16-ounce) can sauerkraut, rinsed and drained	2 tablespoons vinegar
1 (8-ounce) can mushrooms	2 teaspoons dill weed
2-3 medium potatoes, cut in cubes	½ teaspoon pepper
3 medium carrots, chopped	2 slices bacon, cooked and crumbled
1 medium onion, chopped	2 hard-cooked eggs, chopped (optional)
3 stalks celery, cut up	

Put ingredients, except bacon and eggs in crockpot. Cover. Cook on low heat for 10-12 hours or until vegetables are tender. Skim off fat before serving. Sprinkle each serving with bacon and chopped egg.

A Taste of Grace

Depression Potato Soup

This is an updated version of a soup my grandmother served at her boarding house during the Great Depression. It's as inexpensive, filling, and good now as it was then.

3 cups (15 ounces) diced raw
  potatoes
1 cup diced onion
1 cup diced celery
Scant ½ cup (¾ ounce)
  uncooked fine noodles
2 cups water

1½ cups (one 12-fluid-ounce
  can) Carnation Evaporated
  Skim Milk
1 teaspoon dried parsley
  flakes
⅛ teaspoon black pepper

In a large saucepan, combine potatoes, onion, celery, noodles, and water. Cook over medium heat, stirring occasionally, until vegetables are tender, about 15 minutes. Drain, but reserve liquid. Return one cup of reserved liquid and drained vegetables back to pan. Stir in evaporated skim milk, parsley flakes, and black pepper. Lower heat. Simmer 10-15 minutes, stirring occasionally. Serves 4 (1½ cups).

Each serving equals:
Diabetic: 1 starch; 1 skim milk; ½ vegetable.
145 calories; 1gm fat; 4gm protein; 30gm carbohydrate; 103mg sodium; 1gm fiber.
Healthy Exchanges: 1 bread; 1 vegetable; ¾ skim milk.

Diabetic's Healthy Exchanges Cookbook

Cheesy Ham-Potato Soup

¼ cup diced onion
¼ cup diced carrots
¼ cup diced celery
4 large potatoes, diced
3 tablespoons margarine

½ cup diced ham
2 tablespoons cornstarch
4 cups milk
¾ cup cheese

Place all vegetables in a large saucepan. Add small amount of water, butter, and ham, and cook until tender. Mix cornstarch with small amount of milk and shake. Add cornstarch mixture, remaining milk and cheese to vegetables. Cook slowly and stir often until hot.

Colesburg Area Cookbook

Brown Jug Soup

4 teaspoons chicken bouillon
6 cups hot water
1 cup chopped onion
1 cup chopped celery
2 cups chopped potatoes
1 package chopped broccoli
1 package frozen mixed
  vegetables
2 cans cream of chicken soup
1 pound pasteurized process
  cheese spread

Stir the bouillon and hot water together in soup kettle. Add the onion, celery, potatoes, broccoli, and vegetables. Simmer 30 minutes. Add the canned soup and cheese spread. Heat until cheese is melted.

Special Recipes from our Hearts

Gourmet Cream of Zucchini Soup

3 cups sliced onions
3 tablespoons margarine
4 medium zucchini, sliced
4 cloves garlic
1 cup parsley
5 teaspoons chicken bouillon
6-8 cups of water
Dash of pepper

In a large kettle, sauté onions in margarine till transparent. Add rest of ingredients. Cook until tender; cool; run through blender. Terrific with homemade cubed bread, fried in margarine until crusty.
Note: Can add more chicken bouillon to suit your taste.

Oma's (Grandma's) Family Secrets

Canned Cream Soup Substitute

2 cups nonfat dry milk
  powder
¾ cup cornstarch
¼ cup instant chicken or beef
  bouillon

2 tablespoons onion flakes
½ teaspoon thyme
½ teaspoon basil
¼ teaspoon pepper

Blend all ingredients. Store in an airtight container. For each can of soup in a recipe, use ⅓ cup dry mix and 1¼ cups of water. Cook and stir until thick.

For richer tasting sauce, add 1 tablespoon butter, but this will increase the calories from 330 to 430 per can.

Cook of the Week Cookbook

Corn Soup

A South African dish.

1 cup chopped yellow onions
2 ounces oleo
1 cup fresh tomatoes
2 cups canned whole corn

2 cups canned cream-style
  corn
1 can evaporated milk
3 chicken bouillon cubes

Sauté in 4-quart heavy pan the onions in oleo until soft but not brown. Add coarsely diced fresh tomatoes and simmer 3 minutes. Add corn, milk, and bouillon cubes dissolved in 3 cups water. Salt and pepper to taste. Simmer together gently, covered for 15 minutes.

Country Cupboard Cookbook

Velvety Almond Cream Soup

3 tablespoons butter or
  margarine
1 cup chopped celery
½ cup chopped onion
¼ cup all-purpose flour
⅛ teaspoon pepper

4 cups milk
2 teaspoons instant chicken
  bouillon granules
½ teaspoon Worcestershire
  sauce
½ cup sliced almonds

In large saucepan, melt butter or margarine. Add celery and onion, and cook until tender. Stir in flour and pepper. Add milk all at once. Stir in chicken bouillon and the Worcestershire sauce. Cook and stir until soup is thick. Cook and stir one minute more. Serve topped with sliced almonds. Makes 8-10 appetizer servings.

The Taste of the World

Triple-Flavored Wild Rice Soup

⅔ cup wild rice
8 slices bacon, cut up
1 medium onion, chopped
4 cups half-and-half

2 (10¾-ounce) cans cream of
  potato soup
2 cups shredded American
  cheese

Rinse rice well. In a small saucepan bring ½ cup water to boiling. Add rice. Reduce heat; simmer 40 minutes or until tender. Drain, if necessary. Meanwhile, cook the 8 slices of bacon and onion until tender and bacon is crisp. Drain off fat. In large saucepan combine the rice, bacon, half-and-half, condensed soup and cheese. Heat over low heat until cheese melts and mix is heated through. Serve topped with additional bacon pieces, if you like.

Sharing our Best

Oyster Soup

1 pint oysters and juice
¼ cup butter
Salt and pepper

2-3 quarts skim milk
½ pint half-and-half

Place oysters and juice, butter, salt and pepper in small pan. Heat to boiling. Cook until edges of oysters curl. In separate large pan, heat milk and half-and-half. Do not boil. Pour oysters and broth into milk mixture. Heat very slowly.

T.W. and Anna Elliott Family Receipts

Stormy Weather Chili

2 medium onions, diced
1 cup diced celery
2 tablespoons cooking oil
1½ pounds ground beef
4 cups canned tomatoes
1 (15½-ounce) can chili beans

1-2 (15-ounce) cans red kidney beans
Salt and pepper to taste
1 tablespoon sugar
1 bay leaf
2-3 teaspoons chili powder

Sauté onions and celery in cooking oil in large kettle or pressure pan. When golden, stir in ground beef and brown until red is gone. Stir in remaining ingredients, and simmer for one hour. A pressure pan will lower the cooking time. Cook for about 20 minutes at 10 pounds pressure. Put pan under cold running water until pressure is down before trying to open the lid. Remove bay leaf before serving.

Up a Country Lane Cookbook

Salads

Kalona offers an insider's view of Amish and Mennonite life.

Potato Salad

5 pounds potatoes, cooked and diced
9 eggs, hard boiled
1/2 cup onion, diced
1 cup chopped celery
Salt and pepper, to taste

2 1/2 cups salad dressing
1/2 cup sugar
1/2 (12-ounce) can evaporated milk
1/2 cup pickle relish
2 tablespoons mustard

Cook and dice potatoes and eggs. Add onion, celery, and seasonings. In separate bowl, combine salad dressing, sugar, evaporated milk, pickle relish and mustard. Mix until smooth and creamy. Pour over potatoes and mix well. Best if stands overnight or several hours for flavor to work through.

Saint Mary Catholic Church Cookbook

Mom's Potato Salad

Everyone thinks that their mother's potato salad is the best potato salad, but I know I'm right about this one!

4 cups boiled potatoes, cut
4 chopped hard-boiled eggs

1 cup diced celery
6 minced green onions

DRESSING:
1/2 cup mayonnaise
1/4 cup sugar
1 tablespoon vinegar
1 1/2 teaspoons regular mustard

1 teaspoon salt
1/2 teaspoon pepper
1 1/2 teaspoons celery seed

Prepare salad items. Mix dressing ingredients together in bowl or jar. Toss together and chill before serving.

I Love You

In 1992, a 30-foot stainless steel statue of "Immaculate Heart of Mary Queen of Peace" was placed on the Mound of Mary. It is the focal point of the Trinity Heights Development in Sioux City.

Baked German Potato Salad

For a twist on tradition.

2 quarts boiled red potatoes, peeled and sliced

DRESSING:

6 slices bacon, crisp-cooked
1 cup celery, finely chopped
1 cup onion, finely chopped
1 tablespoon cornstarch
$^1/_2$ teaspoon salt
$^1/_2$ teaspoon pepper

$^2/_3$ cup sugar
$^2/_3$ cup cider vinegar
$1^1/_2$ cups water
$^1/_3$ cup chopped fresh
** parsley**
2 tablespoons celery seeds

Preheat oven to 375°. Place potatoes in greased 13x9-inch baking dish. Set aside. Cook bacon until crisp; crumble and set aside. Reserve fat in skillet. If necessary, add additional fat or oil to make $^1/_4$ cup. Stir in celery and onion. Add cornstarch, salt, and pepper and cook 2 minutes. Add sugar, vinegar, and water and stir with whisk. Bring to boil and cook one minute. Add parsley, celery seeds, and reserved bacon, and combine; remove from heat.

Pour warm dressing over potatoes in baking dish. Mix gently. Bake 45 minutes. Makes 10-12 servings.

The Des Moines Register Cookbook

Dutch Lettuce

SAUCE:

(May be made ahead)

1 tablespoon butter	2 egg yolks or 1 egg
1 tablespoon flour	½ cup sugar
½ cup water	½ cup vinegar

Melt butter, add flour, and when well blended, add water and bring to a boil, stirring constantly. Beat egg; add sugar and vinegar. Blend and stir into hot sauce. Let come to a boil.

SALAD:

6 servings hot boiled potatoes	2 teaspoons chopped onion (if desired)
4 hard cooked eggs	6 strips bacon
6 servings coarsely cut lettuce	⅓ cup vinegar
	⅓ cup water

Have ready potatoes, eggs, lettuce, and onion. Dice bacon, fry in skillet until brown; add 3-4 tablespoons of sauce, vinegar, and water. Bring to boil and keep hot. Place a layer of hot potatoes (riced or mashed) in bowl; then a layer of lettuce, 2 sliced hard cooked eggs, and several tablespoons of hot bacon dressing. Add remainder of potatoes, lettuce, and sliced eggs. Pour rest of dressing over this and serve immediately. Serves 6.

Spanning the Bridge of Time

Spinach Salad with Bacon and Apple

DRESSING:

1/4 cup vegetable oil
Freshly ground pepper, to
  taste
3 tablespoons tarragon wine
  vinegar

1 teaspoon sugar
1/8 teaspoon salt
1/2 teapoon dry mustard

SALAD:

1 pound fresh spinach, washed
  and stemmed
5 slices bacon
1/3 cup sliced almonds

3 green onions, including some
  greens, thinly sliced
1 red apple, diced

Combine the dressing ingredients and set aside. Drain and thoroughly chill spinach. Sauté bacon in skillet; remove and drain on paper towels. Discard all but one tablespoon drippings; add almonds and stir over medium heat until browned. Remove and drain on paper towel. Before serving, break spinach into bite-size pieces. Place in bowl. Add green onions, apples, and almonds; crumble bacon on top. Spoon dressing over salad. Serves 8.

Lutheran Church Women Cookbook

Blue Cheese—Artichoke Salad

DRESSING:

1/3 cup olive oil or salad oil
2 tablespoons red wine
  vinegar
4 tablespoons lemon juice, or 6
  tablespoons white wine
  vinegar

1 1/2 teaspoons salt
1/4 teaspoon pepper
1 teaspoon granulated sugar

Mix oil, red wine vinegar, lemon juice, salt, pepper, and sugar.

Salad greens
1 (6-ounce) jar marinated
  artichoke hearts, drained
  and cut into bite-size
  pieces

1 (8-ounce) can water chestnuts,
  drained
2 tablespoons chopped sweet
  red pepper or pimiento
1/4 cup Maytag blue cheese

Place salad greens, artichoke hearts, water chestnuts, sweet red pepper or pimiento, and blue cheese in a large bowl. Toss with dressing. Makes 8-10 servings.

A Cook's Tour of Iowa

Broccoli Salad

1 cup Hellmann's
    mayonnaise
1/3 cup sugar
1 tablespoon vinegar
4 cups broccoli (broken into
    small pieces)
1 cup celery (diced)

1/2 cup green onions with
    tops
1 cup red grapes, halved
1 cup green grapes, halved
2/3 cup diced almonds
8 strips crumbled bacon

Mix mayonnaise, sugar, and vinegar 12 hours before combining with remaining ingredients.

Zion Lutheran Church Cookbook

Broccoli and Cauliflower Salad

Easy to make. Tastes great.

1 head broccoli, broken up
1 head cauliflower, broken
    up
1 small onion, chopped

1 jar Miracle Whip
1/2 cup Bac-Os
1/2 cup Parmesan cheese

Layer broccoli, cauliflower, and onion in large bowl. Then frost with layer of Miracle Whip. Sprinkle Bac-Os and layer of Parmesan cheese; chill overnight. Stir before serving.

St. Joseph's Parish Cookbook

Riviera Salad

1 cup thinly sliced unpeeled
    cucumbers
3/4 cup chopped fresh tomato
1/4 cup finely chopped celery

1/4 cup Kraft Fat Free French
    Dressing
1 tablespoon fresh parsley or 1
    teaspoon dried parsley flakes

In a medium bowl, combine cucumbers, tomato, and celery. Add French dressing and parsley. Toss gently to combine. Cover and refrigerate at least 30 minutes. Toss again just before serving. Serves 2 (1 cup) servings.

Nutritional values per serving: Healthy Exchanges: 2 vegetable, 1/2 slider;
56 Cal; 0gm Fat; 1gm Prot; 13gm Carb; 261mg Sod; 2gm Fiber.
Diabetic: 2 Vegetable.

Dinner for Two

Tomato Salad with Onion and Peppers

Color and texture make this a very appealing dish. And wait until you taste it! This is one of our most requested recipes. We use only garden-grown tomatoes when they are in season. Although "store-bought" tomatoes may be used, they will not have the flavor that homegrown tomatoes have. Yellow tomatoes may also be added. They will add even more color to the salad.

**4 large tomatoes, cut in
  chunks**
¹/₂ green pepper, chopped
1 medium onion, sliced

3 tablespoons sugar
¹/₂ cup vinegar
¹/₂ cup water
Salt to taste

Place tomatoes, green pepper, and onion in a bowl. Sprinkle with sugar and let stand about 15 minutes. Add remaining ingredients and stir thoroughly. Refrigerate at least 4 hours before serving. This will keep several days if refrigerated. Serves 4-6.

German Recipes

Marinated Tomatoes

5 large ripe tomatoes
¹/₄ cup salad oil
1¹/₂ tablespoons lemon juice
¹/₂ clove garlic, minced
¹/₂ teaspoon salt

¹/₂ teaspoon oregano leaves
¹/₈ teaspoon pepper
¹/₂ teaspoon basil
¹/₂ teaspoon marjoram

Peel tomatoes. Cut into thick slices. Combine remaining ingredients. Pour over tomatoes. Chill thoroughly, stirring once or twice. Serves 6-8.

Marcus, Iowa, Quasquicentennial Cookbook

Joseph's Coat

⅓ cup vinegar
Water
¾ cup sugar
2 tablespoons flour
2 teaspoons prepared
   mustard

1 large sack frozen mixed
   vegetables
Chopped onion, to taste
½ cup chopped celery

Put vinegar in measuring cup and add enough water to make ½ cup. Mix sugar with flour and add liquid. Cook, stirring until it thickens; add mustard. Cook mixed vegetables as per directions; add to dressing and cool. Add onion to taste and celery. Mix and store in glass jar. Keeps a long time in refrigerator.

Stirring Up Memories

Marinated Green Beans

¼ cup dairy sour cream
2 tablespoons Italian salad
   dressing
1 (8-ounce) can cut green beans,
   drained

1 tomato, peeled, cubed and
   drained
2 tablespoons finely chopped
   onion

Thoroughly combine sour cream and Italian dressing. Add beans, tomato, and onion; mix well. Chill 3-4 hours before serving. Serve in lettuce cups. Serves 2.

Quasquicentennial / St. Olaf of Bode

Mild Tomato Aspic Salad

1 small package lemon
  Jell-O
³/₄ cup boiling water
1 cup tomato juice
1 teaspoon lemon juice
1 cup finely chopped celery

1 cup finely chopped green
  pepper
¹/₂ cup sliced stuffed olives
Mayonnaise and hard-cooked
  egg slices for garnish

Dissolve the Jell-O in the boiling water, add juices. Refrigerate until mixture begins to thicken, then add remaining ingredients. Pour into mold or pan. Chill until set. Garnish with egg slices and dabs of mayonnaise.

Variation: For luncheon salad, add 1¹/₂ cups cleaned, cooked small shrimp (or two 4¹/₂-ounce cans).

The American Gothic Cookbook

Mandarin Salad

¹/₂ cup slivered almonds
3 tablespoons sugar
¹/₂ cup chopped celery
¹/₂ head romaine lettuce
¹/₂ head iceberg lettuce

2 whole green onions,
  chopped
1 (11-ounce) can mandarin
  oranges, drained
1 crisp apple, chopped

DRESSING:
¹/₂ teaspoon salt
Dash of pepper
2 tablespoons sugar
Dash of Tabasco sauce

¹/₄ cup vegetable oil
1 tablespoon chopped parsley
2 tablespoons vinegar

In a small pan over medium heat, heat almonds and sugar, stirring constantly until almonds are coated and sugar is dissolved. (Watch carefully, as they burn easily.) Cool and store in airtight container. Mix all dressing ingredients and chill. Mix celery, lettuce, and onions. Just before serving, add almonds, oranges, and apple. Toss with dressing. May be prepared early in the day and assembled just before serving.

Madison County Cookbook

Snicker Apple Salad

Sooo simple and sooo good!

1 (8-ounce) Cool Whip
1 (8-ounce) sour cream
6 apples, chopped

4 Snickers bars chopped (can use more)

Mix together, refrigerate and serve. Can be fixed ahead of time.

Fire Gals' Hot Pans Cookbook

Party Apple Salad

3 apples, diced
2 cups celery, diced
1 can crushed pineapple, drained (reserve juice)

1 cup chopped nuts
1 cup whipping cream, whipped

DRESSING:
Juice from pineapple
1 egg
3 tablespoons flour

3 tablespoons sugar
2 tablespoons lemon juice

Boil dressing ingredients until thickened. Cool. Pour over apples, celery, pineapple, and nuts; mix well. Fold in whipped cream.

Centennial Cookbook

Cranberry Salad

4 cups cranberries
2 cups sugar
Mini-marshmallows
1 large can pineapple tidbits

2 cups grapes, cut in half
1/2 pint cream, whipped
1/2 cup walnuts (optional)

Grind cranberries and mix with sugar; let stand overnight in refrigerator. Add miniature marshmallows to absorb moisture. Add drained pineapple tidbits, grapes, and whipped cream. Refrigerate.

Our Heritage

Rhubarb Swirl Salad

3 cups diced, raw rhubarb
¾ cup sugar
1 (3-ounce) package strawberry
  Jell-O

1 (3-ounce) package instant
  vanilla pudding
1½ cups cold milk
1 (8-ounce) carton Cool Whip

Mix rhubarb and sugar in saucepan. Let stand for one hour; then over low heat, simmer until rhubarb is tender. Remove from heat; stir in Jell-O until it is dissolved and syrupy. Prepare the pudding with milk; beat until thick. Add Cool Whip. Blend in rhubarb and lightly swirl. Refrigerate several hours or overnight.

Our Heritage

Congealed Spinach Salad

A colorful addition to a buffet table.

1 (3-ounce) package lemon
  gelatin
1 cup boiling water
1 tablespoon white vinegar
½ cup mayonnaise
¾ cup cottage cheese

Salt and pepper
1 (10-ounce) package frozen
  spinach, thawed and drained
½ cup diced celery
⅓ cup diced onion
12 slices olives (optional)

Dissolve gelatin in boiling water. Add vinegar. Cool a little. Add mayonnaise and cottage cheese, which may be puréed in a processor, and salt and pepper. Blend all. Add other ingredients and mix well. Pour into buttered mold such as a Bundt pan. Yield: 8 servings.

125 Years — Walking in Faith

Yum-Yum Salad

1 package lime Jell-O
½ cup pineapple juice
1 cup whipping cream
1 (12-ounce) carton
  cottage cheese

½ cup nuts
8 marshmallows, diced
1 small can crushed pineapple,
  drained

Boil the lime Jell-O and ½ cup pineapple juice together for 2 minutes and set aside to cool. Whip cream and add to Jell-O mixture which has been cooled. Fold in cottage cheese, nuts, marshmallows, and crushed pineapple.

Centennial Cookbook

Pretzel Salad or Dessert

1 medium package pretzel
  sticks, crushed
1½ sticks oleo, melted
3 tablespoons sugar
1 (6-ounce) package strawberry
  Jell-O
3 cups boiling water

1 (8-ounce) package cream
  cheese, softened
2 (10-ounce) packages frozen
  strawberries
1 cup sugar
1 package Dream Whip

Mix first 3 ingredients together, save ½ cup for top and press remaining portion into bottom of 9x9-inch pan. Mix remaining ingredients together except DreamWhip and put on top of first layer. Add topping. Chill.

A Taste of Grace

Fruit Filled Apricot Ring Salad

1 (3-ounce) package orange
  Jell-O
1 (3-ounce) package lemon
  Jell-O
4 cups apricot nectar

1 (8-ounce) package cream
  cheese
1 cup cream, whipped
1 (11-ounce) can mandarin
  oranges, drained

Dissolve both Jell-Os in 2 cups boiling nectar; add remaining nectar and chill until slightly congealed. Beat cheese until fluffy; add gelatin gradually and mix well. Fold in whipped cream. Line bottom of lightly oiled 2-quart ring mold with ½ oranges (reserve ½ for garnish). Pour apricot mixture into mold and chill firm. Unmold on large serving plate and fill center with filling.

FILLING:
1 (13-ounce) can pineapple
  chunks, drained
1 (11-ounce) can mandarin
  oranges, drained

½ cup toasted shredded
  coconut
1 cup mini-marshmallows
1 cup sour cream

Combine ingredients, reserving a few pineapple chunks and 2 tablespoons coconut for garnish. Chill thoroughly. Serves 8.

The Berns Family Cookbook

Orange Delight Quick Salad

1 package orange Jell-O
1 carton cottage cheese
1 can mandarin oranges
1 small can crushed pineapple,
  drained (reserve juice)

1 cup Cool Whip
1/2 cup mini-marshmallows
Maraschino cherries for
  garnish

Pour dry Jell-O powder over cottage cheese. Now drain a can of mandarin oranges, and pineapple. Mix in thoroughly a cup of Cool Whip. Put in refrigerator. Add mini-marshmallows. Also you can use maraschino cherries for decoration on top.

Favorite Recipes

Tutti Fruiti Salad

1 (8³/₄-ounce) can pineapple
  tidbits
1 (11-ounce) can mandarin
  oranges
1 (17-ounce) can fruit
  cocktail
1/2 cup flaked coconut
  (optional)

2 tablespoons lemon juice
1 package instant lemon
  pudding
2 bananas
Whipped topping, (optional)

In a large bowl combine all fruits (undrained) with the coconut and lemon juice. Sprinkle with the pudding mix and toss lightly. Chill; just before serving, fold in sliced bananas and garnish with topping.

X____ Community Cookbook

Holiday Salad and Dressing

We got this recipe during World War II from a family whose name was Holliday. Thus, we make it at holiday time, and it is a family tradition.

½ pound marshmallows, cut in thirds
½ pound large gumdrops, cut fine (no black ones)
1 (20 or 29-ounce) can cubed pineapple (reserve juice)

1 pound white or red grapes, or 1 can of seeded grapes
½ cup slivered almonds (optional)
1 bottle maraschino cherries, cut in halves

DRESSING:
½ cup sugar
4 tablespoons flour
Juice of 1 lemon

½ teaspoon salt
¾ cup pineapple juice
1 pint whipping cream

Combine salad ingredients. Make dressing in double boiler or heavy pan. Cook all except whipping cream until thick and smooth, stirring constantly. Cool. Whip cream and fold into dressing and fruit. Let stand 12-24 hours.

Note: Prepared topping may be substituted for cream, but does not hold up as well. Small marshmallows tend to melt.

Quasquicentennial / St. Olaf of Bode

Pink Champagne Salad

¾ cup sugar
1 (8-ounce) package cream cheese, softened
2 or 3 bananas, mashed
1 (14-ounce) can crushed pineapple with juice

1 (10-ounce) package frozen strawberries
1 (8-ounce) carton whipped topping
1 cup nuts (optional)

Cream sugar and cream cheese; add bananas, pineapple, and strawberries. Beat well. Fold in whipped topping and nuts. Freeze in a 9x13-inch pan.

Woodbine Public Library

Cabbage and Apple Slaw with Walnuts

Apples and walnuts go together like rhythm and blues, but the cabbage is a delectable and unexpected touch here. You'll be a hit at any fall party if you serve this creamy, crunchy, cold salad that satisfies three palate senses at once. This will provide an unexpected pleasure for an early fall cookout—or with meat loaf anytime at all.

3 cups shredded cabbage	1/2 cup fat-free mayonnaise
1 cup (2 small) cored, unpeeled, finely chopped Red Delicious apples	1 tablespoon skim milk
	1 teaspoon lemon juice
	Sugar substitute to equal 1 tablespoon sugar
2 tablespoons (1/2 ounce) chopped walnuts	

In a large bowl, combine cabbage, apples, and walnuts. In a small bowl, combine mayonnaise, skim milk, lemon juice, and sugar substitute. Add mayonnaise mixture to cabbage mixture. Mix well to combine. Cover and refrigerate at least 30 minutes. Gently stir again just before serving. Serves 4 (3/4 cup).

Each serving equals:
Healthy Exchanges: 1 1/2 vegetable; 1/2 fruit; 1/4 fat; 1/2 slider; 4 optional calories.
62 Cal; 2gm Fat; 1gm Prot; 10gm Carb; 148mg Sod; 2gm Fiber.
Diabetic: 1/2 fruit; 1 free vegetable.

Cooking Healthy with a Man in Mind

Ramen Salad

1 package chicken ramen noodles	4 green onions, diced
3/4 package already-grated cabbage	2 tablespoons sunflower seeds
	1/2 cup sliced almonds

Mix together shortly before serving.

DRESSING:

1/2 cup salad oil	1/2 teaspoon pepper
2 tablespoons sugar	Seasoning packet from noodles
3 tablespoons vinegar	

Mix together and let stand a few minutes. Toss together the salad and dressing. Serve immediately.

First Christian Church Centennial Cookbook

Super Salad

16 ounces macaroni shells or rings
3 large carrots, grated
1/2 head cabbage, shredded
3/4 cup vinegar
1 can sweetened condensed milk
2 cups mayonnaise
1 cup sugar

Cook macaroni until tender. Drain, rinse, and cool. Add carrots and cabbage. Mix together vinegar, condensed milk, mayonnaise, and sugar. Pour over pasta. Best if refrigerated overnight.

Optional: Green pepper and onion may be added.

The Berns Family Cookbook

Macaroni Salad Dressing

An excellent universal dressing for salads.

1 egg
1 cup sugar
2 cups salad oil
3 teaspoons prepared mustard
1 cup mayonnaise
2/3 cup evaporated milk
1/4 cup vinegar
Salt to taste

Combine ingredients well in blender. This will keep several weeks. This dressing can be used for coleslaw by mixing one cup Macaroni Salad Dressing and extra mayonnaise to taste. For apple salad, mix one cup Macaroni Salad Dressing and whipped cream or Cool Whip to taste.

Special Fare by Sisters II

Cucumber Dill Pasta Salad

3 cups cooked pasta
1/2 cup thinly sliced carrots
1/2 cup thinly sliced celery
1 cup parboiled broccoli florets
1 teaspoon dill weed
1 green onion, thinly sliced
1/4 cup chopped onion
1/2 - 3/4 cup bottled cucumber salad dressing
Salt and pepper to taste

Combine all ingredients in a large salad bowl. Chill until serving time. Yield: 4-6 servings.

Generations of Good Cooking

Tuna Salad Supreme

2 cups grated carrots
2 cups finely chopped celery
1/2 cup chopped onion
1 cup mayonnaise

1 can tuna
1 can shoestring potatoes or
   chow mein noodles

Toss together and chill. Just before serving, add potatoes or noodles.

Note: If tuna is washed in hot water in a colander, it will taste more like chicken and have fewer calories.

Thompson Family Cookbook

Chaud Eriod
(Shrimp Salad)

2 (4 1/2-ounce) cans shrimp
1 cup celery, diced
1 cup onion, minced
1 cup cucumbers, diced
1/3 cup capers
2 hard-cooked eggs, chopped
   extra fine

1 envelope unflavored gelatin,
   softened in 1/4 cup cold
   water
1 cup salad dressing
1/4 teaspoon Tabasco sauce
3/4 cup cashews

Rinse shrimp in cold water. Have next 5 ingredients chilled. Soften gelatin in cold water, dissolve in 1/2 cup boiling water, and stir in salad dressing, a little at a time. Add Tabasco and all other ingredients and mold. Serve on lettuce.

The Walnut Centennial Cookbook

Greek Shrimp Salad

2 (6-ounce) packages cocktail
   shrimp
2 medium tomatoes, cut in
   pieces
1 cucumber, unpeeled, sliced
   thin
1/2 red onion, sliced thin
1/4 cup prepared Italian or herb
   dressing

1/2 cup feta cheese, crumbled
1/2 teaspoon dill weed
1/2 tablespoon parsley,
   chopped
Black pepper to taste
1 (2 1/4-ounce) can sliced black
   olives

Add thawed and drained shrimp to all other ingredients. Mix gently. Serve chilled in a bowl on lettuce, spinach, or red cabbage leaves. Serves 4.

Applause Applause

Moroccan Chicken and Wild Rice Salad

Can be made ahead and refrigerated.

DRESSING:

½ cup white wine vinegar
3 tablespoons Dijon mustard
4 or 5 cloves garlic

¼ teaspoon hot pepper sauce
  (Tabasco)
¾ cup salad or vegetable oil

SALAD ITEMS:

2 pounds skinless, boneless
  chicken breasts, cut up
6 green onions, chopped
2 boxes original-flavor Uncle
  Ben's long-grain & wild rice,
  cooked with seasonings

9 ounces shredded carrots
8 ounces pitted dates,
  chopped
6 ounces pecan halves,
  roasted

Combine salad dressing ingredients. Sauté chicken breasts in a little oil until cooked through. Mix salad items, except pecans, with dressings. Chill at least 4 hours. Add pecans (chop, if desired) before serving. This salad can be served chilled or at room temperature. Makes 12 servings.

I Love You

Chicken Salad

3 cups celery, diced
1 small green pepper, diced
6 eggs, boiled and diced
1½ teaspoons salt
½ teaspoon pepper
½ cup green olives, sliced
1 cup crushed pineapple,
  drained well

6 cups cooked chicken, diced
⅓ cup Western-type salad
  dressing (Ranch)
1 cup slivered almonds
1¼ cups Miracle Whip-type
  salad dressing

Day before serving, mix together celery, green pepper, eggs, salt, pepper, olives, and pineapple.

Next morning, pour Western dressing over chicken; let stand one hour. Now mix chicken with other mixture, and add almonds and Miracle Whip dressing; mix well. Serve on lettuce leaf with Chinese noodles on top, or serve on a croissant roll. Serves 15 salads, or more on rolls.

Alta United Methodist Church Cookbook

Card Club Chicken Salad

2 cups cooked chicken, diced
2 cups cooked macaroni
6 diced hard boiled eggs
1 cup cooked, diced carrots
1 can drained peas or frozen
  peas, cooked
2 cups diced celery

1 tablespoon minced onion
¼ cup sliced green pepper
  (optional)
1 jar red pimentos
1 teaspoon sugar
1 teaspoon salt
½ teaspoon pepper

Combine all ingredients.

DRESSING:

1 pint mayonnaise
¼ cup French dressing

⅔ cup evaporated milk
1 cup diced cheese

Combine dressing ingredients. Pour over salad. Can be made ahead and refrigerated. Serve a cupful of salad on a lettuce leaf along with fancy crackers.

The Berns Family Cookbook

Garden Club Salad

8 cups cooked, cubed chicken
  or turkey
1 (16-ounce) can sliced water
  chestnuts
2 pounds grapes, halved
2 cups chopped celery
2 cups slivered almonds

2 cups mayonnaise
1 cup sour cream
1½ teaspoons curry
  powder
2 tablespoons soy sauce
1 (1-pound, 13-ounce) can
  pineapple chunks

Combine turkey or chicken, chestnuts, grapes, celery, and almonds. In separate bowl, combine mayonaise, sour cream, curry powder, and soy sauce. Add to turkey or chicken mixture; stir well. Add pineapple and toss lightly. Serves 12-15 generously. Serve on bed of lettuce. Do not substitute salad dressing for mayonnaise.

St. Joseph's Parish Cookbook

A national historic landmark, the Dubuque Museum of Art is a work of art itself. The old County Jail was built in 1858 and is an excellent example of rare Egyptian Revivalist architecture.

Baked Chicken Salad

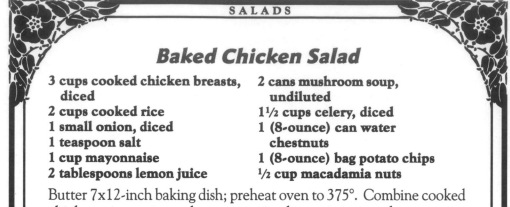

3 cups cooked chicken breasts, diced

2 cups cooked rice

1 small onion, diced

1 teaspoon salt

1 cup mayonnaise

2 tablespoons lemon juice

2 cans mushroom soup, undiluted

1½ cups celery, diced

1 (8-ounce) can water chestnuts

1 (8-ounce) bag potato chips

½ cup macadamia nuts

Butter 7x12-inch baking dish; preheat oven to 375°. Combine cooked chicken, rice, onion, salt, mayonnaise, lemon juice, mushroom soup, celery, and water chestnuts. Pour into baking dish, top with crushed potato chips and nuts and refrigerate over night. Remove from refrigerator one hour before baking. Bake, covered for 40 minutes. Let stand a few minutes before serving. Serves 6-8.

Special Fare by Sisters II

Chicken Salad In-A-Ring

GELATIN SALAD:

2 (3-ounce) packages lime-flavored gelatine

3½ cups water

2 tablespoons lemon juice

1 teaspoon dill leaves

1 cup chopped cucumber

½ cup thinly sliced radishes

CHICKEN SALAD:

4 cans boned chicken

6 tablespoons sour cream

1 cup chopped cucumber

Salt and pepper, to taste

Prepare gelatine with water, lemon juice, and dill as directed on package. Chill until partially set; fold in cucumber and radishes. Pour into 6-cup ring mold; chill 4 hours or until firm. Lightly toss chicken, sour cream, and remaining cucumber. Season to taste. Serve in center of ring using lemon wedges as garnish.

Enjoy

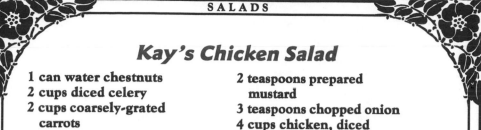

Kay's Chicken Salad

1 can water chestnuts
2 cups diced celery
2 cups coarsely-grated
 carrots
2 cups Miracle Whip
1 cup sour cream

2 teaspoons prepared
 mustard
3 teaspoons chopped onion
4 cups chicken, diced
2 small cans shoestring
 potatoes

Mix first 8 ingredients and refrigerate, covered. Just before serving
add shoestring potatoes. May be made a day before serving. May use
"lite" dressing and sour cream to decrease calorie content.

Armstrong Centennial

Fruited Chicken Salad

1 1/2 cups chicken or turkey,
 cut up
1 (8 1/4-ounce) can green
 grapes, drained or 1 cup fresh
 seedless green grapes
1 (8-ounce) can water chestnuts, drained, chopped
1 (11-ounce) can mandarin
 oranges, drained

1 1/2 cups rotini, cooked
1/2 cup mayonnaise or salad
 dressing
1/2 teaspoon salt or 1 teaspoon
 soy sauce
1/4 teaspoon curry powder

Mix chicken, grapes, water chestnuts, orange segments, and rotini.
Mix remaining ingredients; toss with chicken mixture. Serves 6.

Stirring Up Memories

Sweet Watermelon Pickles

Watermelon
1 cup sugar
1/2 cup vinegar

Stick cinnamon
Whole cloves

Use trimmed watermelon rind and cut into squares. Salt slightly.
Cook in just enough water to cover. Test for doneness (should be
transparent). Pack in jars (do not drain). Cover with syrup made by
boiling sugar, vinegar, cinnamon, and cloves.

New Beginnings Cookbook

West Special Dressing

Something different, a must-try, so good on lettuce.

2 cups mayonnaise
1/4 cup milk
1 tablespoon white vinegar
1 teaspoon garlic powder
1 teaspoon onion powder

1/2 teaspoon salt
1/4 teaspoon pepper
1 tablespoon sugar
2 teaspoons dry parsely

Mix all ingredients well and refrigerate in a covered container. This will keep for weeks.

Note: Use white pepper instead of black pepper in this, as well as other recipes. It is more finely ground and nearly invisible.

Singing in the Kitchen

French Dressing

1 cup vegetable oil
1/2 cup sugar
1/3 cup ketchup
Pinch of salt
1/2 teaspoon paprika

1 small onion, chopped or dried
  onion
1/3 cup vinegar
Juice of 1 lemon
Celery seed

Put all ingredients in blender. Blend well and store in refrigerator.

SEP Junior Women's Club 25th Anniversary Cookbook

Honey Dressing

1/3 cup honey
1/3 cup catsup
1/4 teaspoon salt
1 teaspoon Worcestershire
  sauce

3/4 cup salad oil
3 tablespoons vinegar
Juice of 1 small onion*
2 tablespoons celery seeds

Combine ingredients in the order given, beating well. Serve on fruit or vegetable salads. Makes 1 1/2 cups.

*To prepare onion juice, cut onion and scrape to release juice.

Up a Country Lane Cookbook

Vegetables

Historic Terrace Hill, the Governor's mansion in Des Moines.

Easy Corn on the Cob

For cooking small batches of corn on the cob, no method is easier than microwaving; and it allows the corn to retain its flavor and crispness. Plan on 2-3 minutes for each ear of corn—less time if corn is very tender, a little more if it's not as fresh. As Iowans will tell you, it's important to get the corn from the field to the table as quickly as possible. Also, buy corn still in the husks, because the husks help retain flavor and freshness.

2 large ears of corn, husks **1 teaspoon water**
and silks removed

Place the corn in a microwave-safe dish. Add water and cover with waxed paper or plastic film. Pierce the paper several times and microwave in HIGH for 5-6 minutes. Let stand in microwave for one minute to complete cooking. Remove waxed paper or plastic wrap carefully to prevent being scalded by the steam.

Variation: Many corn lovers believe that microwaving corn in the husks brings out more of the natural corn flavor. Just remove any outer husks that are wilted or soiled and follow the above instructions. The silks will pull away easily after cooking. Serves 2. 0 grams of fat per serving.

New Tastes of Iowa

Skillet Sweet Corn

Cream corn right off the cob.

6 ears corn **½ teaspoon granulated**
6 tablespoons butter **sugar**
½ cup light cream **Ground pepper to taste**
½ teaspoon salt

Husk corn and remove silks. Slice off kernels with a long sharp knife or electric knife. Using the back of a dinner knife, scrape the milky substance from the cob into the corn. Heat butter in a skillet, add corn and milky substance, and cook and stir 3-4 minutes or until desired tenderness. Add cream and seasonings. Stir over low heat for 2-3 minutes. Makes 4 servings.

A Cook's Tour of Iowa

Corn Cheese Casserole

1/4 cup butter
2 cups fresh corn, cut from
   cob
1/2 cup chopped green
   pepper
1/2 cup chopped pimientos
1/2 cup stuffed green olives,
   sliced

1/4 cup chopped parsley
1/4 cup flour
1/2 teaspoon salt
1 teaspoon pepper
2 cups milk
3 eggs, slightly beaten
1 cup shredded Cheddar
   cheese

In a large frying pan melt butter and sauté corn, green pepper, pimientos, green olives, and parsley for 2 minutes. Cover and cook
for 10 minutes. Blend in flour, salt, and pepper. Gradually add milk
and cook, stirring, until thickened. Slowly stir in beaten eggs and
then blend in cheese. Pour mixture into buttered 2-quart casserole.
Set casserole into pan of water and bake, uncovered, at 350° about
25 minutes, or until set. Serve hot. Serves about 8.

License to Cook Iowa Style

Do Ahead Mashed Potatoes

5 medium potatoes (7-8
   ounces each)
2 tablespoons oleo
1/3 cup milk
Salt and pepper

1 egg
1/4 cup milk
2 tablespoons oleo
Paprika

Boil potatoes. Mash while hot, stirring in oleo, milk, salt and pepper. Place in buttered casserole of appropriate size. Beat together
egg, 1/4 cup milk and spread over top of potatoes. Dot with 2 tablespoons oleo and sprinkle with paprika. Refrigerate till needed. Bake
in a preheated 350° oven, uncovered, till hot and brown on top probably 45-60 minutes. Reheating time will vary depending how cold
potatoes are when put in oven. Once you fix them like this for company, you'll never do it any other way.

Special Fare by Sisters II

Easy Twice-Baked Potatoes

8-10 potatoes
1 (8-ounce) package cream
cheese

1 egg, beaten
1 teaspoon salt
1 stick butter

Peel and boil potatoes until done. Drain well and mash. Add cream cheese, egg, salt, and butter. Beat all together. Bake in greased casserole dish 45 minutes at 350°. Can be made ahead and kept in refrigerator until time to bake.

Armstrong Centennial

Company Potatoes

1 (2-pound) bag frozen hash
browns
¼ cup melted margarine
1 teaspoon salt
¼ teaspoon pepper
1 cup sour cream

1 can cream of chicken soup
1 cup milk
2 cups grated cheese
½ cup chopped onions
¾ cup crushed cornflakes
½ cup melted margarine

Mix first 9 ingredients and put in 9x13-inch pan. Before baking, put crushed cornflakes on top, then pour melted margarine on top. Bake at 350° for one hour.

The Orient Volunteer Fire Department Cookbook

Easy Potatoes

2 pounds frozen hash browns
1 can cream of potato soup
1 can cream of Cheddar cheese
soup
2 tablespoons instant minced
onion

1 carton sour cream
1½ cups milk
Parsley flakes
Salt and pepper to taste

Bake in 9x13-inch pan at 350° for one hour. Keep covered for first 45 minutes.

Our Savior's Kvindherred Lutheran Church

Oven-Fried Potatoes

4 large potatoes, unpeeled
¼ cup vegetable oil
1 tablespoon Parmesan
  cheese

½ teaspoon salt
¼ teaspoon garlic powder
¼ teaspoon paprika
⅛ teaspoon pepper

Wash unpeeled potatoes, and cut into wedges. Place skin-side-down in baking dish, or a 9x13-inch pan. Combine remaining ingredients and brush over potatoes. Bake at 375° for one hour, brushing with mixture at 15 minute intervals. Turn potatoes over for last 15 minutes.

New Beginnings Cookbook

Lemon Dill Potatoes

4 large baking potatoes
¼ cup margarine or butter,
  melted
⅓ cup sour cream
2 tablespoons fresh dill (finely
  snipped) or 1½ teaspoons
  dried dill weed

4 teaspoons lemon juice
⅛ teaspoon garlic salt
⅛ teaspoon pepper
Paprika (optional)

Scrub potatoes and prick with fork. Bake in a 425° oven for 40-60 minutes or until tender. Let stand for 5 minutes. Cut potatoes in half lengthwise. Gently scoop out each potato half, leaving a thin shell. Place potato pulp in a large bowl. Add 3 tablespoons melted butter, sour cream, dill or dill weed, lemon juice, garlic salt, and pepper. With electric mixer on low speed, beat until smooth. Pile mixture into potato shells. Place in a 12 x 7½ x 2-inch baking dish. Brush potatoes with remaining melted butter. Sprinkle with paprika, if desired. Bake in a 425° oven about 20 minutes or until light brown. Makes 8 servings.

Stirring Up Memories

Swing to the Big Band sounds of Glenn Miller in Clarinda. The house where the popular orchester leader and hit-maker of the swing era was born has been restored with period furnishings and is open for visitors.

Cheesy BBQ Potato Bake

1 (11-ounce) can Cheddar
  cheese soup
1/3 cup evaporated milk
1/2 cup barbecue sauce
1/2 teaspoon Accent flavor
  enhancer

4 medium potatoes (about 2
  pounds), peeled and thinly
  sliced
1 cup (4 ounces) shredded
  Cheddar cheese

Preheat oven to 375°. In a small bowl, combine the soup, evaporated milk, barbecue sauce, and Accent flavor enhancer. Layer 1/3 of the potatoes into a buttered, shallow, 2-quart baking dish. Top with 1/2 of the soup mixture. Repeat with potatoes and sauce; end with a layer of potatoes. Sprinkle cheese over the top layer of potatoes. Bake for 1 hour or 20 minutes, or until potatoes are tender. Makes 4-6 servings.

Microwave Directions: Layer potatoes, soup mixture and cheese as directed above, in a buttered, shallow 2-quart microwave-safe baking dish. Cover and microwave on HIGH for 30 minutes, turning the dish 3 times. Let stand 10 minutes before serving.

Lehigh Public Library Cookbook

Potato Pie

3 eggs
¾ teaspoon salt
¾ teaspoon pepper
¾ cup milk
3 large potatoes, peeled and
   grated

3 tablespoons flour
¼ teaspoon baking powder
3 tablespoons bacon fat

Beat eggs, salt, and pepper together; add milk and beat lightly. Add grated potatoes, then stir in flour and baking powder. Heat bacon fat in large, ovenproof skillet (iron is best). Pour potato mixture into skillet. Dot with butter. Bake in preheated 400° oven for one hour, or until golden brown. Serve with roast pork and sauerkraut.

Cherished Czech Recipes

Quick Scalloped Potatoes

5 large potatoes, sliced
1 onion, sliced
1 teaspoon salt
Ham or fried bacon

1 can cream of mushroom or
   chicken soup
4 ounces Velveeta cheese

Preheat oven to 325°. Precook potatoes, onions, and salt in water until almost done, but yet very firm (do not overcook). Drain and put into buttered casserole. Add leftover ham or fried bacon, cut in pieces. Add soup and grated cheese which was heated together until melted. Do not use the potato water. Bake at 325° for 30 minutes. Delicious!

Favorite Recipes

Cheese Sauce for Potatoes

2 cups cottage cheese
1 cup sour cream
1 stick margarine
½ package grated Cheddar
   cheese

1 teaspoon seasoning salt
2 green onions (tops and all)
Dash garlic salt
Dash dill weed

Blend in blender. Serve on baked potatoes.

Teresa's Heavenly Cakes and Treasures

Sour Cream and Cheddar Supreme Potatoes

2 pounds sliced potatoes
1/3 cup diced onions
1/4 pound margarine, melted
1/4 cup grated Colby cheese
3/4 cup sour cream

1 1/2 cups chicken gravy
1/2 teaspoon salt
1/2 teaspoon white pepper
1 can Durkee onions

Cook potatoes in water until tender, but firm; drain. Add remaining ingredients, except Durkee onions. Mix well. Place mixture into a 9x9-inch baking dish. Bake in a 350° oven for 20 minutes. Top with Durkee onions, and bake for 5 more minutes. Serves 8.

The Machine Shed Farm Style Cooking

Crunchy Top Sweet Potato Soufflé

3 cups mashed sweet
  potatoes
1 cup white sugar
1/2 cup melted butter or
  margarine

1/3 cup milk
2 eggs, beaten
1 teaspoon vanilla

TOPPING:

1/2 cup brown sugar
1/4 cup flour
1/3 cup butter

1 cup chopped pecans or
  walnuts

Mix potatoes, white sugar, butter, milk, eggs, and vanilla. Place in 2-quart casserole dish. Mix topping ingredients and sprinkle over top of casserole. Bake at 375° 30 minutes. Serves 8-10.

Sharing Traditions from People You Know

Yvonne's Berry-Yam Bake

Sweet potatoes are transformed into festive fare by the addition of cranberries.

½ cup flour
½ cup oatmeal
½ cup brown sugar
1 teaspoon cinnamon
½ cup margarine

1 (34-ounce) can drained, sliced
  yams
2 cups whole cranberries
1½ cups miniature
  marshmallows

Preheat oven to 350°. In small bowl combine flour, oatmeal, brown sugar, and cinnamon. Cut in margarine. Toss one cup of the crumb mixture with yams and cranberries. Place in a lightly greased 1½-quart casserole and top with remaining crumbs. Bake at 350° for 35 minutes. Top with marshmallows and return to oven for about 5 minutes (until marshmallows are melted and lightly browned).

Singing in the Kitchen

Sweet Potato and Cashew Bake

½ cup packed brown sugar
⅓ cup broken cashews
½ teaspoon salt
¼ teaspoon ground ginger
2 pounds sweet potatoes,
  cooked, peeled, and cut
  crosswise into thick pieces

1 (8-ounce) can peach slices,
  well drained
3 tablespoons butter or
  margarine

Preheat oven to 350°. Combine brown sugar, cashews, salt, and ginger. In a 10x6x2-inch baking dish, layer half the sweet potatoes, half the peaches, and half the brown sugar mixture. Repeat layers. Dot with butter or margarine. Bake, covered, in preheated oven 30 minutes. Uncover and bake mixture about 10 minutes longer. Spoon brown sugar mixture over potatoes before serving. Makes 6-8 servings.

A Cook's Tour of Iowa

Carrot Casserole

3 cups cooked, sliced carrots,
  drained (1 pound)
1 can cream of celery soup
1 cup grated processed
  cheese

1-2 tablespoons margarine
½ cup dry bread crumbs

Combine carrots, soup, and cheese. Place in 1-quart casserole. Melt margarine; combine with crumbs. Sprinkle crumb mixture over carrots. Bake at 350° for 20-25 minutes.

St. Paul's Woman's League 50th Anniversary Cook Book

Dill Carrots

1 pound sliced or whole baby
  carrots
1 cup chicken broth
3 tablespoons sugar
1 teaspoon dill weed

¼ teaspoon salt
Dash of white pepper
2 tablespoons heavy cream
1 teaspoon cornstarch
1 teaspoon water

Simmer carrots in chicken stock until tender. Add sugar, dill, salt, white pepper, and heavy cream. Bring to a low boil. Thicken with cornstarch and water mixture. Heat until sauce coats the carrots. Serves 4.

The Machine Shed Farm Style Cooking

Carrots in Dill Butter

8 small carrots
½ cup water
2 tablespoons butter or
  margarine

1 teaspoon sugar
½ teaspoon salt
½ teaspoon dill weed

Scrape and cut carrots in 1-inch pieces. Combine all ingredients in medium saucepan and cover. Heat to boiling, then simmer 25-30 minutes or until carrots are tender and liquid is almost absorbed. Makes 4 servings.

Välkommen till Swedesburg

Marinated Carrots

1 quart sliced, cooked carrots	³/₄ cup vinegar
1 pepper (green or red), sliced	¹/₂ cup oil
1 onion, sliced	¹/₂ teaspoon Worcestershire sauce
1 cup sliced celery	¹/₂ teaspoon dry mustard
1 cup sugar	1 cup tomato soup

Combine first 4 ingredients. Heat next 5 ingredients. Add soup and heat. Pour heated mixture over other mixture. Let stand 24 hours before serving.

Sharing our Best

Carrot Sandwich Filling

1 pound carrots	1 cup Miracle Whip (no substitutions)
1 tablespoon fresh onions	
4 ounces soft butter	¹/₄ teaspoon salt

Peel carrots and grind or shred fine. Grind or mince onion very fine. Mix butter, salad dressing, and salt. Combine with carrots and minced onion.

Applause Applause

Tomato Vegetable Pie

Pastry for 9-inch pie shell	¹/₄ teaspoon basil
³/₄ cup chopped onion	³/₄ teaspoon salt
1 clove garlic, crushed	¹/₈ teaspoon pepper
1 tablespoon oil	2 eggs, beaten
1 (17-ounce) can tomatoes	¹/₂ cup shredded Cheddar cheese
¹/₂ pound zucchini, washed and thinly sliced	
2 tablespoons finely chopped parsley	

Bake pie shell 8 minutes at 425°. Sauté onion and garlic in oil till tender. Add tomatoes, zucchini, herbs, salt and pepper. Simmer, uncovered, for 15 minutes. Allow to cool. Stir beaten eggs into cooled vegetables and pour into pie shell. Sprinkle with cheese, and bake at 375° for 20 minutes. Serves 6.

Recipes from Iowa with Love

Baked Stuffed Tomatoes

2 medium tomatoes (whole)
Salt and pepper to taste
1 teaspoon chives, chopped
2 tablespoons canned
mushrooms, chopped
1 tablespoon dry bread crumbs

2 dots of butter
(½ teaspoon)
2 teaspoons grated Parmesan
cheese

Make a small hollow in each tomato and sprinkle with salt and pepper. Combine the removed bits of tomato with chives, mushrooms, and dry bread crumbs. Fill the tomatoes with the mixture. Dot with butter and sprinkle with cheese. Bake at 375° for 30 minutes. 60 calories per serving.

A Taste of Grace

Stuffed Green Peppers

Green peppers
Salt and pepper to taste
¾ pound ground beef
1 medium onion, chopped

2 tablespoons butter
½ cup canned tomatoes
1 cup cooked rice
Grated Cheddar cheese

If peppers are small, leave them whole and cut off a slice from the stem end. Cut large peppers in half lengthwise. Remove seeds and membrane. Cook in boiling water 3-5 minutes and drain. Sprinkle with salt and pepper and cool. Brown beef and onion in butter. Add tomatoes and rice. Mix well. Stuff peppers generously. Top with Cheddar cheese. Bake 15-25 minutes at 350° until hot and cheese is melted.

The Great Iowa Home Cooking Expedition

Onion Pie

1 cup finely crushed soda
crackers
¼ cup butter, melted
2 cups thinly sliced onions
2 tablespoons butter

¾ cup milk
2 well beaten eggs
¾ teaspoon salt
Dash pepper
¼ cup grated cheese

Mix crackers and melted butter and press in a 9-inch pie plate. Fry the onions in 2 tablespoons butter. Put in the pie shell. Mix milk, eggs, salt and pepper and pour over onions. Top with grated cheese. Bake 350° for 30 minutes.

A Taste of Grace

Mushrooms Florentine

1 clove garlic, chopped
½ cup margarine
1 pound sliced mushrooms
3 packages frozen chopped
  spinach, thawed and drained

1 large onion, chopped
Salt to taste
Pepper to taste
1 cup shredded Cheddar
  cheese

Sauté garlic in ¼ cup margarine; remove garlic and sauté mushrooms. Combine spinach, onion, and remaining margarine. Salt and pepper to taste. Place in a shallow baking dish. Sprinkle with half the cheese. Cover with mushrooms and then sprinkle with remaining cheese. Bake at 350° for 30 minutes. Serves 6-8.

The Taste of the World

Asparagus in the Dutch Way

Typical Dutch dish from the Province of Limburg.

4 pounds fresh asparagus,
  trimmed, steamed 3 minutes
3 pounds peeled new potatoes,
  boiled
2 pounds smoked ham sliced
  ⅛-inch thick and warmed

8 hard-cooked eggs, mashed
1 cup melted butter
1 teaspoon ground nutmeg

Arrange asparagus in center of large oval platter. Arrange boiled potatoes on one end and rolled ham on the other. Sprinkle eggs over top and garnish with melted butter and nutmeg. Serve hot. Serves 8.

The Taste of the World

Creamed Onions

2-4 dozen small white boiling
   onions (depending on size)
1 cup diced celery
4 tablespoons butter
3 tablespoons flour

1 teaspoon salt
Few grains of pepper
1½ cups half-and-half
Slivered almonds
Paprika

Wash and peel onions and cook in boiling salted water until tender. Drain. Cook celery in boiling salted water just until tender-crisp. Drain. Melt butter; stir in flour, salt and pepper. Add half-and-half and heat until thickened, stirring constantly. Arrange alternate layers of onions, celery, almonds, and white sauce in casserole. Sprinkle top with paprika. Bake at 350° until bubbly and lightly browned.

125 Years — Walking in Faith

Spiced Red Cabbage

From the Strawtown Inn, Pella, Iowa.

1 large head red cabbage, very
   finely sliced (about 5 cups)
1 cup chopped, unpeeled, crisp
   tart apples (such as Jonathan,
   Winesap, or McIntosh)
1 tablespoon whole allspice
½ teaspoon salt
¼ teaspoon grated nutmeg

¼ teaspoon ground
   cinnamon
¼ teaspoon freshly ground
   black pepper
¼ cup red wine vinegar
⅓ cup brown sugar
2 tablespoons butter (or more,
   as desired)

Place cabbage in large sauté pan and add enough water to cover. Bring to boil; lower heat and simmer, covered, until cabbage is limp and soft, about 5 minutes. Drain off all but ½ cup water. Add apples; toss and continue cooking until apples are tender, about 15 minutes. Add spices, vinegar, and brown sugar and continue cooking until cabbage and apple mixture is tender and most of liquid is gone. Add butter and serve. Makes 6 servings.

The Des Moines Register Cookbook

Cantonese Celery

4 cups celery pieces
1 can water chestnuts
1 cup cream of chicken soup
½ cup soft bread crumbs

¼ cup toasted slivered
  almonds
4 tablespoons melted butter

Cook celery in small amount of boiling salted water for about 8 minutes. Drain. Mix celery, water chestnuts (drained and thinly sliced), and cream of chicken soup into buttered casserole dish. Toss bread crumbs with almonds in melted butter. Sprinkle on top of casserole. Bake uncovered, 35 minutes at 350°.

Enjoy

Spinach or Broccoli Soufflé

1 (10-ounce) package frozen
  chopped spinach or broccoli
6 eggs, or 2 eggs with 1 carton
  Egg Beaters
¼ pound cheese, cubed

1 pint small-curd cottage
  cheese
¼ cup flour
2 tablespoons oleo, cut small

Thaw and drain spinach or broccoli. Mix remaining ingredients and combine with spinach or broccoli. Bake in greased 9x9-inch pan for one hour at 325°.

Välkommen till Swedesburg

Broccoli and Rice

½ cup celery, chopped
½ cup onion, chopped
2 tablespoons butter
1 can cream of mushroom
  soup

2 packages broccoli, chopped,
  uncooked
¾ cup minute rice
1 (8-ounce) jar Cheez-Whiz

Sauté celery and onions in butter until shiny. Heat soup in pan, then add celery, onions, broccoli, and rice. Mix together and pour into casserole. Add Cheez-Whiz in dabs on top. Bake 45 minutes at 350°.

Appanoose County Cookbook

Spinat
(Spinach)

2 pounds raw spinach
1 pint boiling water
¼ cup lard
¾ cup bread crumbs
1 small onion, chopped fine

1 heaping tablespoon flour
½ teaspoon salt
¼ teaspoon pepper
1 pint beef broth

Cook spinach in boiling water for 5 minutes or until tender. Remove from stove and cool spinach in cold water. Squeeze out all water and run through food chopper. Heat lard over medium heat; add bread crumbs and brown until a golden brown. Stir in onion, then flour, salt and pepper. Add ground spinach and bring to boil. Add beef broth and cook until well blended.

Amana Colony Recipes

Baked Zucchini

3 cups sliced zucchini
2 medium onions, sliced
2 tablespoons margarine
2 tablespoons flour
1 teaspoon salt
Dash of pepper

1 cup milk
1 cup cubed Velveeta cheese
1 package saltine crackers,
   crumbled
1 stick margarine, melted

Cook zucchini and onion in small amount of boiling water until tender. In saucepan, melt 2 tablespoons margarine; blend in flour, salt and pepper. Add milk; cook, stirring constantly until mixture thickens. Combine sauce with cooked vegetables. Place in baking dish. Stir in cubed cheese. Top with cracker crumbs mixed with margarine. Bake at 350° for 20 minutes. Very good!

Community Centennial Cookbook

Many famous people were born in Iowa. Among them are Herbert Hoover, Glenn Miller, Donna Reed, Grant Wood, Meredith Willson, Jerry Mathers (the Beaver), Johnny Carson, John Wayne, Cloris Leachman, the seven Ringling brothers, and Mamie Doud Eisenhower.

Zucchini Bake

3 medium zucchini, grated
1¼ cups seasoned croutons
½ cup sautéed fresh
  mushrooms
½ cup onion, chopped
2 slices bacon, cooked crisp
  and crumbled

½ cup grated Swiss cheese
¼ cup melted butter or
  margarine
1 egg, beaten
½ teaspoon garlic salt
¼ teaspoon pepper

Preheat oven to 350°. Combine ingredients. Place in greased 1½ -
2-quart casserole and bake 40 minutes. Makes 6-8 servings.

The Des Moines Register Cookbook

Zucchini Casserole

2 pounds zucchini squash
¼ cup onion, finely chopped
½ pound bulk sausage
½ cup cracker crumbs, finely
  crushed

2 eggs, slightly beaten
¼ teaspoon ground thyme
½ teaspoon salt
⅓ cup cubed cheese (grated
  Parmesan may be used)

Heat oven to 350°. Wash squash, trim off ends. Cut in thick slices.
Cook in boiling salted water (small amount) for 10 minutes. Drain
and chop squash coarsely. Place onion and sausage in a skillet and
cook until sausage is brown; drain off fat. Combine squash, onion,
sausage, crumbs, beaten eggs, thyme, salt, and half the cheese. Place
mixture in a shallow baking dish or casserole which has been greased.
Sprinkle the remaining cheese over the top. Bake 30-40 minutes.
Serves 4.

Stirring Up Memories

Brown Beans with Bacon

This is a substantial meal for hungry Dutchmen. Sometimes served with warm syrup, honey or sorghum.

1 pound dried brown beans
½ pound bacon
¾ pound onions, peeled and chopped

3 medium-sized potatoes, peeled and sliced
½ pound leeks, sliced
Pepper to taste

Cover the beans with cold water and let soak overnight. Drain and cook in enough water to cover for 1½ - 2 hours or until soft. Drain beans and rinse in cold water. Dice bacon and place in a hot frying pan. When browned, add onion and cook until golden. Add potatoes and leeks and cook until tender. Add the beans; stir and cook until beans have absorbed the bacon drippings. Season to taste. Serves 6.

Dandy Dutch Recipes

Vegetable Loaf

5 tablespoon butter (a little bacon grease is good)
3 tablespoons flour
1 small onion, chopped
2 cups milk or vegetable water
1 teaspoon salt and pepper

1 cup grated cheese
2 eggs, beaten
2 cups cooked string beans
2 cups cooked carrots
2 cups cooked potatoes
1 cup bread crumbs

Melt fat in pan. Add flour, onion, milk, and seasonings. Cook until thick, then add cheese. Take from heat; add eggs. Arrange beans, carrots, and potatoes in layers in greased pan. Pour over white sauce and put buttered crumbs on top. Bake at 350° for 30 minutes.

Armstrong Centennial

Meredith Willson, internationally-renowned composer, immortalized his hometown of Mason City as "River City" in *The Music Man*.

Swiss Vegetable Medley

1 (16-ounce) bag frozen
broccoli, carrots and
cauliflower combination,
thawed and drained
1 (10³/₄-ounce) can condensed
cream of mushroom soup
1 cup (4 ounces) shredded
Swiss cheese

⅓ cup sour cream
¼ teaspoon ground black
pepper
1 (4-ounce) jar chopped
pimento, drained (optional)
1 (2.8-ounce) can Durkee's
French Fried Onions

Combine vegetables, soup, ½ cup cheese, sour cream, pepper, pimento, and ½ can French fried onions. Pour into a 1-quart casserole. Bake covered at 350° for 30 minutes. Top with remaining cheese and onions; bake uncovered 5 minutes longer.

Microwave Directions: Prepare as above. Cook covered on HIGH 8 minutes. Turn after 4 minutes. Top with remaining cheese and onions. Cook uncovered on HIGH one minute or until cheese melts.

St. Paul's Woman's League 50th Anniversary Cook Book

Hot Vegetable Medley

(Microwave)

2 large potatoes, peeled and
sliced
1 cup sliced carrots
1 small onion, sliced
¼ cup water
1 cup milk
2 tablespoons flour

1 teaspoon seasoned salt
¼ teaspoon dry mustard
⅛ teaspoon pepper
1 cup frozen peas
½ cup cubed cheese (Velveeta
or equivalent)

Place potatoes, carrots, onion, and water in 2-quart casserole. Cover and cook on full power 7-8 minutes until potatoes are just about tender. Stir twice. Combine milk, flour, salt, mustard, and pepper. Add to vegetables along with peas. Cook uncovered 5-6 minutes on full power until mixture thickens. Stir twice. Stir in cheese. Cook on full power 1-2 minutes until cheese is melted.

Note: Make this an hour or two ahead of time and put in crockpot on low.

Home Cooking with the Cummer Family

Endive, Amsterdam Style

Endive is one of the most popular vegetables in Holland.

8 bunches endive, cut into
  ⅓-inch slices
Boiling salted water
2 tablespoons butter
2 tablespoons flour

½ cup milk
½ teaspoon nutmeg
½ cup endive stock
Salt and pepper

Cook endive in boiling salted water until tender. Drain, reserving the stock. In a saucepan, melt butter and stir in flour. Gradually add milk, nutmeg, and ½ cup of the stock to make a medium-thick sauce. Season to taste. Arrange endive on a serving platter and cover with the sauce.

Dandy Dutch Recipes

Deluxe Beets

½ cup brown sugar, firmly
  packed
2 tablespoons flour
¼ teaspoon salt
⅓ cup vinegar
1 cup water (or syrup from
  pineapple plus water)

½ cup raisins
1 (9-ounce) can crushed
  pineapple
2 tablespoons butter
2 cups (16 ounces) canned
  beets, drained

Blend sugar, flour, and salt in pan. Add vinegar and water. Add raisins, pineapple, and butter. Cook until thick, stirring. Add beets and heat thoroughly.

Stirring Up Memories

Süsz-Sauere Roterüben
(Pickled Beets)

2 quarts beets
2 cups sugar
2 cups vinegar

2 cups water
2 teaspoons salt, if desired

Boil beets until tender, dip into cold water, peel and quarter. Combine remaining ingredients, bring to boil; add beets and bring to boil again. Fill into sterilized jars and seal.

Amana Colony Recipes

Tomato Chutney

1 pound tomatoes, blanched,
 peeled, and chopped, or 1
 pound canned peeled
 tomatoes, undrained
1 medium onion, finely
 chopped
1-inch piece fresh ginger, finely
 chopped

3/4 cup pitted dates
2/3 cup raisins
2/3 cup currants
1 teaspoon cayenne pepper
1 teaspoon salt
4 tablespoons vegetable oil
1 teaspoon mustard seeds

Place all ingredients except oil and mustard seeds in saucepan and
bring to boil, stirring occasionally. Reduce heat and simmer, uncovered, 1½ - 2 hours or until chutney is thick. Meanwhile, heat oil in
small frying pan. Add mustard seeds and fry, covered, until they
stop popping. Remove pan from heat and tip contents into saucepan with other ingredients. Stir to mix. Refrigerate. Serve with
meat or fish.

The Des Moines Register Cookbook

Frozen Tomato Sauce

20 large tomatoes, peeled and
 cut up
4 large carrots, coarsely
 shredded
3 tablespoons sugar

1 green pepper, chopped
4 large onions, chopped
½ cup chopped parsley
2 tablespoons salt
3/4 teaspoon pepper

Bring to boil and simmer 30 minutes. Cool slightly. Blend at high
speed about one minute. Pour into containers and freeze. Spices
can be added for spaghetti sauce before freezing or after. Can also
be put in jars and processed in boiling water bath. Makes 6 quarts.

Sharing our Best

Lena's End of the Garden Relish

2 cups green tomatoes
2 cups green cucumbers
2 cups green peppers
2 cups red peppers
2 cups onions
½ cup salt
1 quart water
2 cups carrots

2 cups celery
3 cups sugar
3 cups vinegar
2 tablespoons mustard seed
1 can kidney beans, drained and rinsed
1 can lima beans, drained and rinsed

Cut tomatoes, cucumbers, green and red peppers, and onions into small, fine pieces. Let stand overnight in the salt and water mixture. Drain the salt water off in the morning. Now cook carrots and celery (also cut in small diced pieces) until just firm tender, and drain.

Combine sugar, vinegar, and mustard seed and let this come to a boil; add all the cut-up ingredients and bring back to a boil. Add beans and just bring to a boil, (do not overcook so as to keep ingredients from getting mushy). Seal in clean, sterilized Mason jars.

Armstrong Centennial

Also known as "The Pope's Church," the Basilica of St. Francis Xavier in Dyersville is a fine example of true medieval Gothic architecture. It was designated a basilica in 1956. Home to 5,000 parishioners, it has 212-foot twin spires and 64 stained-glass windows.

Seafood, Pasta, Hot Dishes

*The aura is that of quiet magnificence at the Basilica of St. Francis Xavier.
Dyersville.*

Sandy's Spicy Shrimp

½ - 1 teaspoon cayenne (½ is plenty hot)
½ teaspoon black pepper
½ teaspoon salt
½ teaspoon crushed red pepper
½ teaspoon thyme leaves
1 teaspoon dried basil leaves
½ teaspoon dried oregano

2 dozen large or 1 pound medium shrimp
⅓ cup margarine
1½ teaspoons minced garlic
1 teaspoon Worcestershire sauce
¼ cup beer
1 cup diced tomatoes

Combine the first 7 spices; mix with shirmp. Melt butter, sauté garlic; add shrimp, Worcestershire sauce, beer, and tomatoes. Cook until shrimp is done and sauce is somewhat reduced. Serve with rice.

I Love You

Baked Fish and Vegetables

A tasty, healthful way to serve baked fish.

1 pound fish fillets cut into 5 or 6 serving pieces
1 teaaspoon cooking oil
⅛ teaspoon pepper
⅛ teaspoon paprika
⅛ teaspoon oregano
⅛ teaspoon thyme
½ cup shredded or finely cut carrots

¾ cup finely chopped celery
⅓ cup finely chopped green onions
½ cup finely chopped fresh mushrooms
½ cup snipped parsley
1 tablespoon lemon juice

Preheat oven to 350°. Pour teaspoon of oil into 8x8x2-inch baking dish. Rinse fillets under cold water; dry with paper towels and arrange in baking dish. Sprinkle pepper, paprika, oregano, and thyme over fish. Spoon carrots, celery, green onions, mushrooms, and snipped parsley over fish.

Sprinkle the above with one teaspoon lemon juice. Cover tightly with foil and bake 45 minutes to one hour.

Singing in the Kitchen

Poorman's Lobster

3 quarts water
1 medium onion, chopped
Salt, to taste
1/2 cup lemon juice
3 pieces celery, chopped
3 pounds fish fillets in 2-inch
  pieces

1/4 teaspoon paprika
  (optional)
1/2 pound butter or
  margarine

Place water, onion, salt, lemon juice, and celery in a 4-quart pan. Bring to a boil. Add fish and bring back to a boil. Boil for 3 minutes. Drain fish. Sprinkle with paprika if desired. Serve with melted butter.

The Nading Family Cookbook

Tuna Noodle Casserole

My family enjoys this unbaked. When chilled, it is like a cold salad. Be sure noodles are precooked.

2-4 cups noodles or macaroni,
  partially cooked
2 tablespoons diced onion
1 can tuna, do not drain
1 can chicken broth
1 small jar pimiento

1/4 cup diced green pepper
1/4 cup Cheddar cheese, small
  cubes
1/4 cup Monterey Jack cheese,
  small cubes
Salt and pepper, to taste

Combine all ingredients in large casserole. Mix well. Bake 45-50 minutes at 350°, uncovered.

Quasquicentennial / St. Olaf of Bode

Corn and Oyster Casserole

1 cup cream corn
2 eggs, beaten
³/₄ cup canned milk
2 tablespoons chopped green
  pepper

2 tablespoons chopped onion
¹/₄ teaspoon paprika
1 cup coarse cracker crumbs
1 cup oysters, plus liquid
3 tablespoons butter, melted

Use a medium casserole dish. Mix corn, eggs, canned milk, chopped green pepper, onion, paprika, oysters and liquid. Place in casserole dish. Sift crackers over top. Pour butter on crackers. Sprinkle paprika over top. Bake in preheated oven for 30-40 minutes at 350°.

Appanoose County Cookbook

Tuna Burgers

1 (7-ounce) can tuna
1 cup chopped celery
¹/₂ cup Cheddar cheese,
  diced
¹/₂ cup ripe olives, chopped

¹/₄ cup mayonnaise
Salt and pepper to taaste
1 small onion, minced
6 hamburger buns

Combine tuna, celery, cheese, olives, mayonnaise, salt, pepper, and onion. Spread on buns and wrap in foil. Bake at 350° for 10-15 minutes. May freeze. May also use chopped chicken or turkey.

Cook of the Week Cookbook

Ham, Cabbage and Noodle Casserole

1 (8-ounce) package noodles	2½ - 3 cups milk
3 tablespoons butter	3 eggs, well-beaten
½ medium-sized head of	½ teaspoon salt
cabbage, diced	Pepper to taste
2½ cups ground ham	

Cook noodles according to directions, barely tender. Drain and set aside. Melt butter in a skillet and sauté cabbage until tender. In a buttered casserole dish, place a layer of half the noodles and a layer of half the cabbage. Add one layer of all the ham. Add the rest of the cabbage and noodles layered on top. Scald the milk and add slowly to the beaten eggs, beating constantly. Salt and pepper to taste and beat well. Pour over layered ingredients and bake at 350° for about one hour, or until a knife inserted in middle comes out clean.

Cherished Czech Recipes

Cowboy Goulash

The whole family loves this one.

1 package macaroni and cheese	1 can whole corn, drained
dinner	1 (6-ounce) can tomato paste
1 pound hamburger	½ cup water
½ cup chopped green	1 teaspoon salt
pepper	Dash of pepper
¼ cup chopped onion	

Prepare macaroni and cheese as directed. Brown meat, green pepper, and onion. Stir in corn, tomato paste, water, salt and pepper. Add macaroni and cheese and mix well. Simmer 5 minutes. Serves 4-5.

125 Years — Walking in Faith

The town of Fort Atkinson was the site of the only fort ever built by the U.S. government to protect one Indian tribe from another.

Almost Pizza

7 cups thinly-sliced potatoes, about 3 pounds
1 pound lean ground beef
1 (11-ounce) can condensed nacho cheese soup
1 cup milk
1 (10³/₄-ounce) can condensed tomato soup
½ chopped onion
1 teaspoon sugar
½ teaspoon dried oregano, crushed
1 (3½-ounce) package pepperoni or your favorite topping
1-2 cups Mozzarella cheese

Place sliced potatoes in greased 9x13x2-inch baking dish; set aside. Cook ground beef. Drain off fat. Combine cheese soup and milk in saucepan; cook and stir over medium heat until heated through. Mix together tomato soup, onion, sugar, and oregano. Sprinkle meat over potatoes. Pour cheese mixture over all. Top with tomato soup mixture, favorite topping, and Mozzarella cheese. Cover; bake at 375° for 1¼ - 1½ hours. Let stand 5 minutes before serving. Serves 8-10.

Our Heritage

Pasghetti Pizza

1 (16-ounce) package spaghetti
2 eggs
½ cup milk
4 cups shredded Mozzarella
³/₄ teaspoon garlic powder
Salt
1 pound ground beef, browned and drained
1½ teaspoons oregano
1 (32-ounce) jar spaghetti sauce
1 package sliced pepperoni

Break spaghetti into 2-inch pieces. Cook and drain. In large bowl, beat eggs. Add milk, one cup cheese, garlic powder, and salt. Add spaghetti and stir. Spread this mixture into greased 10x15-inch jellyroll pan. Bake 15 minutes at 400°. Spread ground beef over the spaghetti and sprinkle with oregano. Spread the spaghetti sauce over this and then put on the sliced pepperoni. Top with remaining cheese. Lower the oven to 350° and bake 20 minutes until the cheese is bubbly and browned. Let stand 5 minutes before cutting.

Note: Meat is optional. Be sure to cover spaghetti so it doesn't get hard.

Spitfire Anniversary Cookbook

Make Ahead Lasagna

Make several hours or the day ahead, if possible.

1¼ pounds hamburger
1 medium onion, chopped
1 (16-ounce) can tomatoes
1 small can tomato paste
3 small cans water
¼ teaspoon garlic powder
1 teaspoon oregano

1½ tablespoons sugar
1 tablespoon salt
1½ teaspoons Worcestershire
    sauce
1 pound lasagna noodles
    (uncooked)
1 pound mixed cheese, grated

Brown hamburger and onions together; add tomatoes, tomato paste, and water and all seasonings; heat. Build in layers as follows in 9x13-inch pan: ¼ sauce in bottom, ⅓ uncooked noodles, ⅓ cheese, ¼ sauce. Repeat, crisscrossing noodles. Pour last of sauce on top. Cover pan tightly with foil. Bake 45-60 minutes at 325°-350°. Let set ½ hour before serving, covered.

Community Centennial Cookbook

Mexican Lasagna

1 pound ground beef
½ cup onion
1 (16-ounce) can stewed
    tomatoes
1 (8-ounce) can tomato sauce
1 (4-ounce) can chopped green
    chilies

1 package taco seasoning
10 flour tortillas
2-3 packages Cheddar
    cheese

Simmer all ingredients, except tortillas and Cheddar cheese, for 15 minutes. Layer tortillas in 9x13-inch pan. Put ½ cup beef mixture over them. Add cheese, tortilla, beef, and end with cheese. Bake 25-30 minutes at 350°.

Titonka Centennial Cookbook

The word Iowa comes from the American Indian tribe of the same name. Iowa was part of the Louisiana Purchase. Its nickname is The Hawkeye State.

Cheese Spaghetti

1 pound ground beef	2 (15-ounce) jars spaghetti sauce
1/4 cup onion	12 ounces spaghetti

Brown meat and onion. Add sauce and simmer 10 minutes. Cook spaghetti until done and add to meat mixture.

CHEESE SAUCE:

6 tablespoons butter	1 (13-ounce) can evaporated milk
8 tablespoons flour	2 cups shredded Velveeta
1/2 teaspoon salt	4 tablespoons Parmesan
2/3 cup water	cheese

Melt butter; add flour and salt. Add water and milk to make a white sauce. Add Velveeta and stir until melted. Spread 1/2 of meat mixture in a 9x13-inch pan. Pour on Cheese Sauce. Top with other 1/2 of meat mixture. Sprinkle with Parmesan. Bake at 350° for one hour. Let stand 10 minutes and cut into squares.

The Berns Family Cookbook

Spaghetti Bake

1 1/2 - 2 pounds ground beef	2 teaspoons sugar
1 cup chopped onion	1 1/2 teaspoons oregano
1 clove garlic, minced	1 teaspoon salt
1 (28-ounce) can tomatoes cut up	1 teaspoon basil
1 (15-ounce) can tomato sauce	8 ounces spaghetti, broken cooked and drained
1 (4-ounce) can mushroom pieces, drained	1-2 cups shredded Mozzarella cheese
	Parmesan cheese

Brown beef; drain. Put in Dutch oven with the next 9 ingredients. Bring mixture to boiling. Boil gently uncovered 20-25 minutes, stirring occasionally. Stir in cooked spaghetti. Place half of mixture in 9x13-inch baking dish. Sprinkle with Mozzarella cheese. Top with remaining mixture. Sprinkle with Parmesan cheese. Bake 30 minutes at 375°. Serves 12. (May omit the Parmesan and use more Mozzarella.)

Special Recipes from our Hearts

All-At-Once Spaghetti
(Microwave)

1 tablespoon butter	2 (8-ounce) cans tomato
1 large onion, chopped	sauce
3/4 pound ground beef	1 1/2 cups water
1 1/2 teaspoons salt	1 heaping cup small spaghetti
1/4 teaspoon pepper	Grated cheese

Melt butter in an 8x12-inch ceramic baking dish in microwave oven. Add chopped onion. Cook 3 minutes on HIGH, stirring twice. Crumble in beef and cook 4 minutes on HIGH, stirring twice, until it loses its red color. Add salt, pepper, tomato sauce, and water. Cover with Saran Wrap and heat for 4 minutes on HIGH. Turn dish halfway through cooking time. Add spaghetti and cook all 10-12 minutes on HIGH, until spaghetti is tender. Turn dish and mix spaghetti every 3 minutes. Let set, covered, 10 minutes and serve with grated cheese.

Sharing our Best

Spaghetti Pie

6-ounces uncooked spaghetti	1/2 cup chopped onion
2 tablespoons butter	1 small jar spaghetti sauce
1/3 cup grated Parmesan	1 cup cottage cheese
cheese	1/2 cup shredded Mozzarella
2 eggs, well beaten	cheese
1 pound ground beef	

Cook spaghetti until tender; drain. Stir in butter, Parmesan cheese, and eggs. Form crust of spaghetti in 8x8-inch pan. Cook hamburger and onion and add spaghetti sauce. Top spaghetti crust with cottage cheese. Add meat mixture. Bake at 350° for 45 minutes. Top with Mozzarella cheese and return to oven until cheese melts.

Lutheran Church Women Cookbook

Ham Casserole

1 (12-ounce) package
 noodles
1 cup whole kernel corn,
 drained
½ cup chopped green
 pepper

⅓ cup milk
1 cup chopped cooked ham
¾ cup diced cheese
1 can cream of mushroom
 soup

Cook noodles according to package directions. Combine well with remaining ingredients. Turn into greased baking dish. Bake at 375° for 45 minutes.

Celebrating Iowa

Marv's Seafood Pasta

2 tablespoons olive oil
¾ cup chopped onion
¼ cup chopped green
 pepper
¼ cup chopped red pepper
2 large garlic cloves, minced
2 large ripe tomatoes, peeled
 and chopped

¼ cup chopped fresh
 parsley
½ teaspoon salt
½ teaspoon black pepper
1 pound shrimp or crab
16 ounces angel hair pasta
Freshly grated Parmesan
 cheese

Heat the oil in a large saucepan. Add the onion, peppers, and garlic and sauté until glossy. Add the tomatoes, seasonings, and seafood and cook over medium heat for 5 minutes. While the seafood mixture is simmering, cook the pasta according to directions on the package. Drain the pasta and transfer to a large platter. Ladle the seafood sauce over top of the pasta; sprinkle with freshly grated Parmesan cheese. Serves 4. 7 grams of fat per serving.

New Tastes of Iowa

Vegetable Pasta Pie

2²/₃ cups cooked spaghetti (small box)

1½ ounces grated Parmesan cheese

1 tablespoon plus 1 teaspoon margarine

1 teaspoon parsley

Combine the above 4 ingredients in a medium bowl; mix well. Press spaghetti mixture into the bottom and up the sides of a 9-inch pie pan to form a crust; set aside.

FILLING:

1 cup chopped zucchini

½ cup chopped green pepper

3 ounces onion, chopped

½ cup sliced mushrooms

2 tablespoons water

1 clove garlic, minced

1 cup tomato sauce

½ teaspoon oregano

½ teaspoon marjoram

½ cup tomato paste

¼ teaspoon salt

½ teaspoon basil

In a large nonstick skillet combine vegetables, water, and garlic; cook over medium heat, stirring often, about 10 minutes or until vegetables are tender-crisp. Stir in remaining ingredients and simmer 5 minutes. Place over spaghetti pie crust.

TOPPING:

2½ ounces grated Cheddar cheese

1⅓ cups cottage cheese

Combine Cheddar cheese and cottage cheese and top vegetable mixture. Bake at 350° for 30 minutes or until heated throughout and cheese is melted.

Enjoy

Fettuccine Alfredo

3 tablespoons butter

2 tablespoons flour

2 minced garlic cloves

Cayenne pepper, to taste (optional)

³/₄ cup Parmesan cheese

½ cup Romano cheese

1½ cups whole milk

In saucepan, heat butter until melted. Add flour to make roux. Add cayenne pepper, garlic, milk, and cheese. When mixture becomes thick and creamy, pour over hot noodles.

Titonka Centennial Cookbook

Cavatini

1½ pounds ground beef
1 chopped onion
1 chopped green pepper or celery
1 (4-ounce) can mushrooms
1 (15½-ounce) jar spaghetti sauce
1 (15½-ounce) jar pizza sauce
1 teaspoon brown sugar
3 kinds of macaroni (1½ - 2 cups dry)
8 ounces Mozzarella cheese

Brown and drain ground beef. Add onion, green pepper or celery, mushrooms, spaghetti sauce, pizza sauce, and brown sugar. Simmer while cooking macaroni. Add cooked macaroni and put in 9x13-inch pan. Sprinkle Mozzarella on top and bake at 350° for 40 minutes or until cheese is brown.

Home Cooking with the Cummer Family

Cavatelli

14 ounces large shell macaroni
1 pound hamburger
1 pound sausage
Salt and pepper to taste
1 large jar Ragu Sauce
½ jar Ortega Taco Sauce (whatever "hotness" you like)
1 can mushrooms, undrained
2 cups shredded Mozzarella cheese

Cook macaroni. Brown hamburger and sausage; drain and season with salt and pepper. Mix macaroni and meats and put in a 9x13-inch pan. Add sauce and mushrooms. When mixed, cover with cheese and bake at 400° for 30 minutes, until cheese melts.

First Christian Church Centennial Cookbook

Millie's Noodles

3 eggs
Pinch of salt
3 teaspoons water
Flour

Beat eggs, water, and salt together until well mixed. Keep adding flour until dough is real stiff. Roll flat pieces together the long way. Cut 2 rolls together in strips.

The Nading Family Cookbook

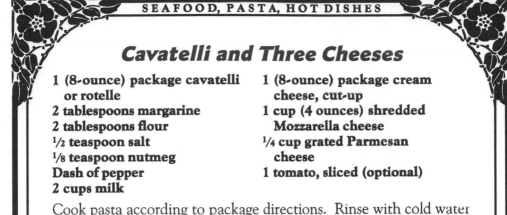

Cavatelli and Three Cheeses

1 (8-ounce) package cavatelli
  or rotelle
2 tablespoons margarine
2 tablespoons flour
1/2 teaspoon salt
1/8 teaspoon nutmeg
Dash of pepper
2 cups milk

1 (8-ounce) package cream
  cheese, cut-up
1 cup (4 ounces) shredded
  Mozzarella cheese
1/4 cup grated Parmesan
  cheese
1 tomato, sliced (optional)

Cook pasta according to package directions. Rinse with cold water and drain; set aside. In saucepan melt margarine. Stir in flour, salt, nutmeg, and pepper. Add milk all at once. Cook and stir over medium heat until mixture is thick and bubbly. Cook and stir for one minute more. Add cream cheese and Mozzarella, stirring until cheeses are melted. Gently fold cooked pasta into cheese sauce. Pour into greased 8x8x2-inch baking dish. Sprinkle with Parmesan cheese and bake at 350° for 30 minutes. Garnish with sliced tomato, if desired. Makes 6 side servings.

Variation: May use light cream cheese, low-fat Mozzarella cheese, and skim milk and they work fine.

Iowa Granges Celebrating 125 Years of Cooking

Skillet Tomato Mac 'n' Cheese

This blend of tomato-y goodness and a traditional, creamy macaroni-and-cheese casserole is something different yet still familiar—a new classic you'll want to enjoy often. I think you'll discover it appeals to the boy in every may.

1³/₄ cups (one 15-ounce can) Hunt's Chunky Tomato Sauce

1 (10³/₄-ounce) can Healthy Request Cream of Mushroom Soup

1 tablespoon dried onion flakes

¹/₂ cup (2.5-ounce jar) sliced mushrooms, drained

1¹/₂ cups (6 ounces) shredded reduced-fat Cheddar cheese

2 teaspoons dried parsley flakes

¹/₄ teaspoon black pepper

3 cups hot cooked elbow macaroni, rinsed and drained

In a large skillet, combine tomato sauce, mushroom soup, onion flakes, and mushrooms. Stir in Cheddar cheese, parsley flakes, and black pepper. Cook over medium heat, stirring often, until cheese melts. Add macaroni. Mix well to combine. Lower heat. Cover and simmer 10 minutes, stirring occasionally. Serves 6 (1 cup).

Hint: 2 cups uncooked macaroni usually cooks to about 3 cups.

Each serving equals:
Healthy Exchanges: 1¹/₃ vegetable; 1¹/₃ protein; 1 bread; ¹/₂ slider; 1 optional calorie.
213 calories; 5gm fat; 13gm protein; 29gm carbohydrate; 853mg sodium; 1gm fiber.
Diabetic: 1¹/₂ starch; 1 vegetable; 1 meat.

Cooking Healthy with a Man in Mind

Corn Noodle Casserole

1 large bag frozen noodles or 3-4 cups cooked noodles

1-2 (16-ounce) cans cream-style corn

³/₄ cup cubed Velveeta cheese

¹/₂ cup melted butter

Mix together and bake at 350° for 40 minutes. Buttered crackers can be put on top.

Generations of Good Cooking

Enchilada Casserole

1½ pounds ground beef
1 cup onion, chopped
1½ teaspoons cumin
2 cloves garlic
4 teaspoons chili powder
1½ teaspoons salt

½ teaspoon pepper
3 cups enchilada sauce
12 corn tortillas
1 pound Monterey Jack cheese
Sour cream

Cook ground beef and onions. Add the next 5 ingredients. Simmer 10 minutes. Pour half of sauce in a 9x13-inch baking dish, then layer 6 tortillas, half of meat mixture ahd half of cheese. Repeat for next layer, starting with sauce. Cover with foil and bake 40 minutes in a 375° oven. Remove foil; bake another 5 minutes. Serve with sour cream.

The Orient Volunteer Fire Department Cookbook

Rice, Corn, Celery Casserole

½ pound American or Cheddar cheese, grated
1 (10-ounce) package frozen corn or 2 cups freshly-cut from cob
2 cups cooked rice
1 cup chopped celery

2 tablespoons melted butter
½ teaspoon salt
⅛ teaspoon paprika
1 cup rich milk (can use whole milk)
2 tablespoons sliced onion (can be sautéed in butter first)

Combine all ingredients, reserving ½ cup cheese to add to the top during last 10 minutes of baking. Bake in casserole for 30 minutes at 350°. Serves 6-8.

Celebrating Iowa

The seven authentic German villages known as Amana Colonies were founded as a religious commune in the mid-1800s by a group from Germany. The people of the Amanas farmed in the European fashion—living in the village and going out to the fields to work, rather than living on separate farms.

Easy Brown Rice

1 stick butter or margarine
1 cup raw rice
2 (10½-ounce) cans beef
  consommé

¼ cup Parmesan cheese

Melt butter or margarine in casserole dish. Add raw rice. Pour 2 cans beef consommé over rice. Sprinkle with generous amount of Parmesan cheese on top. Bake 45 minutes at 350°. Check baking time; may need more moisture if baked longer.

Quasquicentennial / St. Olaf of Bode

He-Man Spanish Rice

1 pound ground beef
½ cup chopped onions
¼ cup chopped green
  peppers
1 teaspoon salt
⅛ teaspoon chili powder

Dash garlic salt
1 can tomato soup
1 can water
1 teaspoon Worcestershire
  sauce
⅓ cup uncooked rice

Brown meat; add remaining ingredients. Cover, cook until rice is tender. Stir often as rice will stick.

Community Centennial Cookbook

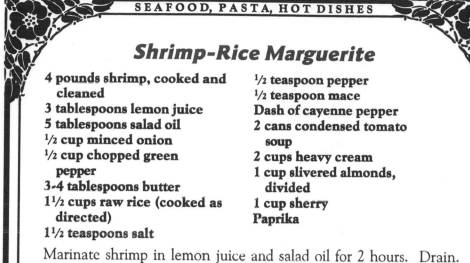

Shrimp-Rice Marguerite

4 pounds shrimp, cooked and cleaned
3 tablespoons lemon juice
5 tablespoons salad oil
1/2 cup minced onion
1/2 cup chopped green pepper
3-4 tablespoons butter
1 1/2 cups raw rice (cooked as directed)
1 1/2 teaspoons salt
1/2 teaspoon pepper
1/2 teaspoon mace
Dash of cayenne pepper
2 cans condensed tomato soup
2 cups heavy cream
1 cup slivered almonds, divided
1 cup sherry
Paprika

Marinate shrimp in lemon juice and salad oil for 2 hours. Drain. Sauté onion and green pepper in butter; add all ingredients except 1/4 cup almonds, few shrimp, and paprika. Mix well. Pour into greased cake pan or large casserole. Top with reserved shrimp, almonds, and sprinkle with paprika. Bake at 350° approximately 45 minutes (until bubbly).

Note: This dish is best if made and let stand overnight or 12 hours before baking, for flavors to blend.

Woodbine Public Library

Chicken and Wild Rice Casserole

1 whole chicken, cooked and deboned
1/2 teaspoon curry powder
1 1/2 teaspoons salt
1 medium onion, diced
1/2 cup diced celery
1 cup dry sherry wine (optional)
2 (6-ounce) packages long-grain and wild rice with seasoning
1 can cream of mushroom soup
1 cup sour cream
1 pound fresh mushrooms, or you may use 2 cans
1/4 cup butter

Cook chicken with curry powder, salt, onion, celery, and sherry. Retain broth for liquid in cooking rice; blend in soup (undiluted) and sour cream. Sauté mushrooms in butter and add to mixture; add chicken. Mix well. Bake, covered, one hour at 350°. Freezes well.

Woodbine Public Library

Broccoli Hot Dish

1 large package frozen chopped
  broccoli
1-2 cups quick rice (cooked)
1 large jar Cheez-Whiz or
  Cheddar cheese soup
1 can sliced water chestnuts
  (optional)

Chopped onion and celery
  (optional)
¼ cup milk
1 can cream of mushroom or
  chicken soup
Crushed potato chips or French
  fried onion rings

Mix all togehter in casserole dish and bake 30-40 minutes at 350°.
Cover with crushed potato chips or onions 15 minutes before done.

Variation 1: For Mexican dish, use jalapeño Cheez-Whiz, but be careful!! May add 2 cups grated cheese. Add ⅔ of it to the casserole; top with remaining.

Variation 2: Combine broccoli, 2 cups rice, onion, 8 ounces Cheez-Whiz and ½ of a half pint of half-and-half.

Country Cupboard Cookbook

Hash Brown Chicken Casserole

1 cooked chicken, boned and
  cut in bite-size pieces
1 (32-ounce) package hash
  brown potatoes
1 can cream of chicken soup
1 pound Cheddar cheese,
  shredded

1 pint sour cream
1 small onion, diced
Salt and pepper, to taste
1 stick margarine
2 cups crushed cornflakes

Mix together chicken and potatoes, soup, cheese, sour cream, onion, salt and pepper; place in a 9x13-inch baking pan. Melt margarine and mix with cornflake mixture. Bake at 350° for 1 - 1½ hours or until bubbly. Serves 12.

Celebrating Iowa

Cheesy Potatoes and Ham

2-3 large Idaho potatoes,
diced
1 can cream of chicken soup
1 cup milk

1 pound Velveeta cheese
¼ cup diced onion
2 cups diced ham

Add potatoes to pan of boiling water; cook until soft. In crockpot, mix soup, milk, cheese, and onion until texture is creamy and smooth. Crockpot should be on high temperature setting. Add cooked potatoes and ham. May serve immediately or may simmer in crockpot for several hours on low temperature setting.

Community Centennial Cookbook

Reuben Potato Casserole

1 (2-pound) bag frozen
hashbrowns
½ pound corned beef, thinly
sliced
1 (16-ounce) can sauerkraut,
drained

Swiss cheese
1000 Island Dressing
Caraway seed (optional)

Fry hashbrowns in skillet until done. Add corned beef. In a 9x13-inch baking dish place the sauerkraut in bottom. Put the potatoes and corned beef over this. Spread 1000 Island Dressing over this. Layer Swiss cheese over the top. Sprinkle with caraway seeds. Bake for 30 minutes at 350°, or microwave on HIGH for 5 minutes.

Generations of Good Cooking

Farmhouse Potatoes 'n' Ham

5-6 large russet potatoes (about
  2½ pounds), peeled and
  thinly sliced
¼ cup butter or margarine
3 tablespoons flour
1⅓ cups milk
2 teaspoons prepared mustard
⅓ cup sweet red onion, minced

1⅓ cups shredded Cheddar
  cheese, divided
1½ cups diced cooked ham
¼ teaspoon salt
⅛ teaspoon pepper
⅓ cup seasoned dry bread
  crumbs

Preheat oven to 350°. Arrange sliced potatoes in 2- to 2½-quart ob-long oven-safe casserole and set aside. Put butter in 4-cup glass measure or microwave-safe bowl. Microwave on HIGH about 45 seconds to melt. Blend in flour, milk, and mustard. Microwave on HIGH 3 minutes. Stir and add onion. Microwave on high until sauce thickens. Add one cup cheese and stir until melted. Fold in ham, salt, and pepper. Pour sauce over potatoes. Sprinkle with remaining ⅓ cup cheese and top with bread crumbs. Bake 50-60 minutes, until potatoes are tender. Makes 6-8 servings.

The Des Moines Register Cookbook

Iowa is tops in the production of oats, corn, popcorn, soybeans, hogs, beef cattle, poultry, and dairy products.

Poultry

The campus of Iowa State University. Ames.

Scalloped Chicken

GRAVY:

1 quart chicken broth without
    fat
1 can cream of mushroom
    soup
1½ teaspoons sage

2 tablespoons chopped onion
1 cup chopped celery
¾ cup chicken fat or butter
4 tablespoons flour or
    cornstarch

Bring gravy ingredients, all but flour, to a boil and thicken with flour or cornstarch.

1 quart cubed stewed
    chicken

1½ quarts toasted bread
    cubes or croutons

Put layer of chicken in bottom of greased 9x13-inch baking pan. Cover with bread cubes. Pour gravy evenly over top. Work gravy down to chicken layer with a fork. Bake until dressing is slightly browned, about 35 minutes at 350°.

Note: If you use flavored croutons, omit the sage in gravy.

Thompson Family Cookbook

French Onion Chicken Bake

One bite of this ultra-easy chicken dish will convince you that healthy food is indeed tasty food. Does it seem too easy to be good? Just smile, and accept all those compliments from your many fans.

2 cups thinly sliced onion
⅓ cup Kraft Fat Free French
    Dressing

16 ounces skinned and boned
    uncooked chicken breasts, cut
    into 4 pieces

Preheat oven to 350°. Arrange onion evenly in bottom of an 8x8-inch baking dish. Place French dressing in a small bowl. Coat chicken pieces in dressing. Arrange chicken evenly over onion. Drizzle any remaining dressing over chicken. Cover and bake 30 minutes. Uncover and continue baking an additional 10-15 minutes. For each serving, place a chicken piece on plate and evenly spoon onion and "sauce" over top. Serves 4.

Each serving equals:
Diabetic: 3 meat; 1 vegetable.
176 Cal; 4gm Fat; 25gm Prot; 10gm Carbo; 247gm Sod; 1gm Fiber.
Healthy Exchanges: 3 Prot; 1 vegetable; ¼ slider; 7 optional calories.

Diabetic's Healthy Exchanges Cookbook

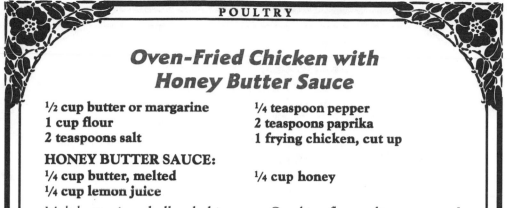

Oven-Fried Chicken with Honey Butter Sauce

¹/₂ cup butter or margarine
1 cup flour
2 teaspoons salt

¹/₄ teaspoon pepper
2 teaspoons paprika
1 frying chicken, cut up

HONEY BUTTER SAUCE:
¹/₄ cup butter, melted
¹/₄ cup lemon juice

¹/₄ cup honey

Melt butter in a shallow baking pan. Combine flour, salt, pepper, and paprika; dip chicken into flour mix and then in the butter, turning each piece. Arrange, skin-side down, in a single layer; bake at 400° for 30 minutes. Turn and pour Honey Butter Sauce over all; bake another 30 minutes at 350° until chicken is tender. To make sauce, melt butter in a saucepan; blend in honey and lemon juice. Do not boil.

Neighboring on the Air

Chicken Dijon

4 skinless, split chicken
 breasts
Salt
2 tablespoons butter or
 margarine
1 tablespoon flour

1 cup milk
¹/₄ cup water
2 tablespoons Dijon mustard
1 tablespoon instant minced
 onion
Chopped parsley

Sprinkle chicken with salt. Heat butter in skillet; brown chicken, meat-side-down, about 4 minutes. Remove chicken from skillet. Stir in flour until smooth; blend in milk, water, mustard, onion, and ¹/₄ teaspoon salt. Heat to boiling, stirring. Return chicken to skillet; spoon sauce over chicken. Reduce heat, cover, and simmer for 12-15 minutes, or until chicken is fork-tender. Sprinkle with chopped parsley and serve with rice.

St. Joseph's Parish Cookbook

Chicken L'Orange

3 chicken breasts
Flour, salt, pepper to dredge
2 tablespoons butter

1 onion, chopped
½ cup water
1½ cups orange juice

Dredge chicken breasts that are deboned and cut in half, in flour, salt, and pepper. Brown in butter in skillet and place in casserole. Sauté onion over medium heat in remaining fat. When the onion is clear, but not brown, pour water in skillet. Pour orange juice over the chicken. Cover and place in a 300° oven and bake 1½ hours. Serve over rice if you prefer, or just as is.

Teresa's Heavenly Cakes and Treasures

Fresh Herb Grilled Chicken

⅓ cup lemon juice
¼ cup oil
2 teaspoons fresh or ½
   teaspoon dried rosemary
½ teaspoon thyme leaves

1 garlic clove, minced
⅛ teaspoon pepper
4 whole chicken breasts,
   skinned, halved, pierced with
   fork

In small bowl, combine ingredients (except chicken); pour over chicken in a 12x8-inch baking dish. Cover and refrigerate for 6-8 hours. Grill 4-6 inches from medium coals for 20-25 minutes.

A Taste of Grace

Holland Cheese Chicken Rolls

4 chicken breasts, skinned and
   boned
¼ pound Edam or Gouda
   cheese, cut into 8 wedges

Flour
2 eggs, beaten
Fine dry bread crumbs
Oil for deep-frying

Cut each chicken breast in half and pound to about ¼-inch thickness. Place wedges of cheese on each half and roll, tucking in the edges and securing with a toothpick. Coat the roll with flour, then dip into beaten egg. Roll in bread crumbs and allow to dry for 10-15 minutes. Heat oil to 325° and fry rolls for about 10 minutes, or until golden. Serves 4.

Dandy Dutch Recipes

Baked Chicken Breast

8 large chicken breast halves
1 package chipped beef
8 slices bacon

1 pint sour cream
2 cans cream of mushroom
soup

Skin and debone chicken. Break up chipped beef in bottom of an 8x12-inch greased baking dish. Wrap bacon around chicken breast. Place on chipped beef. Mix sour cream and soup. Pour over chicken. Bake, uncovered, at 275° for 3 hours.

New Beginnings Cookbook

Crispy Sesame Chicken

1¼ cups cornflake crumbs
¼ cup sesame seeds
¾ teaspoon paprika
¼ teaspoon salt
¼ teaspoon ground ginger
½ cup plain nonfat yogurt

2 tablespoons honey
8 skinned chicken breast
halves
Vegetable cooking spray
2 tablespoons melted
margarine

Combine first 5 ingredients in a large zip-lock plastic bag; set aside. Combine yogurt and honey in a shallow dish; stir well. Coat chicken pieces with yogurt mixture. Place chicken in zip-lock bag and shake to coat. Remove chicken from bag and place on baking sheet coated with vegetable spray. Drizzle with melted margarine. Bake at 400° for 45 minutes or until done.

Applause Applause

Lemon Asparagus Chicken

1 tablespoon oil
4 skinless, boneless chicken
breast halves
1 can cream of asparagus
soup

¼ cup milk
1 tablespoon lemon juice
⅛ teaspoon pepper

Brown chicken in oil on both sides. Remove and place in casserole. After spooning off fat, combine in skillet: soup, milk, lemon juice, and pepper. Heat to boiling. Pour over chicken; cover, and bake 45 minutes to one hour at 325°.

Alta United Methodist Church Cookbook

Chicken Broccoli Vegetable Sauté

2 tablespoons margarine,
    divided
4 skinless, boneless chicken
    breast, halves (about 1
    pound)
1 cup cut-up broccoli

½ cup thinly sliced carrots
1 cup sliced mushrooms
1 can cream of broccoli soup
⅓ cup milk
⅛ teaspoon pepper

In skillet over medium heat, in one tablespoon hot margarine, cook chicken 10 minutes or until browned on both sides. Remove chicken; keep warm.

In same skillet, in remaining margarine, cook broccoli, carrots, and mushrooms 5 minutes, stirring often. Stir in soup, milk, and pepper. Heat to boiling. Return chicken to skillet. Reduce heat to low, simmer 5 minutes or until chicken is fork tender. Makes 4 servings. Good served with rice.

Home Cooking with the Cummer Family

Chicken Cordon Bleu

12 ounces breast of chicken
    pounded out to make 8 filets
1 cup bread crumbs
⅛ teaspoon basil
⅛ teaspoon garlic
⅛ teaspoon pepper
¼ teaspoon salt
½ stick butter
2 tablespoons flour

1 cup milk
1 (8-ounce) can mushrooms
⅛ teaspoon pepper
⅛ teaspoon thyme
8 ounces ham (1-2-ounce slice
    per serving)
8 ounces Swiss cheese
    (1-2-ounce slice per serving)

Blend together bread crumbs, basil, garlic, pepper, and salt and toast in oven at 350° for 6 minutes. Dip chicken in milk, then dip in bread mix; cover completely. Place chicken in pan and fry to light brown. Place one slice ham and one slice cheese between 2 pieces of chicken; do same with rest of ham, cheese, and chicken to form 4 servings. Place chicken in pan and cook at 350° for 20-30 minutes. Heat butter until melted, stir in flour, add milk and heat. Stir until thickened. Add additional flour as necessary to thicken. Add mushrooms, pepper, and thyme; mix and heat until warm. When chicken is done, pour sauce over it and serve. Serves 4.

Sharing Traditions from People You Know

Chicken a la King

¼ cup onion, chopped
½ cup red bell pepper, chopped
½ cup green bell pepper, chopped
2 tablespoons butter or margarine

1 (10-ounce) can cream of chicken soup
⅓ - ½ cup milk
1½ cups cooked chicken or turkey, cubed
2 tablespoons pimento, diced
Dash of pepper

Cook onion and pepper in melted butter or margarine until tender. Blend in soup and milk; add chicken, pimento and pepper. Heat slowly; stir often. Serve over hot biscuits or toast. Yield: 3-4 servings.

Cookin' for Miracles

Chicken Enchiladas

2 cans cream of chicken soup
1 (8-ounce) carton sour cream
1 can diced green chilies
8 ounces shredded Cheddar cheese

1 (6-ounce) can sliced black olives
3 chicken breasts (skinned, deboned, cooked and diced)
8 flour tortillas

Combine soup, sour cream, chilies, ½ the cheese, and ½ the olives. Divide mixture into 2 halves. Add chicken to one bowl, setting other bowl aside. Use chicken mixture to fill tortillas (either fold them as enchiladas or roll them up like crepes) and put in greased 9x13-inch pan, seam-side-down. Pour remaining soup mixture over all. Top with remaining cheese and olives. Bake at 350° for 30-40 minutes. Serves 6.

Iowa Granges Celebrating 125 Years of Cooking

Chicken Casserole

2-3 pounds chicken
1 (16-ounce) package tortilla chips
1 can nacho cheese soup
1 can Cheddar cheese soup
1 medium jar picante sauce

1 medium brick Mozzarella cheese, shredded
3 small cans mushrooms
1 can pitted olives, sliced
1 medium brick Cheddar cheese, shredded

Skin chicken and boil until done. Let cool and cut into bite-size pieces. Grease a 9x13-inch casserole pan. Crumble enough tortilla chips to cover bottom of pan, then coarsely layer chicken on top. Mix soups and picante sauce and dot over chicken, using ½ of mixture. Cover with Mozzarella cheese. Cover with Cheddar cheese. Cover with crumbled tortilla chips. Bake at 375° until bubbly, about 45 minutes to one hour. Serve with sour cream and sauce, if desired.

The Orient Volunteer Fire Department Cookbook

Tea Room Chicken

1 (6-ounce) package wild rice mix, cooked
1 (16-ounce) package frozen chopped broccoli
3 cups cooked diced chicken
1 cup shredded Velveeta cheese
1 cup fresh mushrooms, sliced

½ cup mayonnaise
1 can cream of mushroom soup
¼ teaspoon dry mustard
¼ teaspoon curry powder
Parmesan cheese
½ cup cracker crumbs
1 tablespoon butter

In a 9x13-inch pan, layer rice, broccoli, chicken, cheese, and mushrooms. In a separate bowl combine mayonnaise, soup, mustard, and curry powder. Pour over chicken mixture. Sprinkle with Parmesan cheese. Sauté crackers with butter and sprinkle over cheese. Bake at 350° for 30-45 minutes or until bubbly.

Madison County Cookbook

Chicken Casserole

1 (7-ounce) package macaroni (don't cook)
1 chicken, cooked, boned and cut into pieces
2 cans cream of chicken soup
2 cups milk
1/2 pound Velveeta cheese, cubed
1 can mushroom pieces
1 small onion, chopped fine
2 hard boiled eggs, chopped fine (optional)
Crushed potato chips

Mix all ingredients, except potato chips, and pour into a greased 9x13-inch pan. Cover and refrigerate overnight. Use crushed chips as topping. Bake covered for one hour at 350°.

Note: The above is the "basic" recipe. For the "Funeral Casserole" double the macaroni, chicken, soup, milk, and cheese.

First Christian Church Centennial Cookbook

Chicken Essex

2 cups diced, cooked chicken
2 (10½-ounce) cans cream of mushroom soup
1 (13-ounce) can chicken broth or broth from cooked chicken
1 (2-ounce) jar pimiento, diced
1/2 pound grated Cheddar cheese
2 cups elbow macaroni, uncooked
1 soup can milk
1 small onion, finely chopped
1/2 green pepper, finely chopped
1 (5-ounce) can water chestnuts, thinly sliced
1/2 teaspoon salt

Combine all together in order given. Mix well and pour into a well-greased 9x13-inch pan. Cover with foil and refrigerate overnight. When ready to bake, remove foil and bake in a 350° oven for one hour. Equally good made with tuna, turkey, or ham.

Lutheran Church Women Cookbook

Margery's Chicken 'n' Niffles

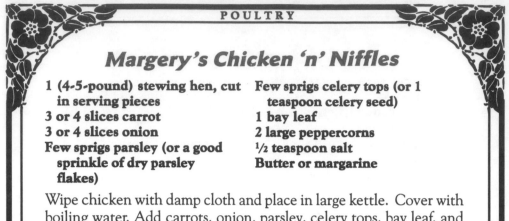

1 (4-5-pound) stewing hen, cut in serving pieces
3 or 4 slices carrot
3 or 4 slices onion
Few sprigs parsley (or a good sprinkle of dry parsley flakes)
Few sprigs celery tops (or 1 teaspoon celery seed)
1 bay leaf
2 large peppercorns
½ teaspoon salt
Butter or margarine

Wipe chicken with damp cloth and place in large kettle. Cover with boiling water. Add carrots, onion, parsley, celery tops, bay leaf, and peppercorns. Cover and simmer for 2-3 hours or until meat begins to loosen from the bone. Add salt during the last hour of cooking. When tender, remove chicken from broth, place on platter, brush with butter or margarine, and keep hot in oven at 300°.

NIFFLES:

1 cup biscuit mix
½ teaspoon salt
2 eggs
¼ cup cold water

Combine biscuit mix and salt in bowl. Make a well in center and add whole eggs. Pour in water and work with fork to make a soft batter, adding more water if necessary. Drop pieces of batter, about a teaspoon at a time, into the simmering chicken broth. Cook for 5 minutes. Take niffles from broth with a slotted spoon and place in a serving dish. You can't make them all at once, but probably half of the batter can be cooked at one time. Thicken the broth with a little flour and serve from a gravy boat.

Neighboring on the Air

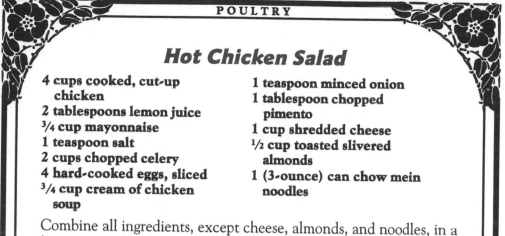

Hot Chicken Salad

4 cups cooked, cut-up
  chicken
2 tablespoons lemon juice
³/₄ cup mayonnaise
1 teaspoon salt
2 cups chopped celery
4 hard-cooked eggs, sliced
³/₄ cup cream of chicken
  soup

1 teaspoon minced onion
1 tablespoon chopped
  pimento
1 cup shredded cheese
¹/₂ cup toasted slivered
  almonds
1 (3-ounce) can chow mein
  noodles

Combine all ingredients, except cheese, almonds, and noodles, in a large mixing bowl. Pour into a 9x13x2-inch pan. Top with cheese, almonds, and noodles. Refrigerate, covered, overnight. Bake at 350° for 30-35 minutes or until lightly browned and bubbly. Yields 8 large servings.

T.W. and Anna Elliott Family Receipts

Iowa's Grilled Turkey Tenderloin

State Fair recipe from Iowa Turkey Foundation.

1 pound turkey tenderloins
  (³/₄ - 1-inch thick)
¹/₄ cup Kikkoman soy sauce
¹/₄ cup vegetable oil
¹/₄ cup dry sherry
2 tablespoons lemon juice

2 tablespoons dehydrated
  onion
¹/₄ teaspoon ginger
Dash of black pepper
Dash of garlic powder

Blend all ingredients together in shallow pan for marinade with turkey tenderloins or steaks. Add turkey, turning to coat both sides. Cover and marinate in refrigerator several hours, turning occasionally. Grill over hot coals, 6-8 minutes per side depending on thickness.

Turkey steaks are done when there is no pink in center of meat. Do not overcook. Serves 3-4. Serve on fresh buns.

SEP Junior Women's Club 25th Anniversary Cookbook

Glazed Turkey Breast

This is the easiest way I know to have beautiful slices of moist turkey breast for a delicious low-fat main course.

1 (6 to 7-pound) turkey
  breast
1/3 cup honey

1 tablespoon dry mustard
1 (6 1/2-ounce) can frozen apple
  juice (undiluted)

Preheat the oven to 325°. Remove the skin from the turkey breast and insert a meat thermometer into the center of the breast. Combine the honey, dry mustard, and apple juice. Place the turkey breast in a large roasting pan. Baste the entire breast generously with the apple juice mixture. Cover the turkey breast and bake for one hour. Uncover and bake for another hour or until meat thermometer registers 180°. Baste frequently after removing cover from turkey. Remove from the oven and allow to cool for 15-20 minutes before slicing. Serves 8-10. 4 grams of fat per serving.

New Tastes of Iowa

Crock-Pot Dressing

1 cup butter
3 cups onion, chopped
3 cups celery, chopped
3/8 cup parsley sprigs,
  chopped
3 (4-ounce) cans sliced
  mushrooms
18-20 cups dry bread cubes
2 1/4 teaspoons sage

2 1/4 teaspoons salt
1 1/2 teaspoons thyme
3/4 teaspoon pepper
3/4 teaspoon marjoram
1 1/2 teaspoons poultry seasoning
4 1/2 - 6 cups chicken broth
3 well-beaten eggs

Melt butter in a skillet and sauté onion, celery, parsley, and mushrooms. Pour over bread cubes in a large bowl. Add all seasonings and mix well. Pour in enough broth to moisten. Add beaten eggs and mix together well. Pack lightly into a 6-quart slow-cooker. Cover and cook on HIGH for 45 minutes. Reduce to low for 4-8 hours.

Visitation Parish Cookbook

Turkey and Spinach Burgers

The spinach, herbs, and apricot preserves add a special flavor to these turkey burgers. They are delicious topped with grilled onions or a combination of fresh pineapple slices, onion, and green pepper slices.

1½ pounds ground turkey	**¼ cup chopped parsley**
1½ cups packed fresh	**2 tablespoons apricot**
spinach, washed, dried, and	**preserves**
cut into small pieces	**1 teaspoon freshly ground**
1 cup minced onions	**pepper**
½ cup whole wheat bread	**¼ teaspoon salt**
crumbs	

Combine turkey, spinach, onions, bread crumbs, parsley, apricot preserves, pepper, and salt in a large bowl and blend well. Cover bowl and refrigerate several hours.

Form turkey mixture into 6 patties. Over hot coals, place burgers on a grilling grid coated with nonstick vegetable spray. Cover grill and cook 9-11 minutes, turning burgers every 3 minutes.

Per serving: 255 Cal; 22.1g Prot; 13.6g Carbo; 12.0g Fat; 42% Cal. from Fat; 1.1g Fiber; 230mg Sod; 58mg Chol.

The Lowfat Grill

Quail Stuffed with Oysters

1 crushed saltine per each	**Worcestershire sauce**
quail	**Quail**
4 oysters per each quail	**Melted butter**
Salt and pepper	**Sprigs of parsley**

Preheat oven to 350°. Roll saltines into fine crumbs. Season oysters with salt, pepper, and Worcestershire sauce. Dip oysters into cracker crumbs and place 4 oysters (or as many as possible) into each quail. Score quail and brush with melted butter. Bake 1½ - 2 hours at 350°. Garnish with parsley and serve.

Wildlife Harvest Game Cookbook

Stuffed Grouse or Partridge

1 grouse or partridge	1 cup cooked rice
½ teaspoon poultry seasoning	2 tablespoons chopped onion
	¼ cup chopped mushrooms
1 tablespoon chopped green pepper	Salt and pepper to taste
	2 slices of bacon

Soak bird in salted water (2 tablespoons salt to 1 quart water) for one hour. Dry thoroughly. Combine remaining ingredients except bacon. Stuff bird; close opening with a skewer. Wrap bird with bacon, place in covered roaster and bake at 375° for one hour. Remove cover toward end of roasting period to crisp bacon and brown bird.

Wildlife Harvest Game Cookbook

 Winterset is the birthplace of Marion Robert Morrison, better known as "the Duke," John Wayne.

Meats

Birthplace of a legend—John Wayne. Winterset.

Iowa Chops
(Stuffed)

½ cup whole kernel corn
½ cup bread crumbs
Pinch of salt and pepper
¾ tablespoon parsley
Pinch of sage
½ tablespoon chopped
  onion

½ cup diced apple
1 tablespoon milk (whole)
2 Iowa pork chops (thick
  cuts)

In a bowl combine ingredients until well mixed. Cut a slit in the side of chop and stuff with the mixture. In a separate bowl, combine the basting ingredients and blend until smooth. In frying pan, brown the stuffed chops and then bake in a 350° oven for about one hour, basting the chops often with sauce.

BASTING SAUCE:
¼ cup honey
¼ cup mustard
¼ teaspoon rosemary leaves

½ teaspoon salt
Pinch of pepper

Spanning the Bridge of Time

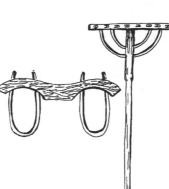

Stuffed Glazed Chops

The stuffing adds a tenderness and flavor which enhances this delicious entrée.

APPLE STUFFING:

½ cup celery, diced
¼ cup (2 ounces) melted
  margarine
3 cups croutons

½ cup apple juice
⅓ cup raisins
⅓ pound apples, peeled, cored
  and sliced

APPLE GLAZE:

1/3 cup brown sugar

¼ cup apple juice

STUFFED CHOPS:

4 (13-ounce) center-cut rib chops

Combine all stuffing ingredients together and toss. In saucepan, combine Glaze ingredients. Bring to a boil, reduce heat, and simmer ½ hour. Preheat oven to 350°. Split chops in half by making one cut from meat-side to bone. Leave connected at bone. Stuff each chop with approximately ¾ cup Apple Stuffing. Bake approximately 45 minutes to internal temperature of 165°. Brush with Glaze last 15 minutes. May be covered with foil, if browning too fast.

The Machine Shed Farm Style Cooking

Mary Ellen Wall's Stuffed Iowa Chops

1 tablespoon butter
¼ cup chopped celery
¼ cup chopped onion
2 cups coarse bread crumbs
1 egg, beaten
¼ teaspoon salt
½ teaspoon sage

½ cup chicken giblets, ground
  or chopped (optional)
Enough milk or chicken broth
  to moisten dressing
4 Iowa chops, 1¼ - 1½
  inches thick, with pockets cut

Preheat oven to 325°. In a small skillet, melt butter. Add celery and onion and sauté until tender. Mix with bread crumbs, egg, salt, sage, and giblets and moisten with milk or broth. Fill pockets of chops and fasten together with toothpicks. Sear chops in a hot skillet with a little fat, then place them in a baking dish. (Remaining dressing can be added around the sides of the chops.) Bake one hour covered, then 20 minutes uncovered. Makes 4 servings.

A Cook's Tour of Iowa

Pork Chops a' la McKee

Tender chops with a wonderful sauce.

4 butterfly pork chops
2 tablespoons flour, seasoned
  with salt and pepper
1 tablespoon oil
1 lemon, sliced

1 medium onion, sliced
1 medium green pepper,
  sliced
2 cups tomato juice

Make 3 small slashes around edge of each pork chop to keep from curling. Dust with seasoned flour and brown lightly in moderately hot oil. Place meat in baking dish. Arrange one slice each of lemon, onion, and green pepper on each chop. Tuck any remaining slices around the sides. Pour tomato juice over the top, cover and bake at 325° for one hour. Serves 4.

Recipes from Iowa with Love

Pork Chops with Dressing

4 pork chops, browned
6 slices bread, cubed
1/4 cup onion, minced
1 egg, beaten
1/4 cup butter, melted
3/4 cup broth or water

1/2 teaspoon poultry
  seasoning
3/4 cup celery, diced fine
1 can cream of mushroom
  soup
1/2 can milk

Brown pork chops and place in greased pan. Mix all other ingredients except soup and milk and place on top of chops. Combine soup and milk and pour over dressing. Bake at 325° for 1 hour 30 minutes. Yields 4 servings.

Marcus, Iowa, Quasquicentennial Cookbook

Pork Chop Corn Bake

4 pork chops
1 tablespoon shortening
3/4 teaspoon salt
1/8 teaspoon pepper
1 (16-ounce) can whole-
  kernel corn, drained
Milk
3/4 cup coarse cracker
  crumbs

1 tablespoon prepared
  mustard
1 egg, slightly beaten
2 tablespoons sugar
1 tablespoon instant minced
  onion

Brown pork chops in melted shortening in heavy skillet over low heat. Sprinkle with salt and pepper. Drain liquid from corn, measure, and add enough milk to make one cup. Stir corn and liquid together with remaining ingredients. Spoon into greased 1½-2-quart casserole and place browned pork chops on top of corn mixture. Bake at 350° for 50-60 minutes.

Neighboring on the Air

Pork Chop 'n' Potato Bake

6 pork chops
Vegetable oil
Seasoned salt (may use plain
  salt)
1 can cream of celery soup
1/2 cup milk
1/2 cup sour cream

1/4 teaspoon black pepper
1 (24-ounce) package O'Brien
  or hash brown potatoes
  (thawed)
1 cup (4 ounces) shredded
  Cheddar cheese
1 can French fried onions

Brown pork chops in lightly greased skillet. Sprinkle with salt; set aside. Combine soup, milk, sour cream, pepper, and ½ teaspoon salt. Stir into potatoes. Last add ½ cup cheese, ½ can French fried onions. Spoon mixture into a 9x13-inch pan. Arrange pork chops over potatoes. Bake covered at 350° for 40 minutes. Top with remaining cheese and onions. Uncover, bake 5 minutes longer. Makes 6 servings.

Zion Lutheran Church Cookbook

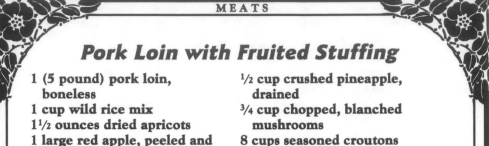

Pork Loin with Fruited Stuffing

1 (5 pound) pork loin, boneless	½ cup crushed pineapple, drained
1 cup wild rice mix	¾ cup chopped, blanched mushrooms
1½ ounces dried apricots	
1 large red apple, peeled and finely chopped	8 cups seasoned croutons
	8 ounces chicken broth

Place pork loin in large pan, fat-side-up and slice almost through lengthwise. Prepare rice according to package directions. Combine with remaining ingredients, adding chicken broth to moisten. Fill cavity of pork loin with stuffing and cover with foil. Bake covered in a 350° oven for 1½ hours, removing foil last 20 minutes to brown meat. Meat thermometer should register 155°-160° when done. Slice into 12 servings and top with Glaze. Serves 12.

GLAZE:

2 tablespoons margarine	¼ teaspoon dried thyme leaves
2 tablespoons flour	⅛ teaspoon cracked black pepper
1 tablespoon onion	
1 tablespoon dried minced parsley	10 ounces chicken broth
	¼ cup dry white wine

Sauté margarine, flour, and onion until lightly browned. Add remaining ingredients and simmer until thickened.

Sharing Traditions from People You Know

Stuffed Pork Loin

1 (2-4-pound) boneless pork loin

Butterfly the boneless pork loin and lay out flat. Pile Sage Dressing in center and roll up, tie, season with salt, pepper, sage, and garlic salt. Roast in preheated oven at 325° for 1½ hours to internal temperature of 160°. Let stand to cool 15 minutes, slice and serve. Any unused stuffing may be placed in baking dish and baked (cover or not) with pork roast.

SAGE DRESSING:

1 cup celery, diced	½ cup butter, melted
½ cup onion, diced	1 pint chicken stock
1 pound bread crumbs	1 tablespoon sage

The Machine Shed Farm Style Cooking

Pork Loin Roulade

4 boneless center pork loin slices, about 1 pound
1/2 red bell pepper, cut into strips
1/2 green pepper, cut into strips
1 tablespoon cooking oil
2/3 cup orange juice
2/3 cup bottled barbecue sauce
1 tablespoon Dijon mustard

Place cutlets between 2 pieces of clear plastic wrap. Pound with a mallet to about 1/4-inch thickness. Place several red and green pepper strips crosswise on each pork portion; roll up jellyroll style. Secure rolls with wooden toothpicks. In a large skillet, brown the pork rolls in hot cooking oil. Drain fat from pan. Combine remaining ingredients and add to skillet. Bring mixture to boiling; reduce heat. Cover and simmer 10-12 minutes or until pork is tender. Remove toothpicks. Serves 4.

License to Cook Iowa Style

Indonesian Pork Tenderloin

The fabulous balance of the kecap manis (sweet soy sauce) and honey with the garlic and crushed red pepper in this marinade elevates pork tenderloin to a gourmet experience. The marinade would also enhance the flavor of lamb or chicken.

MARINADE:

1/4 cup each honey mustard and kecap manis (sweet soy sauce)
1 tablespoon rice vinegar
2 large cloves garlic, minced
1/8 teaspoon crushed red pepper
1 pork tenderloin (1 1/2 pounds)

Combine honey mustard, kecap manis, rice vinegar, garlic, and red pepper in a nonmetal dish (or a 1-gallon reclosable plastic bag). Add pork tenderloin and turn to coat all over. Cover dish and refrigerate several hours or overnight.

Prepare a grill with a drip pan in the center of the lower grate and place an equal number of briquettes on both sides of pan. When coals are hot, place pork (reserve marinade) directly over drip pan and cook, covered, 20-25 minutes, or until a meat thermometer registers 150° - 155°, turning pork occasionally and brushing with reserved marinade the last 10 minutes of cooking time. Allow pork to sit for 5 minutes before carving it into thin slices.

Per serving: 234 calories; 33.5g protein; 14.0g carbohydrates; 5.8g fat; 22.4% calories from fat; 0.0g fiber; 427mg sodium; 107mg cholesterol

The Lowfat Grill

Fruited Roast Pork

1 (3-pound) pork roast
1 cup red cooking wine
1 cup cranberries
1/2 cup cranberry juice or
   cocktail

1/2 cup honey
1 teaspoon dried mustard
1/2 cup apricot preserves
1/2 teaspoon pepper

Mix all ingredients and "dump" over meat. Roast, covered, at 350°
until meat thermometer registers done (180° - 185°), about 2½ hours.

From the Cozy Kitchens of Long Grove

Harvest Barbecued Pork Roast

1 (4-5-pound) pork roast
3/4 cup barbecue sauce

1 (10-ounce) jar pure apple
   jelly

Roast meat approximately 3 hours. Heat sauce and jelly. Stir to
blend well. Baste meat with half of the sauce during last half hour of
roasting time. Serve remaining sauce with sliced meat. Takes 2½ -
3 hours at 325°. Serves 8-10.

Cook of the Week Cookbook

Pork Chop Casserole

6 pork chops
Salt and pepper to taste
1 tablespoon butter
6-8 potatoes, peeled and
   sliced

6 slices cheese
1 can cream of celery soup
1¼ cups milk

Trim fat off chops; salt and pepper and brown in one tablespoon
butter. Slice ½ of potatoes in bottom of small roasting pan. Top
with cheese slices; add rest of the sliced potatoes. Top with the
browned chops. In the same fry pan that you browned chops, add
the soup and milk; heat to boiling. Pour over the chops. Bake,
covered, at 350° for about one hour.

Fontanelle Good Samaritan Center
Commemorative Cookbook

Zucchini Pork Dish

1 pound ground pork	6 (5-inch) long zucchini
1/2 teaspoon garlic salt	1/4 cup fine dry bread
3 tablespoons grated Parmesan	crumbs
cheese	Salt and pepper
1 cup sour cream	6 ounces Mozzarella cheese

Put pork in frying pan over medium heat. Cook pork, stirring until pink color is gone. Drain. Stir in garlic salt, 2 tablespoons Parmesan cheese and sour cream. Set aside. Cut zucchini into slices and coat with bread crumbs mixed with salt and pepper. Grease 2-quart shallow baking dish and place half of zucchini slices in bottom of dish. Spoon pork over top and cover with remaining zucchini slices. Bake covered at 350° for 35 minutes. Remove and place Mozzarella cheese slices on top and put remaining Parmesan cheese on top. Place back in oven and bake uncovered 10 minutes longer.

Generations of Good Cooking

Sweet Ham Loaf

2 pounds ground smoked	1 cup milk
ham	1 cup bread or cracker
1 1/2 pounds ground pork	crumbs
2 beaten eggs	1 teaspoon baking powder

Mix ingredients together. Bake in 350° oven. When starts to brown, baste with the glaze.

GLAZE:

1 1/2 cups brown sugar	1 tablespoon ground mustard
1/2 cup vinegar	1/2 cup water

Cook above ingredients for 5 minutes. Pour over meat and baste occasionally. Bake for 2 hours.

Our Savior's Kvindherred Lutheran Church

Ham Balls

1 pound ground beef (or
  pork)
1 pound ground ham
1 egg
1 cup graham cracker
  crumbs

½ cup milk
1 can condensed tomato soup
1 tablespoon dry mustard
1 cup brown sugar

Mix the beef and ham, egg, crumbs, and milk. Shape into walnut-size balls. Put in a 9x13-inch baking dish. Combine remaining ingredients and pour over ham balls. Bake one hour at 350°, basting at least twice.

Fontanelle Good Samaritan Center
Commemorative Cookbook

Hot Ham Buns

Poppy seeds give them a special flavor; try to use rye buns.

¼ cup soft butter or
  margarine
2 tablespoons prepared
  horseradish mustard
2 teaspoons poppy seed
2 tablespoons finely chopped
  onion

4 rye hamburger buns, split
4 thin slices boiled ham (can use
  baked)
4 slices Swiss cheese

Mix butter, mustard, poppy seed, and onion; spread generously on both cut surfaces of buns. Tuck a slice of ham and cheese in each bun. Arrange on baking sheet. Do not wrap in foil. Bake at 350° for about 15 minutes or until sandwiches are hot. Makes 4 sandwiches.

Note: Do not wrap in foil. Baking the sandwiches unwrapped results in a deliciously crisp outside with a tasty filling.

Singing in the Kitchen

BBQ Ribs

2 tablespoons liquid smoke
1 cup catsup
2 tablespoons Worcestershire
  sauce
1/4 cup vinegar (wine vinegar is
  best)
1 teaspoon salt
1 teaspoon chili powder

1 cup water
1/2 teaspoon celery seed
1/4 teaspoon pepper
1/2 cup brown sugar, firmly
  packed
4 pounds lean spareribs,
  parboiled

Stir all sauce ingredients together. Pour over ribs and bake for 2½ hours at 325°.

Spitfire Anniversary Cookbook

Barbecued Beef Sandwiches

1 cup onion, chopped
1 cup water
1 cup ketchup
1/2 cup brown sugar
1 teaspoon Worcestershire
  sauce

1 teaspoon horseradish
1/2 teaspoon salt
1/2 teaspoon pepper
1/2 teaspoon chili powder
5-6 cups sliced roast beef

Combine all but beef and simmer until onions are tender. Add sliced roast beef to sauce. Simmer a little longer.

Marcus, Iowa, Quasquicentennial Cookbook

Barbecued Brisket

1 (3-4-pound) brisket
1 onion
1 bay leaf

Water to cover
Barbecue sauce

Put the brisket in a roaster along with the onion and bay leaf. Cover with water and bring to a boil. Salt and pepper lightly and cook until meat is half done, one hour or so. Take brisket out of roaster, place onto a cutting board and let stand 30 minutes. Then slice. Cover the bottom of a baking dish with barbecue sauce and put sliced meat on top. Cover the sliced brisket with barbecue sauce and cover with aluminum foil. Bake 3/4 - 1 hour. If meat seems a little dry, just add more barbecue sauce. You can use any good barbecue sauce (like K.C. Masterpiece). It freezes well.

T.W. and Anna Elliott Family Receipts

Memorial Day Roast

1 (5-7-pound) beef roast (use a good cut of boneless meat)
1 can cream of mushroom soup
Pepper
1 envelope Lipton Dry Onion Soup Mix
2 cups water

Have meat cut about 2½ inches thick. Put on rack (flat one preferred) in roaster. Spread cream of mushroom soup evenly on top of meat. Sprinkle with black pepper. Sprinkle with onion soup mix. Pour water in roaster, not over meat. Put in 325° oven for 5 hours.

(Note: If you think meat isn't tender, rub with 2 tablespoons vinegar before adding cream of mushroom soup.)

Quasquicentennial / St. Olaf of Bode

Beef Roast

(Mock Prime Rib)

1 (5-pound) boneless rump roast
1 can beef broth
1 package Good Seasons Italian Dressing Mix
1 (10-ounce) package au jus mix

Place roast in slow cooker. Mix beef broth, dressing mix and au jus mix. Pour over roast. Cover and cook 8-10 hours on low setting. Broth may be thickened for gravy.

Applause Applause

Best Meat in Iowa

Sirloin or chuck roast
1 teaspoon ginger
1 teaspoon dry mustard
2 tablespoons dark molasses
½ cup soy sauce
¼ cup oil
3 cloves garlic, cut up (or 2 teaspoons garlic salt)

Cut meat into cubes. Mix all ingredients and place cubes of meat in mixture. Let stand in refrigerator for 24 hours or 5 hours if in a hurry. Broil or grill for best results.

A Taste of Grace

Italian Beef Pot Roast

1 (4-pound) beef roast
1 tablespoon flour
1 teaspoon salt

1 teaspoon ground ginger
$^1/_2$ teaspoon pepper

SAUCE:

1 can tomato sauce
1 can mushrooms
$^1/_2$ cup Burgundy

1 can pitted black olives
$^1/_3$ cup soy sauce
1 onion, sliced

Flour a 4-pound beef roast in the flour, salt, ground ginger, and pepper mixture. Mix together the tomato sauce, mushrooms, Burgundy, black olives, and soy sauce; bring to a boil. Pour mixture over meat; add onion. Bake, covered, at 350° for 2½ hours, or for 6 hours on low, in crockpot.

Saint Mary Catholic Church Cookbook

Glazed Country Steak

The 1990 Iowa Beef Cook-Off winning recipe.

1½ pounds boneless beef
  chuck shoulder steak, cut
  into serving-size pieces
$^1/_4$ cup flour
$^1/_2$ teaspoon salt
$^1/_4$ teaspoon pepper
2 tablespoons vegetable oil
$^1/_4$ cup dry white wine
1 clove garlic, finely chopped

$^1/_4$ cup tomato juice
1 teaspoon parsley flakes
$^1/_2$ cup beef broth
1 small onion, chopped
2 cups cubed raw potatoes
1 cup carrot chunks
2 tablespoons brown sugar
1 cup raisins

Combine flour, salt and pepper; pound into steak. In skillet, brown steak pieces on both sides in oil. Pour off drippings. Add wine, garlic, tomato juice, parsley flakes, beef broth, and onion. Cook, covered, over low heat for 30 minutes. Add potatoes and carrots; cook 30 minutes more. Sprinkle with brown sugar and raisins; simmer 15 minutes, or until meat is tender. Serve on platter encircled with vegetables. Makes 4-6 servings.

Lehigh Public Library Cookbook

Pepper Steak

1½ pounds round steak, cut
   into thin strips
¼ cup oil
2 cloves garlic
1 cup chopped onion
1 tablespoon soy sauce
1 tablespoon Worcestershire
   sauce

1 teaspoon salt
¼ teaspoon pepper
1 cup green pepper, chopped
½ cup celery, chopped
1½ tablespoons cornstarch
1¼ cups water

Brown beef in hot oil; add onion, garlic, soy sauce, Worcestershire sauce, salt and pepper. Cook for 20 minute, or until vegetables are tender. Combine cornstarch and water and add to meat mixture until thickened. Serve over hot rice.

Spitfire Anniversary Cookbook

Nana's Swiss Steak

This was the Swiss steak contest winner!

6 tablespoons flour
2 teaspoons salt
¼ teaspoon pepper
2 pounds round steak, cut
   1-inch thick
4 medium onions
6 tablespoons shortening,
   divided

½ cup chopped celery (about 2
   ribs)
1 clove garlic, minced
¾ cup chili sauce
¾ cup water
1 green pepper (optional)

Combine flour, salt and pepper; rub into both sides of steak, or pound in with meat mallet. Cut into 8 portions. Peel and slice onions. Preheat skillet and add half of shortening, then onion; brown lightly. Remove from skillet. Add remaining shortening. Brown steak on both sides. Reduce heat. Add celery, garlic, chili sauce and water; cover and simmer one hour. Cut green pepper into slices. Add pepper and onions to meat and cover with foil and bake at 350° for 2 - 2½ hours. Makes 8 servings.

Return Engagement

Stir-Fry

1 - 1½ pounds pork or beef
(stir-fry cut)
1-2 tablespoons oil
1 - 1½ tablespoons ginger
5 cups diagonally sliced
vegetables (celery, onion,
carrots, mushrooms, broccoli,
water chestnuts)

1 small soup can chicken or
oriental broth
2-3 tablespoons soy sauce
¼ cup flour

Coat the meat with flour. Heat up oil in a wok or fry pan. Cook meat until brown, adding ginger. When meat is cooked, add vegetables. Combine the soup, soy sauce, and flour. Add to meat and vegetables until mixture thickens and vegetables are semi-soft. Cook time: 15-20 minutes from start to finish. Serves 4 people. Enjoy.

Note: You may add any fresh vegetables.

125th Anniversary Celebration Cook Book

Maytag Steak Au Poivre

4 (8-ounce) beef tenderloin
filets
4 teaspoons crushed
peppercorns
1½ teaspoons kosher salt
1 tablespoon Worcestershire
sauce

1 tablespoon lemon juice
1 tablespoon hot pepper
sauce
¼ cup butter
¼ cup plus 2 tablespoons
Maytag blue cheese
¼ cup brandy

Rub steaks with crushed peppercorns. Heat 10-inch skillet over medium heat, add kosher salt and heat until it just starts to brown. Add steaks and cover with lid. Cook 2 minutes, turn steaks, cover and cook 2 minutes more. Remove lid, top steaks with butter; add Worcestershire, lemon, and pepper sauce. Add ¼ cup blue cheese and brandy. Flame brandy, reduce heat to low while constantly shaking pan to swirl sauce until slightly thickened. Place steaks on plates, top with sauce and remaining blue cheese and serve. Serves 4.

Sharing Traditions from People You Know

Salisbury Steak

1 pound lean ground beef
1 cup dry bread crumbs
1 egg
1 teaspoon salt

⅛ teaspoon pepper
2 tablespoons minced onion
¼ cup finely chopped celery

SAUCE:
1 can mushroom soup
½ cup water or juice of
  mushrooms

1 small can mushrooms

Combine meat, crumbs, egg, salt, pepper, onion, and celery. Shape into medium-sized oblong steak patties. Using a small amount of margarine, brown in skillet. Place in casserole. Mix the sauce ingredients together and pour over the steaks. Bake at 350° for one hour or until done. Serves 6-8.

Centennial Cookbook

Sizzling Steak Fajitas

¾ pound flank steak
2 teaspoons chili powder
⅛ teaspoon pepper
⅛ teaspoon cayenne pepper
2 teaspoons cumin
⅛ teaspoon garlic powder
¼ teaspoon salt
4 flour tortillas

1 teaspoon vegetable oil
2 cups sliced onion
⅓ cup green pepper
⅓ cup red pepper
⅓ cup yellow bell pepper
1 tablespoon lime juice
¼ cup sour cream

Trim fat from steak. Slice diagonally across grain into thin strips. Combine steak with spices in Ziploc bag. Seal and shake to coat. Heat tortillas.* Heat one teaspoon oil in large non-stick skillet over medium-high heat. Add steak, onion, and bell peppers. Sauté 6 minutes, or until steak is done. Remove from heat, stir in lime juice. Divide mixture evenly among tortillas and roll up. Serve with sour cream. Garnish with green salsa. Makes 4 servings.

*Heat each tortilla 15 seconds in hot non-stick skillet. Or wrap 4 in damp paper towel and sandwich between two salad plates; microwave on HIGH 40 seconds.

Woodbine Public Library

Italian "Carne Pane"
(Meat Loaf)

This was a 1995 Iowa State Fair Blue Ribbon Winner.

⅓ cup olive oil
1 cup chopped onions
1 cup sweet Italian peppers, chopped
½ cup green peppers, chopped
7 garlic cloves, minced
½ teaspoon basil
½ teaspoon oregano
½ teaspoon thyme
1 teaspoon Sweet Italian Seasoning
1 pound Italian sausage

1 pound lean ground beef
1 teaspoon salt
1 teaspoon black pepper
1/2 cup spaghetti sauce
3 eggs, beaten
½ cup Italian style bread crumbs
½ cup grated Italian Parmesan cheese
½ cup Italian tomatoes, drained or ½ cup dried tomatoes
Mozzarella cheese, shredded

In a large non-reactive skillet, warm the olive oil over medium heat. Add the onions, sweet peppers, green peppers, garlic, basil, oregano, thyme, and Italian seasoning; cover and cook for 10 minutes, stirring once or twice. Remove from heat and set aside to cool.

Preheat oven to 350°. Meanwhile in large bowl, combine the Italian sausage, ground beef, salt, pepper, spaghetti sauce, eggs, bread crumbs, Parmesan cheese, and tomatoes and mix thoroughly. Combine onion-seasoning mixture and mix. Place in meat loaf pan and top with Mozzarella cheese.

Bake the meat loaf for about 1½ hours at 350°, or until an instant-reading thermometer inserted into the center of the loaf registers 160°. Let the meat loaf rest on a rack for 10 minutes before slicing.

Note: May wish to drain fat by removing meat loaf from baking dish.

Enjoy

Beef Stroganoff

1 pound ground beef
1 teaspoon salt
1 teaspoon pepper
1 clove garlic (or garlic salt)
2 (8-ounce) cans tomato sauce
1 cup sour cream

1 (3-ounce) package cream
  cheese
½ cup chopped onions
1 (8-ounce) package noodles,
  cooked
1 cup Cheddar cheese, grated

Brown ground beef. Add salt, pepper, garlic, and tomato sauce. Simmer for 20 minutes. Mix together in a bowl the sour cream, softened cream cheese, and onions. Finally, layer noodles, ground beef mixture, sour cream mixture and repeat. Top with Cheddar cheese. Bake at 350° for 20 minutes. (Be careful not to overbake because the noodles will dry out.)

Lutheran Church Women Cookbook

Steak Stroganoff

2 tablespoons all-purpose
  flour
1 tablespoon dried parsley
  flakes
¼ teaspoon black pepper
2 (4-ounce) lean, minute or
  cube steaks

½ cup thinly sliced onion
½ cup (one 2.5-ounce jar)
  sliced mushrooms, undrained
3 tablespoons No-Fat Sour
  Cream
1 tablespoon skim milk

Spray a large skillet with butter-flavored cooking spray. In a shallow dish, combine flour, one teaspoon parsley flakes, and black pepper. Evenly coat steaks, one at a time in flour mixture. Place steaks in prepared skillet. Brown steaks about 4 minutes on each side. Lower heat. Add onion and undrained mushrooms. Cover. Simmer about 12-15 minutes, or until onion is tender.

Remove meat from skillet and cover to keep warm. Stir sour cream, skim milk, and remaining 2 teaspoons parsley flakes into onion mixture. Continue cooking, stirring occasionally, until mixture is heated through.

For each serving, place one piece of steak on plate and evenly spoon sour cream mixture over top. Serves 2.

Nutritional values per serving:
Healthy Exchanges: 3 Prot, 1 Vegetable, ¼ Slider, 5 Optional calories.
226 Cal; 6gm Fat; 28gm Prot; 15gm Carb; 263mg Sod; 2gm Fiber.
Diabetic: 3 Meat, 1 Vegetable, ½ Starch.

Dinner for Two

Stromboli

1 pound ground beef
1/2 cup diced onion
1/2 cup diced green pepper
2 medium cloves garlic,
   minced
1 (15 1/2-ounce) jar Prego (with
   mushrooms) Spaghetti Sauce

2 (8-ounce) packages
   refrigerated crescent rolls
4 slices (4 ounces)
   Mozzarella

Cook beef, onion, and green pepper with garlic until beef is browned and vegetables are tender. Spoon off fat. Stir in spaghetti sauce. Cool to room temperature.

On floured surface, roll each package of rolls to 11x9-inch rectangle. Arrange 2 slices cheese in center of each and 1/2 beef mixture. Starting at long edge, roll up. Pinch seams. Place both rolls 3 inches apart on cookie sheet. Bake at 350° for 30 minutes. Let stand 5 minutes for easier slicing. Makes 6 servings.

Trinity Lutheran Church Centennial Cookbook

Barbecued Hamburger Crispies

1 pound ground beef
1 egg
1 cup Rice Krispies
1 teaspoon salt
1/4 teaspoon pepper

1 tablespoon chopped onion
3 tablespoons brown sugar
1/4 cup ketchup
1/8 teaspoon nutmeg
1 teaspoon dry mustard

Combine beef, egg, 3/4 cup Rice Krispies, salt, pepper, and onion. Mix brown sugar, ketchup, nutmeg, and dry mustard. Add half of sauce to beef mixture. Shape meat into balls; place in muffin pans. Top balls with remaining sauce and sprinkle with remaining Krispies. Bake at 400° for about 30 minutes. Yields 12 meatballs.

Note: You can substitute ground pork for the ground beef and 1/8 teaspoon cloves for the nutmeg.

St. Joseph's Parish Cookbook

Stuffed Hamburger

1 pound ground beef
1 teaspoon salt
1/4 teaspoon pepper
1/2 cup oatmeal
1 egg
1/4 cup Miracle Whip
1 beef bouillon cube
1 cup water

1/4 cup chopped celery
1/2 cup chopped onion
1/4 teaspoon salt
1/2 teaspoon sage
5 slices bread, cubed
1 can cream of mushroom
  soup
1/2 cup milk

Mix well the first 6 ingredients and pat into a 9x13-inch pan. Dissolve bouillon cube in water; add celery, onion, salt, sage, and bread cubes. Mix well and spread over meat. Mix soup and milk; pour over all. Bake 45 minutes at 375°.

Spitfire Anniversary Cookbook

Birds' Nests

1 pound ground or chopped
  beef
1 tablespoon finely chopped
  onion
1 tablespoon finely chopped
  parsley

Pepper, salt, nutmeg to taste
2 tablespoons butter or
  margarine
4 eggs

Mix meat with onion, parsley, and seasonings. Divide into four equal portions and shape into rings. Heat butter in large skillet and brown the rings on one side. Turn. Break one egg into each, taking care that the egg whites do not spill over the meat. Cover, and fry over moderate heat until egg whites are firm.

Note: Great served with creamed spinach and strips of bread, fried golden brown.

Dutch Touches

Manhattan Meatballs

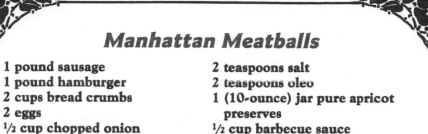

1 pound sausage	2 teaspoons salt
1 pound hamburger	2 teaspoons oleo
2 cups bread crumbs	1 (10-ounce) jar pure apricot
2 eggs	preserves
½ cup chopped onion	½ cup barbecue sauce
2 tablespoons chopped parsley	

Combine, meat, crumbs, eggs, onion, and seasonings. Mix lightly. Heat oven to 350°. Shape into meatballs, brown in oleo and drain. Place in casserole dish or crockpot. Combine preserves and barbecue sauce. Pour over meatballs; bake 30 minutes or on low in crockpot, stirring occasionally. Can be made ahead and frozen.

Mom's Favorite Recipes

Swedish Meatballs

½ cup onion	1 egg
1 tablespoon butter	½ teaspoon sugar
½ cup bread crumbs	1½ teaspoons salt
1 cup milk	¼ teaspoon ginger
1 pound ground beef	Dash of pepper and nutmeg
¼ pound ground pork	

Brown onion in butter. Soak bread crumbs in milk. Mix onions and milk mixture with meats, egg, sugar, salt, ginger, pepper, and nutmeg. Form into meatballs and brown in skillet. When brown, put in casserole.

GRAVY:

2 tablespoons flour	¼ cup water
1 can beef consummé soup	¼ teaspoon instant coffee

After all the meatballs are browned, add flour to drippings in the skillet; add soup, water, and instant coffee. Pour this gravy over meatballs and bake in oven until bubbly!

Community Centennial Cookbook

Meat Balls

3 pounds ground beef
1 large can evaporated milk
½ teaspoon garlic salt
2 cups quick oatmeal
1 medium-size onion,
   finely chopped

½ teaspoon pepper
2 teaspoons salt
2 eggs
2 teaspoons chili powder

Combine all of the ingredients in a large bowl. Mix well using hand. Form into small balls. Brown under broiler, no longer than 10 minutes. Must be watched very, very closely. As you remove balls from the broiler, place them in a large baking pan; set aside. (May use a large electric skillet.)

SAUCE:

2 cups ketchup
2 cups brown sugar
1 tablespoon Liquid Smoke

½ teaspoon garlic salt
½ cup onion, chopped
½ cup water

Combine all ingredients in a heavy saucepan. Bring to a boil. Pour sauce over meat balls. Bake at 350° for one hour.

Note: You may keep baking temperature lower and simmer for a longer time. Watch very carefully so that the meat balls do not stay above the sauce and dry out.

Cookin' for Miracles

Pizza Burgers

2 pounds ground beef
1 teaspoon oregano
1 small onion, diced
1 teaspoon pepper
½ pound Velveeta cheese

1 (11-ounce) pizza sauce
1 (6-ounce) can tomato paste
10 hamburger buns
Cheddar and Mozzarella
   cheeses, grated

Brown ground beef with oregano, onion, and pepper added. Drain off grease and add cheese, pizza sauce, and tomato paste. Heat till cheese is melted. Let cool. Put open buns on baking sheet. Divide pizza mixture among the buns and sprinkle with grated Cheddar and Mozzarella cheese. It takes about ¼ pound of each kind. Heat oven to 350° and warm Pizza Burgers for 20-30 minutes. These can be made ahead of time and frozen.

Special Fare by Sisters II

Cranberry Meat Balls

2 pounds ground beef
1 cup cornflake crumbs
1/3 cup parsley flakes
2 eggs
2 tablespoons soy sauce

1/4 teaspoon pepper
1/2 teaspoon garlic powder
1/3 cup catsup
3 tablespoons instant minced
  onion

SAUCE:
1 (1-pound) can jellied
  cranberry sauce
1 (12-ounce) bottle chili
  sauce

2 tablespoons brown sugar
1 tablespoon lemon juice

Combine ground beef, cornflake crumbs, parsley, eggs, soy sauce, pepper, garlic powder, catsup, and onion. Mix well. Form into meat balls and arrange in 9x12-inch pan. Combine cranberry sauce, chili sauce, brown sugar, and lemon juice in a saucepan. Heat until melted. Pour over meat balls. Bake, uncovered, for 30-45 minutes in a 350° oven.

Lutheran Church Women Cookbook

Ground Nut Stew

This is a favorite of many Pella residents when it is served at the Central College Auxiliary's annual Foreign Food Fair. A West African recipe.

2 pounds ground beef
1 onion, chopped fine
¼ teaspoon thyme
¼ teaspoon oregano
¼ teaspoon black pepper
¼ teaspoon cayenne pepper
1 large can tomato paste

1 tablespoon Worcestershire
  sauce
½ cup catsup
2 cups beef bouillon
½ cup crunchy peanut
  butter
Cooked rice

Fry in a large skillet the ground beef and onion. Add the spices; tomato paste, Worcestershire sauce, catsup, and bouillon. Simmer 30 minutes. Cook rice according to directions on the package. One half hour before serving stir the peanut butter into the meat mixture. Heat thoroughly and serve over rice with side dishes.

The Taste of the World

Danish Dumplings

1 stick margarine
7 heaping tablespoons flour

2 eggs
Salt

Beat until firm, drop by spoonfuls into stew; cook 15 minutes or until done.

Enjoy

Four-Hour Stew

1 pound beef stew meat
1 package Lipton Onion Soup
  Mix
1 can tomato soup
1 can cream of mushroom
  soup

2 cans water
6 carrots
4 large potatoes
3 stalks celery
½ cup frozen peas

In large Dutch oven put stew meat, onion soup mix, tomato soup, cream of mushroom soup, and water. In 350° oven bake without lid for 2 hours. Then add vegetables (your choice—vegetables can vary with taste, use your imagination), stirring, and bake with lid on for 2 more hours (4-hour stew). No salt and pepper, no thickening for gravy. Very easy, very good!

Country Lady Nibbling and Scribbling

Beef Stew

This is a great farm favorite . . . perfect for refueling after a long day in the field.

2 pounds lean beef, cut into 2-inch pieces	1 cup diced carrots
1 quart water	1 cup diced celery
4 bouillon cubes	½ cup diced onion
1 tablespoon Kitchen Bouquet	¼ cup frozen corn (optional)
2 cups diced potatoes	½ cup frozen peas (optional)
	½ cup frozen cut green beans (optional)

This recipe is good, as there is no need to brown meat before cooking. Put meat into kettle. Cover with water, bouillon cubes and Kitchen Bouquet. Bring to boil and simmer until tender (about 2 hours). Add more water, if necessary. Add potatoes, carrots, celery, and onion. Bring to boil and simmer about 20 minutes. Add corn, peas, or green beans, if desired. Return to boil and simmer additional 10 minutes. Drain liquid and reserve for gravy. Add more water if necessary, to make at least 3 cups stock. Melt ⅓ cup fat (butter, margarine, vegetable oil, or fat skimmed from stock) in pan. Add 6 tablespoons flour. Bubble for about one minute, stirring constantly. Add stock. Heat until thickened, stirring constantly. Pour over stew. Serve over baking powder biscuits. (If you prefer more gravy in stew, ratio is 2 tablespoons flour, 2 tablespoons fat, 1 cup liquid.)

The Machine Shed Farm Style Cooking

Beef Hash with Corn Muffin Mix

1 can beef hash	3 tablespoons grated Parmesan cheese
½ cup chopped onion	½ teaspoon salt
1 egg, beaten	
1 (8½-ounce) package corn muffin mix, prepared by directions	

Mix hash, onion, and egg. Prepare muffin mix; add cheese and salt. Spread ½ of muffin mix into a greased 8x8-inch pan. Spread hash mixture next. Top with remaining batter. Bake at 400° for 25 minutes in preheated oven. Good with gravy or creamed peas on top when served.

Generations of Good Cooking

Mince Meat

3 pints ground (precooked)
   roast beef
5 pints chopped apples
4½ cups sugar
1 cup molasses
½ cup vinegar
2 cups water

1 pound currants
2 pounds raisins
3 tablespoons cinnamon
1 tablespoon salt
2 tablespoons cloves
1 tablespoon nutmeg

Mix well and cook slowly until apples are tender, then seal in jars or freeze as you prefer.

Cook of the Week Cookbook

Beef or Deer Jerky

1 pound very lean steak
4 tablespoons soy sauce
4 tablespoons Worcestershire
   sauce
1 tablespoon ketchup or BBQ
   sauce

¼ teaspoon garlic powder
½ teaspoon salt
½ teaspoon ground pepper
¼ teaspoon onion salt

Cut steak into ¼-inch strips with the grain. Marinate overnight in mixture of remaining ingredients. Drain meat. Lay flat on trays (cookie sheets). Don't overlap. Bake at 145° for 6-10 hours. Turn at least once while drying. Ready when it bends like green willow without breaking.

Trinity Lutheran Church Centennial Cookbook

Soy-Garlic Marinade

Good for pork, beef, chicken or deer.

¼ cup salad oil
¼ cup soy sauce
2 tablespoons catsup

1 tablespoon vinegar
¼ teaspoon pepper
2 cloves garlic, crushed

Mix all ingredients. Marinate meat for 24 hours. Makes ¾ cup.

Trinity Lutheran Church Centennial Cookbook

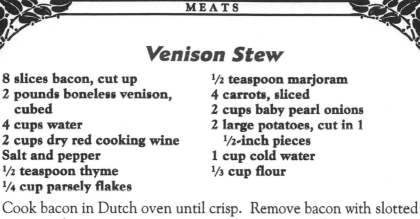

Venison Stew

8 slices bacon, cut up
2 pounds boneless venison,
  cubed
4 cups water
2 cups dry red cooking wine
Salt and pepper
½ teaspoon thyme
¼ cup parsely flakes

½ teaspoon marjoram
4 carrots, sliced
2 cups baby pearl onions
2 large potatoes, cut in 1
  ½-inch pieces
1 cup cold water
⅓ cup flour

Cook bacon in Dutch oven until crisp. Remove bacon with slotted spoon and reserve. Brown venison in bacon grease about 7 minutes. Add 2 cups water, wine, and spices. Heat to boiling. Reduce heat and simmer until tender. Stir in carrots, onions, and potatoes. Heat to boiling. Reduce heat and simmer until vegetables are tender. Shake cold water and flour in tightly covered shaker. Slowly stir into stew. Heat to boiling, stirring constantly. Boil and stir one minute. Sprinkle with bacon.

The Great Iowa Home Cooking Expedition

Czech Goulash

2 tablespoons butter
1 large onion, finely cut
4 cloves
4 whole allspice
1 bay leaf
1 tablespoon brown sugar

2 tablespoons vinegar
2 pounds beef (cut in small
  cubes)
2 tablespoons flour
Water

Melt butter in a skillet. Add onion. When onion is golden brown, add cloves, allspice, bay leaf, brown sugar, and vinegar. Add meat. Let simmer until tender. Add flour and brown. Add enough water (while stirring) to make thick gravy.

Generations of Good Cooking

Grant Wood's Cabbage Rolls

Grant Wood's own recipe, a favorite.

8 large cabbage leaves	1 teaspoon salt
1 pound bulk, ground sausage	½ cup tomato juice
	2 cups boiling water
2 cups cooked rice (or mashed potatoes)	3 tablespoons vinegar
	2 tablespoons sugar

Pour boiling water over the cabbage leaves and let stand about 4 minutes, then drain. Mix well the sausage, rice (or potatoes) and salt. Place meat mixture in equal portions on each cabbage leaf. Roll from stem end, folding in the sides, to wrap meat in leaf. Tie each bundle with string or fasten with toothpicks. Place rolls in kettle and cover them with the tomato juice, boiling water, and vinegar. Add sugar. Simmer until tender about one hour.

The American Gothic Cookbook

Bohemian Beef Dinner

1 cup flour (for dredging)	1 teaspoon dill weed
1 teaspoon salt	1 teaspoon caraway seed
¼ teaspoon pepper	1 teaspoon paprika
2 pounds stewing beef, cubed	½ cup water
2 tablespoons oil	1 cup sour cream
2 medium onions, chopped	1 (27-ounce) can sauerkraut
1 clove garlic, minced	Paprika for top

Mix flour, salt and pepper. Dredge beef in mixture and brown in hot oil. Pour off drippings. Add onions, garlic, dill weed, caraway seed, paprika, and water to the meat. Cover loosely and cook slowly for 2 hours until meat is tender. Stir in sour cream and heat through, but do not boil. Heat sauerkraut in a saucepan, drain and place on a platter. Serve meat mixture over sauerkraut. Sprinkle with paprika. Serves 6-8.

Cherished Czech Recipes

Cakes

The Grotto of the Redemption in West Bend is a composite of nine separate grottos portraying the life of Christ in stones and gems.

Hot Milk Cake

2 eggs	1 teaspoon baking powder
1 cup sugar	1 tablespoon butter
1 cup sifted flour	1/2 cup hot milk
1/8 teaspoon salt	1 teaspoon lemon flavoring

Beat eggs until light and lemon colored and thick. Add sugar and continue beating about 5 minutes. Fold in combined dry ingredients. Heat butter and milk together and add all at once and fold in quickly, no more than one minute. Add flavoring. Pour into a waxed paper-lined 8x8-inch square pan and bake at 350° for 30 minutes. For cup-cakes, bake in paper-lined cups for about 20 minutes. The cake will pull away from the side of the pan more than most cakes, but that is normal. This is excellent plain or frosted with a thin powdered sugar glaze. Makes 9 pieces.

Up a Country Lane Cookbook

Peanut Butter Frosting

1/2 cup oleo	Powdered sugar (enough to
1/4 cup milk (add more if	make spreadable frosting)
desired)	1/2 cup peanut butter
1/4 teaspoon vanilla	

Soften oleo and add milk and vanilla. Gradually add powdered sugar until it's frosting that's spreadable, then add peanut butter. Very good over angel food cake.

Mom's Favorite Recipes

The Buffalo Bill Museum in LeClaire is a memorial tribute to their native son, William F. "Buffalo Bill" Cody. One of the homesteads of the Cody family in nearby Princeton was built in 1847 by Buffalo Bill's father. The restored house with buffalo, covered wagon and stagecoach can be viewed there.

Edna's Fresh Apple Cake

4 cups chopped tart apples
2 cups granulated sugar
2 eggs
1/2 cup vegetable oil
1 teaspoon vanilla
2 cups all-purpose flour
2 teaspoons baking soda
2 teaspoons cinnamon
1/2 teaspoon salt
Whipped cream or your favorite
   frosting (optional)

Preheat oven to 350°. In a large bowl, combine apples and sugar; let stand 30 minutes. In another bowl, beat together eggs, vegetable oil, and vanilla. Sift together flour, baking soda, cinnamon, and salt. Thoroughly combine all 3 mixtures. Pour into a greased and floured 9x13-inch pan. Bake in preheated oven 50-60 minutes, or until knife inserted in middle comes out clean. Serve warm or cold with whipped cream or your favorite frosting. Makes 10-12 servings.

A Cook's Tour of Iowa

Cream Frosting

5 tablespoons flour
1 cup milk
1 cup sugar
1/2 cup Crisco
1/2 cup butter or oleo
3 teaspoons vanilla

Cook flour and milk until thick on stove. Stir constantly to prevent lumping. Set aside to cool. Beat until fluffy the sugar, Crisco, butter, and vanilla. Add cooled flour mixture. Beat again until it resembles whipped cream.

Trinity Lutheran Church Centennial Cookbook

Applesauce Cake

½ cup butter
1 cup sugar
1 egg, beaten lightly
1 teaspoon vanilla
1¾ cups flour
1 teaspoon soda
1½ teaspoons cinnamon

½ teaspoon cloves
1 cup hot applesauce (may be
  cold)
1 cup chopped raisins (can be
  whole)
¼ cup nutmeats

Cream together the butter and sugar; fold in lightly-beaten egg and vanilla. Add flour, soda, and spices, and blend; fold in applesauce, raisins, and nuts. Spread batter in greased 9x13-inch cake pan and sprinkle top of unbaked cake with granulated sugar; bake for ½ hour in 350° oven.

Armstrong Centennial

Carrot-Apple Cake

1½ cups sugar
1½ cups vegetable oil
3 eggs
2 teaspoons vanilla
2 cups sifted flour
2 teaspoons cinnamon
1 teaspoon each baking soda,
baking powder and salt

2 cups shredded carrots
1 cup coarsely-chopped
apples
1 cup raisins
1 cup chopped pecans

Combine first 4 ingredients in a large bowl. Blend. Add sifted dry ingredients to first mixture and mix. Stir in remaining ingredients. Bake in 2 greased and paper-lined 9-inch pans or a 9x13-inch pan. Bake at 350° for 35-45 minutes. Cool 10 minutes. Frost with Pecan Cream Cheese Frosting.

PECAN CREAM CHEESE FROSTING:
2 (3-ounce) packages cream
cheese, softened
1 tablespoon milk
2 teaspoons vanilla

Dash of salt
1 pound powdered sugar
½ cup chopped pecans

Blend first 4 ingredients thoroughly. Beat in sugar until smooth and spreading consistency. Fold in nuts. This makes a lot of frosting and will frost top and sides of layer cake.

Lutheran Church Women Cookbook

Apple Goodie

3 cups sliced or diced apples
¾ cup white sugar
¼ teaspoon soda
¼ teaspoon baking powder
⅓ cup melted butter
1 rounded tablespoon flour

Salt and cinnamon to taste
¾ cup oatmeal
¾ cup flour
¾ cup brown sugar, firmly
packed

Combine apples and white sugar and put in buttered 8x8-inch Pyrex pan. Mix soda, baking powder, melted butter, flour, and salt and cinnamon to taste. Spread over top of apples. Combine remaining ingredients and crumble over the top. Bake 30-40 minutes at 350°. Cut in squares and serve with hard sauce or whipped cream.

Neighboring on the Air

Polynesian Cake

This is a special cake.

1 cup oil	2 teaspoons cinnamon
1¼ cups sugar	2 teaspoons baking powder
3 eggs	1 small can crushed pineapple,
2 teaspoons vanilla	drained
2 small jars strained carrots*	½ pound coconut
2 cups flour	1 cup chopped nuts

Beat oil, sugar, eggs, vanilla, and carrots in mixer. Add dry ingredients that have been sifted together 2 times. Add pineapple, coconut, and nuts. Bake in greased Bundt pan 350° for 50-55 minutes. Frost with Cream Cheese Frosting.

CREAM CHEESE FROSTING:

1 (3-ounce) package cream cheese, softened	1 teaspoon vanilla
2 tablespoons butter	2-3 cups powdered sugar

Combine; thin with a little cream to make it spread nicely.

Note: *Can use 1 cup cooked mashed carrots or grated carrots.

Oma's (Grandma's) Family Secrets

Mandarin Orange Cake

1 cup sugar	1 teaspoon baking soda
1 cup flour	½ teaspoon salt
1 egg	1 teaspoon vanilla
1 can mandarin oranges, drained	

Combine all ingredients in bowl; beat 2½ - 3 minutes. Bake 30-35 minutes in 350° oven in an 8-inch buttered pan.

TOPPING:

1 cup brown sugar	4 tablespoons milk
4 tablespoons butter	

Bring topping mixture to a boil; pour over cake. Serve warm.

Colesburg Area Cookbook

Banana Marshmallow Cake

During baking, marshmallows melt like flowers over top of cake.

2½ cups sugar
1 cup shortening
4 egg whites
3 cups flour
1½ teaspoons baking
  powder
2 cups mashed bananas

6 tablespoons buttermilk or
  sour milk
1 teaspoon vanilla
¾ cup nuts (optional)
¾ cup raisins (optional)
16 marshmallows

Cream sugar and shortening together in a large bowl. Add rest of ingredients except marshmallows, and mix thoroughly. Place marshmallows in a greased and floured 9x13-inch pan in rows 2 inches apart. Pour batter over the marshmallows. Smack pan smartly on counter until tops of marshmallows show through batter. Bake at 350° for one hour. Makes 18 pieces.

Recipes from Iowa with Love

Myrtle's Famous Banana Cake

1³/₄ cups sugar
½ cup butter
2 eggs, beaten
½ cup buttermilk

1 teaspoon baking soda
1 cup mashed bananas
2¼ cups sifted cake flour
1 teaspoon vanilla flavoring

Cream together the sugar and butter. (High-grade margarine can be substituted for the butter if you prefer, but that is something Myrtle would never do.) When mixture is light and fluffy, add the eggs and continue beating until smooth. Dissolve the baking soda in the buttermilk and stir into batter. Add bananas, cake flour, and flavoring. Mix well and pour into 2 greased and floured (8-inch) pans or one (9x13-inch) baking pan. Bake at 350° for 30-45 minutes. Can make 4-6 cupcakes as well as the flat cake, for this makes a generous amount of batter. The cupcakes take about 20 minutes to bake. Can frost with Brown Sugar Frosting. Makes about 20 servings.

BROWN SUGAR FROSTING:
3 tablespoons brown sugar, packed
3 tablespoons butter
3 tablespoons cream

1½ cups powdered sugar
1 teaspoon vanilla flavoring
Dash of salt

Heat brown sugar, butter, and cream together over low heat, stirring until well blended and sugar is dissolved. Remove from fire and stir in remaining ingredients, using enough powdered sugar to make of spreading consistency. When smooth and creamy, frost the cake.

Up a Country Lane Cookbook

Rhubarb Cake

1 yellow cake mix
3 cups rhubarb, cut up
1½ cups sugar

Small carton whipping cream
(not whipped)

Prepare cake mix according to directions and pour into greased Bundt pan. Top with rhubarb, sugar, and then whipping cream. Bake 350° for 50 minutes.

Enjoy

Tomato Soup Cake

3 cups flour	2 eggs
1 tablespoon baking powder	1 (10¾-ounce) can tomato
1 teaspoon cinnamon	soup
1 teaspoon nutmeg	¾ cup water
1 teaspoon cloves	1 teaspoon baking soda
¾ cup shortening	¾ cup raisins
1¼ cups sugar	¾ cup walnuts

Mix together flour, baking powder, and spices; set aside. Cream shortening and sugar thoroughly; add eggs, one at a time, beating well after each addition. Combine soup, water, and baking soda and add alternately with dry ingredients, beating after each addition. Add raisins and nuts. Pour into an angel food cake pan and bake in 350° oven for one hour. Frost with Cream Cheese Icing. Serves 10-12.

CREAM CHEESE ICING:

1 (3-ounce) package cream	2 cups powdered sugar
cheese	2 tablespoons milk
½ teaspoon vanilla extract	

Soften cream cheese; add cream cheese and vanilla to powdered sugar and moisten with milk. Mix until creamy. Cake freezes well.

Sharing Traditions from People You Know

Corn Cake

1 can cream-style corn	2¼ cups flour
½ cup brown sugar	1 teaspoon baking soda
¾ cup sugar	1 teaspoon salt
3 eggs	1 teaspoon cinnamon
1 cup oil	½ cup raisins
1 tablespoon baking powder	½ cup chopped nuts

Mix corn and sugars. Add eggs and oil. Beat well. Mix dry ingredients. Add and mix well. Stir in raisins and nuts. Put in sprayed 9x13-inch pan. Bake at 350° for 30-35 minutes. Cool well.

FROSTING:

4 tablespoons oleo	¼ cup milk
½ cup brown sugar	2-3 cups powdered sugar

Bring oleo and sugar to a boil over medium heat. Take from heat. Stir in milk. Stir in powdered sugar. Frost cooled cake.

Quasquicentennial / St. Olaf of Bode

Poppy Seed Cake

1 package white cake mix	¼ cup poppy seeds
1 package instant coconut	½ cup oil
pudding mix	1 cup hot water
4 eggs	

Mix all together 4 minutes. Pour into 2 greased bread pans. Bake at 350° for 40 minutes.

Variation: Can use lemon cake mix or lemon instant pudding mix.

Visitation Parish Cookbook

Pistachio Cake

1 white cake mix
1 cup oil
1 cup 7-Up
3 eggs

1 package instant pistachio
   pudding
1 teaspoon almond extract

Mix all ingredients together well. Grease and flour a Bundt pan or a 9x13-inch pan. Bake at 350° for 30-35 minutes.

The Great Iowa Home Cooking Expedition

Angel Food Cake

2¼ cups egg whites
   (approximately 16 whites)
1 teaspoon almond extract
¾ teaspoon salt

2 teaspoons cream of tartar
2½ cups sugar
1⅞ cups cake flour

Preheat oven to 375°. Beat egg whites until stiff but not dry. Add almond extract, salt, and cream of tartar when whites are foamy. Beat in 1½ cups sugar, a small amount at a time after whites are stiff.

Sift the cake flour with the remaining one cup of sugar several times, then sprinkle the mixture a little at a time over the egg whites, folding this in very carefully. Pour batter into an ungreased 10-inch tube pan. Bake at 375° for about 45 minutes.

7-MINUTE FROSTING:
1½ cups sugar
¼ cup water
2 egg whites

1 tablespoon syrup
1 teaspoon almond extract

Put the above in the top of a double boiler and cook over heat, beating with mixer at the same time. Cook about 7 minutes.

Favorite Recipes

At one time there were nineteen covered bridges in Madison County; there are currently six.

Special Lemon Cake

1 package yellow cake mix	¾ cup Wesson oil
4 eggs	1 package lemon Jell-O,
1½ teaspoons lemon	dissolved in 1 cup hot water
extract	

Mix well. Bake in a moderate 350° oven. When done, prick with fork.

TOPPING:

1½ cups powdered sugar	2 tablespoons lemon juice

Mix well and put on top of the warm cake. It will sink through the pricked holes.

Lehigh Public Library Cookbook

Lemon Pudding Cake

1 egg, separated	3 tablespoons all-purpose
2 tablespoons lemon juice	flour
½ cup skim milk	¼ teaspoon salt
½ cup Sugar Twin or Sprinkle	1 cup hot water
Sweet	

Preheat oven to 325°. In a medium bowl, beat egg yolk with a wire whisk until frothy. Add lemon juice, skim milk, Sugar Twin, flour, and salt to egg yolk. Mix well until mixture is smooth. Set aside. In another medium bowl, beat egg white with an electric mixer until stiff peaks form. Fold egg white into egg yolk mixture. Evenly divide batter between 2 (1-cup) custard dishes. Pour hot water into an 8x8-inch baking dish and arrange custard dishes in baking dish. Bake 45-50 minutes. Serve warm. Serves 2.

Healthy Exchanges: ½ Protein (limited), ½ bread, ¼ skim milk, ¼ slider, 4 optional calories.
127 Cal; 3gm Fat; 6gm Prot; 19gm Carb; 34mg Sod; 0gm Fiber.
Diabetic: 1 Starch, ½ Meat.

Dinner for Two

Sunshine Lemon Cake

The intense lemon flavor in this two-layered cake frosted with a luscious lemony frosting is sure to please lemon fans!

LEMON CAKE:

2 cups bread flour
³/₄ cup granulated sugar
1 tablespoon baking powder
¹/₄ teaspoon salt
1 (6-ounce) jar pear baby food
1 cup skim milk

1 teaspoon vanilla
1 tablespoon finely grated lemon peel
¹/₈ teaspoon lemon oil
4 egg whites, at room temperature
¹/₄ cup granulated sugar

Preheat oven to 350°. Combine flour, ³/₄ cup granulated sugar, baking powder, and salt in a large mixing bowl.

Combine pears, milk, vanilla, lemon peel, and lemon oil in a small bowl and blend well.

In mixing bowl of electric mixer, beat egg whites on moderate speed until they are foamy. Gradually add ¹/₄ cup granulated sugar, one tablespoon at a time, beating well after each addition. Increase speed to high and beat until stiff peaks form but are not dry. Add lemon mixture to egg whites and beat on moderate speed to lightly blend. Add lemon and egg white mixture to dry ingredients and quickly mix with a fork to blend. Pour batter into 2 (8-inch) round cake pans that have been coated with vegetable spray. Bake for 25 minutes, or until cake tester inserted into center of cakes comes out clean. Cover cakes with waxed paper and cool on cake racks for 10 minutes. Remove cakes from pans, re-cover with waxed paper, and cool completely.

LEMON FROSTING:

2 tablespoons each fat-free and light margarine, at room temperature
2 tablespoons fresh lemon juice

1 tablespoon finely grated lemon peel
3 cups powdered sugar

In mixing bowl of electric mixer, beat margarines until smooth. Add lemon juice, lemon peel, and 2 cups of the powdered sugar and beat until blended. Add the remaining one cup powdered sugar and beat until light and fluffy. Makes 16 servings.

Nutritional analysis per serving: 202 Cal; 4% Cal from Fat; 3g Prot; 46g Carbo; 1g Fat; 0g Fiber; 128mg Sod; 0mg Chol.

101 Great Lowfat Desserts

Sour Cream Lemon Pound Cake

1 cup butter	3 cups flour
3 cups sugar	½ teaspoon soda
6 eggs	½ teaspoon salt
¼ cup lemon juice	1 cup sour cream
1 tablespoon grated lemon rind	

Cream butter and sugar. Add eggs one at a time, beating well after each. Add lemon juice and rind. Mix flour, soda, and salt together and add alternately with sour cream to the creamed mixture. Pour into greased and floured 10-inch angel food pan (16-cup size). Bake at 325° for 1 hour and 30 minutes, or until it tests done. Cool 15 minutes before turning out on rack to cool. If desired, a Lemon Glaze can be poured over cake.

LEMON GLAZE:

2 cups powdered sugar	2 tablespoons grated lemon rind
¼ cup melted butter	¼ cup lemon juice

Mix all ingredients together and beat until of spreading consistency.

Variations: Orange juice and grated orange rind can be substituted for lemon; ¼ cup poppy seed to ½ cup finely chopped pecans or walnuts can be added.

German Recipes

Pumpkin Jellyroll

3 eggs	1 teaspoon ginger
1 cup sugar	2 teaspoons cinnamon
½ teaspoon nutmeg	⅔ cup pumpkin
1 teaspoon lemon juice	1 teaspoon baking powder
¾ cup flour	Chopped nuts (optional)

FILLING:

1 cup powdered sugar	4 tablespoons soft oleo
2 (3-ounce) packages cream cheese	½ teaspoon vanilla

Line a 10x15-inch jellyroll pan with foil, and spray with cooking spray. Beat eggs for 5 minutes and add rest of ingredients. Pour mixture in foil-lined pan and bake at 375° for 15 minutes. Turn onto a kitchen towel that has been sprinkled with powdered sugar. Pull foil off and roll in towel to cool, starting at narrow end. When cool, unroll, spread with filling and roll up again.

125 Years — Walking in Faith

Aunt Darlene's Black Bottom Cupcakes

These keep well, and are excellent for picnics or traveling—less messy.

FILLING:

1 (8-ounce) package cream
  cheese, softened
1 egg, unbeaten
1/3 cup sugar
1/8 teaspoon salt
1 (6-ounce) package chocolate
  chips

Combine cream cheese, egg, sugar, and salt in mixing bowl; mix well. Stir in chocolate chips, and set aside.

BATTER:

1 1/4 cups flour
1 teaspoon baking soda
1 teaspoon salt
1 cup sugar
1/4 cup cocoa
1 cup water
1/3 cup cooking oil
1 tablespoon vinegar
1 teaspoon vanilla

In large mixing bowl, sift together flour, soda, and salt; add sugar and cocoa. Add water, cooking oil, vinegar, and vanilla. Beat well, until combined. Place paper baking cups into muffin tins. Fill 1/3-full with chocolate batter. Top each one with one heaping teaspoon of the cream cheese mixture. Sprinkle with sugar and chopped almonds (optional). Bake at 350° for 30-35 minutes. Makes about 24 cupcakes.

Lehigh Public Library Cookbook

Double Chocolate Cupcakes

These cupcakes taste a lot like brownies. If you have any chocolate lovers in the house, this should quickly become their "best of the best!"

1½ cups all-purpose flour
½ cup Sugar Twin or Sprinkle
  Sweet
¼ cup unsweetened cocoa
1 teaspoon baking soda
½ teaspoon salt
½ cup unsweetened orange
  juice

⅓ cup water
3 tablespoons vegetable oil
1 tablespoon white vinegar
1 teaspoon vanilla extract
¼ cup (1 ounce) mini-chocolate
  chips

Preheat oven to 375°. Spray a 12-cup muffin pan with butter-flavored cooking spray or line with paper liners. In a medium bowl, combine flour, Sugar Twin, cocoa, baking soda, and salt. Make a well in center of mixture. In a small bowl, combine orange juice, water, oil, vinegar, and vanilla extract. Add liquid mixture to dry ingredients, stirring just until moistened. Fold in chocolate chips. Fill prepared muffin cups ⅔ full. Bake 12 minutes or until a toothpick inserted in center comes out clean. Remove from pan immediately and allow to cool on a wire rack. Serves 12.

Each serving equals:
Diabetic: 1 starch; 1 fat.
108 Cal; 4gm Fat; 2gm Prot; 16gm Carb; 197mg Sod; 1gm Fiber.
Healthy Exchanges: ¾ fat; ⅔ bread; ¼ slider; 7 optional calories.

Diabetic's Healthy Exchanges Cookbook

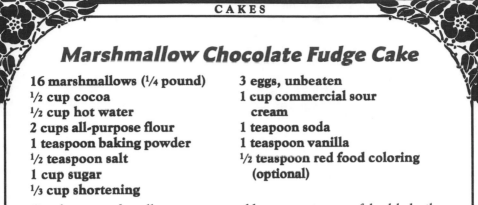

Marshmallow Chocolate Fudge Cake

16 marshmallows (¼ pound)
½ cup cocoa
½ cup hot water
2 cups all-purpose flour
1 teaspoon baking powder
½ teaspoon salt
1 cup sugar
⅓ cup shortening

3 eggs, unbeaten
1 cup commercial sour cream
1 teapoon soda
1 teaspoon vanilla
½ teaspoon red food coloring (optional)

Combine marshmallows, cocoa, and hot water in top of double boiler. Let stand over hot water until marshmallows melt. Do not cook. Stir until smooth; cool. Sift together flour, baking powder, and salt, and set aside. Add sugar gradually to shortening, creaming well. Blend in eggs, beating well after each one. Combine sour cream and soda, and add alternately with the dry ingredients. Blend well after each addition. Mix vanilla and food coloring into chocolate mixture and blend into batter. Turn into two well-greased and lightly floured 8-inch layered pans. Bake in 350° oven for 30-35 minutes. Cool and frost with favorite frosting.

Teresa's Heavenly Cakes and Treasures

Cherry Chocolate Cake

1 package chocolate cake mix
3 eggs

1 (21-ounce) can cherry fruit filling

Combine cake mix, eggs, and cherry fruit filling. Mix until well blended. Pour into a greased and floured 9x13-inch pan. Bake at 350° for 35-40 minutes, or until cake springs back when lightly touched.

FROSTING:

1 cup sugar
5 tablespoons butter or margarine

⅓ cup milk
1 (6-ounce) package semi-sweet chocolate pieces

In a small saucepan, combine sugar, butter, and milk. Bring to a boil, stirring constantly, and cook one minute. Remove from heat. Stir in chocolate pieces until melted and smooth. Spread over cooled cake.

Alta United Methodist Church Cookbook

Hot Fudge Pudding Cake

1 cup all-purpose flour
¾ cup sugar
2 tablespoons cocoa
2 teaspoons baking powder
¼ teaspoon salt
½ cup milk
2 tablespoons shortening,
  melted

1 cup finely-chopped nuts
  (optional)
1 cup brown sugar, packed
¼ cup cocoa
1¾ cups hot water

Heat oven to 350°. Measure flour, sugar, 2 tablespoons cocoa, baking powder, and salt into bowl. Blend in milk and shortening; stir in nuts. Pour into ungreased 9x9x2-inch pan. Stir together brown sugar and ¼ cup cocoa; sprinkle over batter. Pour hot water over batter. Bake 45 minutes. While hot, cut into squares; invert each piece onto plate or bowl. Spoon sauce on top. Great with ice cream.

Spitfire Anniversary Cookbook

Radio Cake

1 cup sugar
2 tablespoons butter
2 tablespoons cocoa
¼ cup boiling water
1 cup sour milk or buttermilk

1⅓ cups flour
1 teaspoon soda
½ teaspoon salt
1 teaspoon vanilla

To the creamed sugar and butter, add the cocoa mixed with boiling water. Then add sour milk, flour, soda, salt, and vanilla. Beat together and bake in 2 greased and floured pans in 350° oven 25 minutes.

FILLING:
1½ tablespoons cocoa
1½ tablespoons cornstarch
⅔ cup sugar

¾ cup water
½ teaspoon vanilla

Mix dry ingredients, then water, and cook until thick and creamy. Spread between layers and use any desired icing for top.

Neighboring on the Air

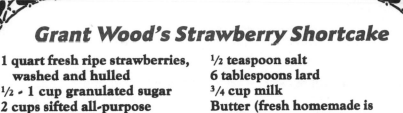

Grant Wood's Strawberry Shortcake

1 quart fresh ripe strawberries,
  washed and hulled
1/2 - 1 cup granulated sugar
2 cups sifted all-purpose
  flour
3 teaspoons baking powder

1/2 teaspoon salt
6 tablespoons lard
3/4 cup milk
Butter (fresh homemade is
  best)
Rich country cream

Place strawberries in a bowl and bruise and chop with a silver spoon. Cover with sugar to suit and let stand at room temperature to bring out the juice. Make a biscuit dough as follows. Preheat oven to 425°. Sift together flour, baking powder, and salt. Cut in lard. Add milk and mix lightly, the less the better. Spread out in a greased pie tin with a spoon. Bake in hot oven until done (12-20 minutes).

Carefully break biscuit dough into 2 layers, using a fork to separate them. Lay top layer to one side (remove with a pancake turner if necessary). Butter the bottom layer and cover with crushed strawberries. Butter the top layer and put back on the strawberries. Top the cake with more strawberries. Cut in huge slices and serve with country cream. Makes 6-8 servings.

A Cook's Tour of Iowa

French Chocolate Cake

1/2 cup butter
2 cups sugar
1 cup sour cream
1/2 cup cocoa
3/4 cup hot coffee

2 cups sifted cake flour
1/2 teaspoon soda
1/2 teaspoon salt
3 egg whites, stiffly beaten

Cream butter and sugar; add sour cream and cocoa dissolved in coffee, flour, soda, and salt. Fold in egg whites. Bake at 350° (moderate oven). Bake layers for 25-30 minutes; square or oblong for 35-40 minutes.

Teresa's Heavenly Cakes and Treasures

Iowa is bordered by six states: Illinois, Minnesota, Wisconsin, South Dakota, Nebraska, and Missouri.

Better Than Sex Cake

A very good, but rich, cake!

1 German chocolate cake
  mix
1 jar butterscotch-caramel ice
  cream topping

1 can condensed milk
8-12 ounces whipped topping
2 chocolate covered toffee
  candy bars

Make cake in 9x13-inch pan according to package directions. While warm, poke holes in cake with a meat fork. Heat topping and milk and pour over warm cake. Let cool, then spread whipped topping on top. Sprinkle with crushed chocolate covered toffee bars. Refrigerate. Better if made the day before serving.

The L.o.V.E Chocolate Cookbook

Pigout Cake

1 yellow cake mix
1 package instant milk
  chocolate pudding

2 cups lukewarm water
2 egg whites, slightly
  whipped

Put in greased 13x9-inch pan. Bake 25-35 minutes at 350°. Cool and frost.

FROSTING:
¼ cup softened margarine
1 cup powdered sugar
1 (8-ounce) carton Cool
  Whip

Heath or Skor candy bars,
  crushed

Mix margarine and powdered sugar. Fold in Cool Whip. Frost cake and sprinkle crushed Heath or Skor candy bars on top. Refrigerate.

Home Cooking with the Cummer Family

Watergate Cake

1 package white cake mix
1 package pistachio pudding
   (instant)
3 eggs

1 cup vegetable oil
½ cup chopped nuts
1 cup Canada Dry Club Soda

Mix cake mix and pudding mix, add eggs, oil, nuts, and soda; mix until well blended, beat 4 minutes. Bake at 350° for 45 minutes.

FROSTING:

2 envelopes of Dream Whip
1½ cups milk
1 package pistachio pudding
   (instant)

Coconut
Nuts, chopped

Blend Dream Whip and milk until it stands in peaks; add pudding mix, beat until light and fluffy, frost cake. Cover with cocount and nuts.

Mom's Favorite Recipes

Tropical Delight

1 white cake mix
1 (3-ounce) package
   orange-pineapple Jell-O
4 eggs
3 teaspoons flour

⅔ cup salad oil
½ cup juice from fruit
1 can mandarin oranges
½ cup crushed pineapple
½ cup coconut

GLAZE:

1 cup powdered sugar
2 tablespoons lemon juice

Rind from 1 orange, grated

Mix for 4 minutes the cake mix, Jell-O, eggs, flour, oil, and ½ cup juice. Cut the oranges in half and thirds. Stir in the oranges, pineapple, and coconut. Bake in a greased 9x13-inch pan for 45-50 minutes at 350°. Mix Glaze ingredients. With a meat fork, punch cake all over and pour the Glaze over the hot cake.

From the Cozy Kitchens of Long Grove

Punch Bowl Cake

1 angel food cake mix (or 1 "boughten" cake)
2 small boxes vanilla regular pudding
1½ quarts fresh strawberries, sliced
1 (16-ounce) box frozen strawberries, thawed
1 (15-16-ounce) jar strawberry glaze
1 can crushed pineapple, drained
1 (16-ounce) carton whipped topping

Make cake as directed and bake. While cake is baking, make up pudding so cake and pudding can cool. After cake is baked and cool, crumble half into the bottom of a punch bowl. Mix the berries and the glaze together. Then to the cake in the bowl, add half of the pudding, pineapple, berries/glaze and whipped topping. Repeat the layers. Cover and refrigerate at least overnight.

First Christian Church Centennial Cookbook

Strawberry Fluff

1 medium-size angel food cake
2 small packages strawberry Jell-O
1½ cups hot water
1 cup cold water
2 (10-ounce) packages frozen strawberries
½ pint whipping cream, whipped

Arrange bite-size pieces of cake in a 9x13-inch pan. Make Jell-O with hot water; add cold water and frozen berries. Let stand until slightly congealed. Add the whipped cream; mix well. Pour over cake and stir a little to be sure all of cake pieces are covered. Put in refrigerater and let set. Serves 15.

Cookin' for Miracles

Snowballs

The final word of advice in preparing Snowballs for New Year's Eve is, "Remember that resolutions about your diet don't start until tomorrow!"

1 cup boiling water	**Oil or shortening for deep**
¹/₂ cup butter	**frying**
1 cup flour	**Sweetened whipped cream**
¹/₄ teaspoon salt	**Powdered sugar**
4 eggs	

Combine water and butter. Add flour and salt. Stir over low heat until mixture forms a ball, leaving the sides of the pan. Add eggs one at a time, beating vigorously after each addition.

Heat oil. Drop in rounded tablespoons of dough. When fully puffed and golden, remove balls and drain thoroughly. With the point of a pastry bag, make a small hole in each ball and fill with sweetened whipped cream. Roll in powdered sugar; stack in a mound to serve. Makes 12.

Dutch Touches

Home Style Dutch Crullers

(Poffertjes)

In The Netherlands, Poffertjes, small, light and fluffy crullers, will be made and available for sale (as are Olie Bollen) at Market Days or Carnivals. Special iron molds are used on such occasions. This delicacy is served with powdered sugar. Poffertjes are available at Pella's Tulip Time.

4 tablespoons sugar	**1 cup hot water**
1 teaspoon salt	**1 cup flour**
4 tablespoons fat	**3 eggs**
1 teaspoon grated orange rind	

Put sugar, salt, fat, rind, and water in saucepan. Heat to boiling point. Add flour and mix well. Cook until thick (like cream puffs) stirring constantly. Cool slightly. Add one egg at a time, beating hard after each addition. Press through pastry bag onto well greased square of heavy paper (one at a time). Turn paper upside down and let cruller drop into hot fat. Fry 6-7 minutes until well puffed and a delicate brown. Drizzle with powdered sugar, or ice with plain powdered sugar icing.

The Taste of the World

Orange Push-Up Cheesecake

The best ice cream I can remember from childhood is those orange push-ups, so I just had to invent a dessert that recalled the scrumptious taste beloved by all kids—and the men they grew up to be! This tastes amazingly like the dream dessert you remember.

2 (8-ounce) packages fat-free cream cheese

1 (4-serving) package sugar-free instant vanilla pudding mix

1 (4-serving) package sugar-free orange gelatin

2/3 cup nonfat dry milk powder

1 cup unsweetened orange juice

3/4 cup Cool Whip Lite

1 (6-ounce) shortbread pie crust

2 tablespoons flaked coconut

In a large bowl, stir cream cheese with a spoon until soft. Add dry pudding mix, dry gelatin, dry milk powder, and orange juice. Mix well using a wire whisk. Blend in 1/4 cup Cool Whip Lite. Spread mixture evenly into pie crust. Refrigerate at least one hour. Cut into 8 servings. Top each serving with one tablespoon Cool Whip Lite and one teaspoon coconut.

Each serving equals:
Healthy Exchanges: 1/2 bread; 1/2 protein; 1/4 skim milk, 1/4 fruit; 3/4 slider; 11 optional calories.
205 Cal; 5gm Fat; 12gm Prot; 28gm Carb; 554mg Sod; 1gm Fiber.
Diabetic: 1 1/2 starch; 1 fat; 1/2 meat.

Cooking Healthy with a Man in Mind

Quick Lemon Cheesecake

CRUST:

1¼ cups graham cracker
  crumbs

¼ cup sugar
6 tablespoons melted butter

Combine crumbs, sugar, and butter. Press firmly on bottom and sides of a 8-inch-square pan or 9-inch-round pie pan. Chill while preparing filling.

FILLING:

1 (8-ounce) package cream
  cheese, softened
2 cups milk
1 tablespoon sugar

½ teaspoon vanilla
1 (3¾-ounce) package instant
  lemon pudding

Beat cream cheese until soft. Blend in ½ cup milk. Add remaining milk, sugar, vanilla, and pudding mix; mix well. Pour into crust. Chill until firm. Garnish with whipped cream and strawberries or cherries.

St. Joseph's Parish Cookbook

Cheese Cake

1¼ cups graham cracker
  crumbs
1 cup + 2 tablespoons sugar
3 tablespoons margarine or
  butter, melted

19 ounces cream cheese,
  softened
1 teaspoon lemon juice
¼ teaspoon vanilla
3 eggs

Heat oven to 350°. Mix cracker crumbs, 2 tablespoons sugar, and butter or margarine. Press into bottom of 9-inch springform pan. Bake 10 minutes; cool.

Heat oven to 300°. Beat cream cheese in large mixing bowl. Add 1 cup sugar gradually, beating until fluffy. Add lemon juice and vanilla. Beat in one egg at a time. Pour over crumb mixture. Bake until center is firm, about one hour. Cool to room temperature. Refrigerate at least 3 hours, but no longer than 10 days. Loosen edge of cheese cake with knife before removing side of pan. Top with a can of pie filling if desired.

The Orient Volunteer Fire Department Cookbook

Turtle Cheesecake

CRUST:

5 tablespoons melted unsalted
butter
1/4 cup sugar

1 1/4 cups (5 ounces) graham
cracker crumbs

Cover bottom of 10-inch springform pan with foil; wrap around edge; replace side of pan. Mix crust ingredients and press into springform pan and half way up sides. Refrigerate 10 minutes.

FILLING:

16 ounces cream cheese,
softened
1 cup sweetened, condensed
milk
3 grade-A large eggs, room
temperature

4 ounces semi-sweet chocolate
(imported), melted
1/2 cup caramel sauce
1/2 teaspoon cornstarch in 1/2
teaspoon water
1/2 cup chopped pecans, roasted

Beat cream cheese until smooth. Add milk gradually, then blend in eggs. Divide in half and add melted chocolate to half, blending well. Alternate spooning in plain and chocolate batter. Mix caramel sauce with cornstarch and water; drizzle over cheesecake batters. Run spatula through to marble.

Bake at 300° for 55 minutes. Batter will rise some around the edges, but not in the middle. Put directly into refrigerator, covered loosely with light cardboard cover. Refrigerate overnight. Remove from pan and foil. Place on serving plate and sprinkle with pecans. Makes 12-16 servings.

Return Engagement

Iowa Dirt Cake

1/2 cup butter
1 cup sugar
1 (8-ounce) package cream
cheese
2 packages chocolate or
vanilla instant pudding

3 1/2 cups milk
1 (12-ounce) container
Cool Whip
1 (20-ounce) package Oreo
Cookies, crushed

Blend butter, sugar, and cream cheese. Mix pudding with milk and fold in Cool Whip. Fold in cream cheese mixture. Put 2/3 of crushed Oreos in a 9x13-inch pan. Pat down. Cover with Cool Whip mixture. Sprinkle remaining Oreos on top. Refrigerate to set. You may want to decorate with gummy worms.

Fire Gals' Hot Pans Cookbook

Cookies and Candies

*Little Brown church, made famous by the song, "Little Brown Church in the Vale."
Nashua.*

Apple Pie Bars

CRUST:

2½ cups flour
1 tablespoon sugar
1 teaspoon salt
1 cup soft lard

⅔ cup milk
1 egg yolk, slightly beaten (save white for glaze)

Mix flour, sugar, salt, and lard with pastry blender. Then add milk and slightly beaten egg yolk. Mix all together and divide for bottom and top crusts. Roll out bottom crust and shape into a 12x15-inch cookie sheet pan with sides.

FILLING:

1½ cups sugar
2 tablespoons flour

1 teaspoon cinnamon
5 cups apples

Combine sugar, flour, and cinnamon; mix with apples. Put apple mixture on bottom crust in pan. Then roll out second crust and put on top of apple mixture. Make fluted edges and cut slits in it. Slightly whip one egg white and spread over crust. Bake at 400° for 30-40 minutes or until golden brown and bubbly. Glaze with powdered sugar frosting while still warm.

T.W. and Anna Elliott Family Receipts

Fresh Apple Bars

4 cups apples (chop or dice thin)
2 cups flour
2 teaspoons cinnamon
1 teaspoon soda
½ teaspoon salt
2 cups sugar

2 eggs
1 cup salad oil
1 teaspoon vanilla
1 teaspoon burnt sugar flavoring
½ cup walnuts

Peel, core and dice apples. Sift dry ingredients together in mixing bowl. Add eggs and all liquids at the same time and mix well (will be very thick). Add apples and nuts and mix lightly. Spread into a 10x15-inch jellyroll pan. Bake at 350° for 45 minutes.

May be frosted, but is very good plain or with whipped topping or ice cream.

Fontanelle Good Samaritan Center
Commemorative Cookbook

Yummy Cherry Bars

2 cups flour
2 cups quick oatmeal
1/2 teaspoon soda
1 1/4 cups sugar
1/2 cup chopped pecans

1 3/4 cups melted butter
1 (21-ounce) can cherry pie
   filling
1 cup miniature
   marshmallows

In a large bowl combine flour, oatmeal, soda, sugar, pecans, and butter. Mix at low speed, scraping sides of bowl often until crumbly (2 or 3 minutes). Reserve 1 1/2 cups crumb mixture, and spread remaining mixture evenly in 13x9-inch pan that is buttered. Bake at 350° for 12-15 minutes, until brown at edges. Gently spoon pie filling over crust and sprinkle with marshmallows, then remaining crumbs. Return to oven for 25 minutes or until lightly browned. Cool.

Iowa Granges Celebrating 125 Years of Cooking

Pumpkin Bars

2 cups sugar
1 cup cooking oil
4 eggs
1 3/4 cups pumpkin
2 cups flour

2 teaspoons baking powder
1 teaspoon soda
1/2 teaspoon salt
2 teaspoons cinnamon

ICING:

Cream sugar and oil. Add eggs and pumpkin; beat well. Add dry ingredients and mix thoroughly. Spread batter in greased 17x11-inch cookie sheet and bake at 350° for 25 minutes. Cool, and frost with Cream Cheese Icing.

CREAM CHEESE ICING:

1 (3-ounce) package cream
   cheese
6 tablespoons butter or
   margarine

1 teaspoon vanilla
1 tablespoon milk
1 3/4 cups powdered sugar

Cream together cream cheese and butter. Stir in vanilla and milk; add powdered sugar and beat until mixture is smooth.

St. Joseph's Parish Cookbook

Bohemian Chewy Bars

FIRST LAYER:

¹/₂ cup oleo	1 cup flour

SECOND LAYER:

¹/₂ cup coconut	¹/₄ teaspoon baking powder
1¹/₂ cups brown sugar	¹/₂ teaspoon salt
1 cup pecans, chopped	2 eggs, beaten
2 tablespoons flour	1 teaspoon vanilla

FROSTING:

1¹/₂ cups powdered sugar	¹/₄ teaspoon lemon flavoring
2 tablespoons oleo	2 tablespoons orange juice
2 teaspoons lemon juice	

Combine ingredients for first layer and pat into 9x13-inch pan. Bake until light brown, about 10 minutes in a 350° oven. While first layer browns, combine all ingredients for second layer. Spoon over baked crust and return to 350° oven for 20 minutes more. Cool. Combine ingredients for frosting. If a little more liquid is needed to make spreading consistency, use lemon or orange juice. Frost cooled bars and sprinkle top with nuts, if desired. Cut into bars or squares. Very good!

Iowa Granges Celebrating 125 Years of Cooking

Sour Cream Bars

1³/₄ cups rolled oats	1 cup margarine or butter,
1³/₄ cups flour	softened
1 cup brown sugar	¹/₂ teaspoon butter flavoring
1 teaspoon baking soda	

Combine and mix like pie crust. Reserve half of the mixture for topping. Pat other half into a 9x13-inch pan. Bake for 15 minutes at 350°.

4 egg yolks or whites, beaten	2 cups raisins
1¹/₂ cups (or less) white	Dash cinnamon
sugar	2 teaspoons vanilla
3 tablespoons cornstarch	Dash salt
2 cups sour cream	

Mix together in saucepan. Boil over low heat, stirring for 5-10 minutes. Pour over baked crust. Top with remaining crumbs and return to oven to bake for 30-45 minutes at 350°. Cut into bars. Freeze well.

First Christian Church Centennial Cookbook

World's Best Cookie Bars

LAYER 1:

1 cup flour   ¼ cup sugar
½ cup butter

Mix with pastry blender and press into 9x13-inch pan. Bake at 375°
for 10 minutes.

LAYER 2:

1 cup graham cracker   ½ cup chocolate chips
  crumbs   ½ cup chopped nuts
1 teaspoon baking powder   (optional)
1 can Eagle Brand milk

Melt together and pour over crust. Bake at 325° for 25 minutes. Cool.

LAYER 3:

½ cup butter, softened   1 teaspoon vanilla
1½ cups powdered sugar

Whip, and frost.

New Beginnings Cookbook

Czech composer Antonin Dvorak spent the summer of 1893 in Spillville. He
worked on his "New World Symphony" in what is now the Bily Clock Museum,
where hand-carved clocks (by Czechoslovakian brothers Frank and Joseph Bily)
can be seen.

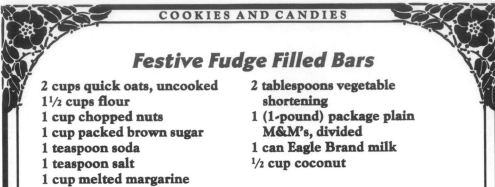

Festive Fudge Filled Bars

2 cups quick oats, uncooked
1½ cups flour
1 cup chopped nuts
1 cup packed brown sugar
1 teaspoon soda
1 teaspoon salt
1 cup melted margarine

2 tablespoons vegetable
shortening
1 (1-pound) package plain
M&M's, divided
1 can Eagle Brand milk
½ cup coconut

Mix together first seven ingredients to resemble coarse crumbs. Reserve 1½ cups; press remaining crumb mixture into bottom of 9x13-inch pan. Bake at 375° for 10 minutes.

Melt vegetable shortening with 1½ cups plain M&M's in heavy pan or microwave, stirring and pressing with spoon to break up chocolate mixture. This mixture will be almost melted and pieces of color coating remain. Remove from heat and stir in Eagle Brand milk and mix well. Spread over partially baked crust within ½-inch of edge. Combine reserved crumb mixture and approximately one cup M&M's and coconut. Sprinkle on top and press. Continue baking 20-25 minutes.

Appanoose County Cookbook

Mound Bars

Easy and very good! Tastes just like the candy bar!

2 cups graham cracker
crumbs
½ cup butter, melted
½ cup sugar
1 cup sweetened condensed
milk

2 cups coconut
1 (6-ounce) package chocolate
chips
1 (6-ounce) package butterscotch
chips

Mix graham cracker crumbs, butter, and sugar. Line bottom of 9x13-inch pan and bake for 10 minutes. Combine condensed milk and coconut and spread over crust. Bake at 350° for 15 minutes. Melt chocolate and butterscotch chips and spread on warm bars.

The L.o.V.E Chocolate Cookbook

Cinnamon Bars

³⁄₄ cup oil	¹⁄₂ teaspoon salt
¹⁄₂ cup honey	1 teaspoon cinnamon
2 cups flour	1 egg
1 cup sugar	1 teaspoon vanilla
1 teaspoon baking soda	1 cup nuts

Mix oil and honey. Add dry ingredients, then add egg, vanilla, and nuts. Pour on greased cookie sheet and bake at 350° for 20 minutes.

GLAZE:

2 tablespoons margarine	1 teaspoon vanilla
2 cups powdered sugar	2 tablespoons water

Spread while warm and cut into bars.

Iowa Granges Celebrating 125 Years of Cooking

Moon Bars

1 cup water	1 (8-ounce) package cream
1 stick oleo	cheese, softened
1 cup flour	1 (8-ounce) carton Cool
4 eggs	Whip
2 packages instant vanilla	Chocolate syrup
pudding	Nuts (optional)

Boil water and oleo. Add flour and stir well. Add eggs one at a time. Stir well. Bake at 400° for 30 minutes in jellyroll pan. Cool. Mix pudding according to directions. Add softened cream cheese. Mix and put on baked crust. Cool. Add Cool Whip. Drizzle with chocolate. Top with nuts if desired.

Trinity Lutheran Church Centennial Cookbook

Delta Bars

¹/₂ cup shortening	1 teaspoon baking powder
1 cup sugar	¹/₂ teaspoon salt
1 egg, separated	1 cup brown sugar
1 teaspoon vanilla	¹/₂ cup nuts or coconut
1¹/₄ cups flour	

Heat oven to 375°. Mix shortening, sugar, egg yolk, and vanilla well. Stir in dry ingredients and mix thoroughly. Spread in greased 13x9x2-inch pan. Beat egg white until foamy; gradually beat in brown sugar. Continue beating until mixture is stiff and glossy. Fold in nuts and/or coconut. Spread mixture over dough in pan. Bake about 25 minutes. Cut while warm into 2-inch squares.

Välkommen till Swedesburg

Triple Good Raisin Bars

FILLING:

2 cups raisins	1 tablespoon grated lemon
1 cup sweetened condensed	peel
milk	1 tablespoon lemon juice

Cook raisins, condensed milk, lemon peel and juice, just until mixture begins to bubble. Cool slightly.

CRUST:

1 cup margarine	1 cup flour
1²/₃ cups brown sugar	¹/₂ teaspoon baking soda
1¹/₂ teaspoons vanilla	1 cup chopped nuts
2¹/₂ cups oatmeal	

Beat margarine, brown sugar, and vanilla. Add remaining ingredients and blend until crumbly. Reserve 2 cups of mixture and press remaining mixture into a 9x13-inch pan. Pour raisin filling over this and spread remaining crumbs over filling. Bake at 350° for 25-30 minutes.

St. Joseph's Parish Cookbook

Pen Pal Brownies

2 sticks oleo
9 tablespoons cocoa
2 cups sugar
3 eggs

1 teaspoon vanilla
1/2 teaspoon salt
1 1/2 cups flour
Nuts (optional)

Melt oleo and mix with cocoa; cool. Add sugar and mix. Beat in eggs and add vanilla and salt. Stir in flour and also nuts, if desired. Spread mixture into an 11x15-inch pan that has been sprayed with Pam. Bake at 350° for 20-25 minutes.

Note: Bake for 20 minutes for more "fudgy" texture. Frost, if desired.

Iowa Granges Celebrating 125 Years of Cooking

Snicker Bars

2 cups chocolate chips
1/2 cup butterscotch chips
1/2 cup creamy peanut butter
1 cup sugar
1/4 cup milk
1/4 cup margarine

1 cup marshmallow creme
1 teaspoon vanilla
1 1/2 cup dry-roasted
   peanuts
40 caramels
4 tablespoons water

Melt and spread 1 cup chocolate chips, 1/4 cup butterscotch chips, and 1/4 cup creamy peanut butter in buttered 9x13-inch pan. Cool. Boil 1 cup sugar, milk, and margarine for 5 minutes to soft ball stage. Add marshmallow creme, 1/4 cup peanut butter, and vanilla. Pour over first layer. Sprinkle peanuts over 2nd layer. Mix together caramels and hot water, melt and pour over peanuts. Melt 1 cup chocolate chips, 1/4 cup butterscotch chips, and 1/4 cup creamy peanut butter and spread over caramel layer re;aining. Cool and cut into squares.

Trinity Lutheran Church Centennial Cookbook

Buddy Holly gave his last concert at the legendary Surf Ballroom in Clear Lake, home to big band and rock n' roll entertainers for nearly 50 years. February 3, 1959 is known as "the day the music died." On that day Buddy Holly, Richie Valens, and the Big Bopper died in a plane crash near Clear Lake.

Butter Brickle Bars

1 yellow cake mix	1 slightly beaten egg
1/3 cup oleo	

Mix like pie crust and pat into a 15x10-inch jellyroll pan.

1 (6-ounce) package butter brickle chips (Heath bars)	1 can sweetened condensed milk
1½ cups chopped pecans	

Mix and dot over top of crust. Bake at 350° for 20 minutes.

The Berns Family Cookbook

Salted Nut Roll Bars

1 package yellow cake mix	1 egg
1/3 cup butter	Miniature marshmallows

Mix together cake mix, butter, and egg. Press into a 9x13-inch pan and bake at 350° for 12-18 minutes. Remove from oven and sprinkle with marshmallows. Return to oven for 1-2 minutes. Cool while preparing topping.

TOPPING:

2/3 cup corn syrup	2 cups Rice Krispies
1/4 cup margarine	2 cup salted peanuts
2 teaspoons vanilla	
1 (12-ounce) package peanut butter chips	

In pan heat syrup, margarine, vanilla, and chips until melted and smooth. Stir in cereal and nuts. Immediately spoon warm topping over marshmallows and spread.

Madison County Cookbook

West Branch is the birthplace of President Herbert Hoover, the 31st President of the United States. There is a National Historical Site and Presidential Library there.

Paddington's Peanut Logs

A favorite for children of all ages.

1 cup butter, melted
2 cups graham cracker crumbs,
   finely crushed
1¼ cups creamy peanut butter

2 cups powdered sugar
1 (12-ounce) package chocolate
   chips

Blend all ingredients except chocolate chips thoroughly. Mixture will be very stiff. Roll and shape into 1½-inch flat-sided logs. Refrigerate for one hour. Melt chocolate chips in a double boiler, stirring with a rubber spatula. Using tongs, dip and roll logs in chocolate until completely covered. Place coated logs on wax paper-covered cookie sheet. Chill. Makes 72.

Recipes from Iowa with Love

Nuss Plätzchen
(Nut Cookies)

6 egg whites
2¼ cups sugar
Dash of cinnamon
2 cups finely chopped filberts
   or hazelnuts

2 cups flour
1 teaspoon baking powder

Beat egg whites until stiff; gradually add sugar and cinnamon and stir until well blended. Add nuts and flour sifted with baking powder. Drop by teaspoons onto greased baking sheet and bake in 325° oven for 12-15 minutes.

Amana Colony Recipes

Cream Cheese Brownies

1 package German chocolate
cake mix
1 (8-ounce) package cream
cheese, softened

1 egg
½ cup sugar
½ cup milk chocolate chips

Heat oven to 350°. Grease and flour jellyroll pan. Prepare cake mix as directed on package. Pour batter into pan. Mix remaining ingredients. Drop by tablespoonfuls onto batter. Cut through batter with knife for marbled effect. Bake until cake tests done in center, 25-35 minutes.

Special Recipes from our Hearts

Dump Brownies

2 cups sugar
1¾ cups flour
1 cup oil
5 eggs
1 teaspoon vanilla

½ cup cocoa
½ teaspoon salt
1 (6-ounce) package chocolate
chips

Dump all ingredients, except chips, in a mixing bowl. Mix well until blended. Pour into a greased 9x13-inch pan. Top with chocolate chips. Bake in a 350° oven for 20-25 minutes.

If you are low on chocolate chips, frost with Never Fail Chocolate Frosting.

Fontanelle Good Samaritan Center
Commemorative Cookbook

Never Fail Chocolate Frosting

1½ cups sugar
6 tablespoons milk
6 tablespoons butter (oleo)

½ cup chocolate chips
1 teaspoon vanilla

Just bring to a boil, sugar, milk, and butter/oleo. Then boil one minute. Add chocolate chips and vanilla. Beat until right consistency for frosting. Will frost a 9x13-inch cake. Delicious on Dump Brownies.

Fontanelle Good Samaritan Center
Commemorative Cookbook

Zucchini Brownies

2 cups shredded zucchini	1½ teaspoons soda
1½ cups oil	⅓ cup cocoa
2 cups flour	2 teaspoons vanilla
1 teaspoon salt	½ cup chopped nuts

Combine in order given. Pour into greased 9x13-inch pan. Bake at 350° for 30-35 minutes.

X____ Community Cookbook

S'Mores

3/4 cup light corn syrup	1 small box Golden Grahams
3 tablespoons margarine	cereal
1 (12-ounce) package	3 cups miniature
chocolate chips	marshmallows
1 teaspoon vanilla	

Grease a 13x9x2-inch rectangular pan. Heat syrup, margarine, and chocolate chips together until boiling, stirring constantly. Remove from heat; stir in vanilla. Pour chocolate mixture over cereal (in a bowl). Toss until coated. Fold in marshmallows, one cup at a time. Press into pan with back of a buttered spoon. Let stand one hour. Cut into 2-inch squares. Store at room temperature.

The Nading Family Cookbook

Lemon Squares

1 cup butter or margarine
2 cups flour
½ cup powdered sugar
4 eggs, beaten
2 cups sugar

4 tablespoons flour
6 tablespoons real lemon
  juice
1 teaspoon baking powder
½ teaspoon salt

Cream together butter and flour. Add powdered sugar. Press into a 9x13-inch cake pan. Bake at 350° for 20 minutes. While mixture is baking, add sugar, flour, lemon juice, baking powder, and salt to beaten eggs. Mix well. After crust is finished baking, spread egg mixture on top. Bake an additional 30 minutes. Remove from oven; sprinkle with powdered sugar. Cool and cut into 1-inch squares.

Fire Gals' Hot Pans Cookbook

Double-Chocolate Sugar Cookies

1 (12-ounce) package
  semi-sweet chocolate chips,
  divided
1 cup butter or margarine,
  softened
1 cup sugar
1 large egg

2 tablespoons milk
1 teaspoon vanilla extract
3 cups flour
1 tespoon baking powder
½ teaspoon baking soda
½ cup sugar

Melt one cup chocolate chips in a heavy saucepan over low heat. Reserve remaining chocolate chips and set aside. Beat butter at medium speed with electric mixer until fluffy. Gradually add one cup sugar, beating well. Add egg, milk, and vanilla, mixing well. Add melted chocolate, mixing until blended. Combine dry ingredients, except ½ cup sugar, and add to butter mixture, mixing well. Add remaining chocolate chips. Roll dough into balls, one tablespoon at a time. Roll balls in ½ cup sugar. Place on cookie sheet. Bake at 400° for 8-10 minutes. (Cookies will be soft and will firm up as they cool.) Yields 4½ dozen cookies.

The L.o.V.E Chocolate Cookbook

Caramel-Filled Chocolate Cookies

Well worth the effort.

2½ cups flour
¾ cup unsweetened cocoa
1 teaspoon soda
1 cup sugar
1 cup firmly-packed brown
sugar
1 cup oleo or butter, softened
2 teaspoons vanilla

2 eggs
1 cup chopped pecans
48 Rolo chew caramels
(9-ounce package)
1 tablespoon sugar
4 ounces vanilla-flavored candy
coating (if desired)

Heat oven to 375°. In a bowl, combine flour, cocoa, and soda; mix well. In a large bowl, beat one cup sugar, brown sugar, and oleo until fluffy. Add vanilla and eggs; beat well. Add flour mixture; blend well. Stir in ½ cup pecans. For each cookie, with floured hands, shape about a tablespoon of dough around one caramel, covering completely. In a small bowl, combine remaining ½ cup pecans and one tablespoon sugar. Press one side of each ball into mixture. Place nut-side-up on ungreased cookie sheet. Bake at 375° for 7-10 minutes, or until lightly cracked. Cool 2 minutes. Melt candy coating, stirring constantly. Drizzle over cookies.

Alta United Methodist Church Cookbook

Cookie Mix

1 cup white sugar
½ cup dry milk
1 teaspoon salt
½ teaspoon soda

1 cup brown sugar
4 cups flour
3 teaspoons baking powder
1½ cups shortening

Mix all together, except shortening. Cut shortening in and store in the refrigerator in an airtight container. When ready to bake, mix in 3 tablespoons water to 2 cups of mix. Add flavoring and nuts, or raisins, or chips, or coconut. Bake at 350° for 10-12 minutes.

Lehigh Public Library 1994 Cookbook

Chocolate Chip Pudding Cookies

3$\frac{1}{3}$ cups flour
1$\frac{1}{2}$ teaspoons baking soda
1$\frac{1}{2}$ cups butter or margarine,
  softened
1 cup firmly packed brown
  sugar
$\frac{1}{2}$ cup sugar

1 (6-ounce) package vanilla
  flavor instant pudding
1$\frac{1}{2}$ teaspoons vanilla
3 eggs
3 cups chocolate chips
$\frac{1}{2}$ cup chopped nuts

Mix flour with baking soda. Combine butter, the sugars, pudding mix, and vanilla in a large bowl; beat until creamy and smooth. Beat in eggs. Gradually add flour mixture; then stir in chips and nuts. Drop by rounded teaspoonfuls onto ungreased baking sheet. Bake at 375° for 8-10 minutes. Makes about 10 dozen.

Thompson Family Cookbook

Unbaked Peanut Butter Cookies

1$\frac{1}{2}$ cups sugar
1$\frac{1}{2}$ pints peanut butter
1$\frac{1}{2}$ cups white corn syrup

1$\frac{1}{2}$ quarts cornflakes or Rice
  Krispies

Mix all ingredients together. Drop by small ice cream scoop onto wax paper. This makes a very large amount. Good for sending to school with children.

Mom's Favorite Recipes

Diabetic Applesauce Cookies

1²/₃ cups flour
½ teaspoon salt
1 teaspoon cinnamon
½ teaspoon cloves
½ teaspoon nutmeg
1 teaspoon baking soda
½ cup margarine

1 egg
2 tablespoons liquid artificial
   sweetener
1 cup unsweetened apple sauce
⅓ cup raisins
1 cup oatmeal

Preheat oven to 350°. Sift flour, salt, cinnamon, nutmeg, cloves, and soda together. Mix margarine, egg, and sweetener until light and fluffy. Add flour mixture and applesauce alternately, mixing well after each addition. Fold in raisins and oatmeal. Drop by level tablespoon onto greased cookie sheet. Bake about 15-18 minutes until golden brown.

Special Recipes from our Hearts

Mom's Pineapple Drop Cookies

1 cup white sugar
1 cup brown sugar
1 cup butter or oleo
2 eggs, beaten
1 (16-ounce) can crushed
   pineapple with juice

4 cups flour
1 teaspoon salt
1 teaspoon baking soda
1 teaspoon baking powder
1 cup chopped nuts (optional)

Combine sugars and oleo. Add eggs and pineapple. Add dry ingredients. Add nuts, if desired, last. Drop by teaspoonful on cookie sheet. Bake at 350° for 12 minutes.

May frost with a simple powdered sugar frosting, but add some squeezed orange juice and pulp.

SEP Junior Women's Club 25th Anniversary Cookbook

The Hitchcock House in Lewis is a restored station on the Underground Railroad. It now features special exhibits and country music events.

Orange Slice Cookies

2 cups flour, divided
1 pound orange slice candies,
   cut fine
1½ cups brown sugar

½ cup margarine
2 eggs
1 teaspoon soda
½ cup coconut

Put ½ cup flour on orange slices so they don't stick together. Mix sugar, margarine, and eggs. Add 1½ cups flour with soda, coconut, and orange slices. Make in balls, press down with fork.   When doubling recipe, use only one pound orange slices.

Home Cooking with the Cummer Family

Cashew Cookies

½ cup butter or oleo
1 cup brown sugar
1 egg
½ teaspoon vanilla
2 cups flour

¾ teaspoon soda
¾ teaspoon baking powder
¼ teaspoon salt
⅓ cup sour cream
1¾ cups whole cashews

Cream butter and sugar. Add remaining ingredients. Drop by teaspoon on ungreased cookie sheet. Bake at 350° for 10 minutes. Makes 4 dozen.

CASHEW COOKIE FROSTING:
½ cup butter
3 tablespoons cream

¼ teaspoon vanilla
2 cups powdered sugar

Brown butter; cool slightly. Add remaining ingredients and beat until spreading consistency.

Titonka Centennial Cookbook

Elk Horn is the site of the largest Danish settlement in the United States. The authentic Danish windmill, built in Denmark in 1848, was reassembled in Iowa.

Krakalinger
(Dutch Figure-Eights)

4 cups flour
2 teaspoons baking powder
1½ cups butter

1 egg
1 cup milk
Sugar

Sift together flour and baking powder. Cut in butter and then add egg and milk as though making pastry. Roll dough out on sugar, working in as much sugar as possible. Cut into strips and make in figure-eights. Place on buttered cookie sheet and bake at 375° just until lightly browned (9-10 minutes).

Armstrong Centennial

Dutch Letters

. . .especially for Christmas. The strips are formed into the shape of the first letter of your last name or of your friends. Then give for a gift, as was done traditionally in Holland.

ALMOND PASTE:

4 eggs
2 teaspoons almond flavoring
2-3 cups powdered sugar

$1\frac{1}{2}$ cups almonds, chopped fine

Beat eggs, saving the white of one egg. Stir in almond flavoring. Add powdered sugar and almonds. Refrigerate 2 hours or overnight.

PASTRY:

$1\frac{1}{4}$ cups lard or shortening
2 cups flour

Pinch of salt
3 tablespoons water

Blend lard or shortening, flour, and salt with pastry blender. Stir in water, one tablespoonful at a time. Roll out on lightly floured board and cut into 4-inch-wide strips. Place almond paste along center of each strip, and fold over the dough. To seal, moisten the long edge of each strip with egg white.

Length of individual filled strips will be determined by size of letters to be shaped. Cut filled strips, seal ends and place strips on cookie sheet, seam-side-down. Form into letters, pressing edges securely together. Brush tops with lightly beaten egg white.

Bake at 425° for 10 minutes. Prick holes in top of each letter and return to oven. Bake at 350° an additional 15 minutes, or until lightly browned. Letters may be topped with powdered sugar icing, if desired.

Dutch Touches

Almond Cookies
(Bitterkoekjes)

¹/₂ pound almond paste   **³/₄ cup sugar**
2 egg whites, unbeaten

Mix ingredients together with a fork. Drop by teaspoon onto greased cookie sheet. Bake at 300° for 20 minutes. Remove from cookie sheet promptly to prevent sticking.

Dutch Touches

Dutch Handkerchiefs

2 cups flour   **1 egg white**
1 cup butter   **1 cup sugar**
¹/₄ cup water   **1 teaspoon almond flavoring**

Cut butter into flour. Add water gradually as if making a pie crust. Roll very thin and cut into 4-inch squares. Beat egg white until stiff. Fold in sugar and flavoring. Place about 2 teaspoonfuls of the egg white mixture into the center of each square and fold the corners toward the center of the square. Place on a greased cookie sheet and bake at 350° until lightly browned.

Dandy Dutch Recipes

Pride of Iowa Cookies

1 cup brown sugar   **1 teaspoon baking powder**
1 cup white sugar   **¹/₂ teaspoon salt**
1 cup shortening   **1³/₄ cups oatmeal**
2 eggs   **¹/₂ cups nuts (optional)**
1³/₄ cups flour   **1 cup chocolate chips**
1 teaspoon soda   **¹/₂ cup coconut (optional)**

Cream sugars, shortening, and eggs. Sift flour, soda, baking powder, and salt. Add oatmeal, then stir into creamed mixture. Add nuts, chips, and coconut. Bake at 350° for 10-12 minutes.

Country Cupboard Cookbook

Ladyfingers

8 egg yolks
½ pound sugar
8 egg whites

2 cups sifted flour
Powdered sugar

Beat egg yolks and sugar till light and foamy. Beat egg whites until stiff, then add to yolk mixture. Add sifted flour, and stir until smooth. Pour batter into floured finger molds or on waxed paper pressed into finger forms. Bake on cookie sheet in slow (300°) oven for 1 hour. Dust with powdered sugar.

Cherished Czech Recipes

Scotchies

1 cup sugar
1 cup white Karo syrup

1 cup peanut butter
6 cups Rice Krispies

FROSTING:
1½ cups chocolate chips

Combine sugar and Karo syrup and bring to a boil, stirring until sugar is dissolved. Remove from heat and stir in peanut butter. Have the 6 cups Rice Krispies in a large bowl and pour syrup over Rice Krispies. Stir until all coated and press lightly into 9x13-inch pan. Melt chips together in microwave and spread on bars. When cool, cut in squares.

Cookin' for the Crew

Cookie Brittle

1 cup oleo
1 cup sugar
1 teaspoon salt
1 teaspoon vanilla

2 cups unsifted flour
1 cup nutmeats
1 (6-ounce) package chocolate
  chips

Grease a 10x15-inch pan. Mix all and pat dough into pan. Bake 20-25 minutes at 375°, or until edges turn brown. Cool in pan or rack. When cooled, break into pieces.

Spitfire Anniversary Cookbook

Fudge

4½ cups sugar
1 tall can evaporated milk
1 cup (2 sticks) butter or
  margarine
3 (6-ounce) packages
  semi-sweet chocolate chips

1 (8-ounce) jar marshmallow
  creme
1½ cups pecans

Combine the sugar and milk. Bring to a boil, stirring to dissolve sugar. After mixture reaches a full rolling boil, cook for 11 minutes, stirring constantly. Remove from heat; add the butter, chocolate chips and the marshmallow creme. Stir in nuts. Pour into a shallow foil-lined pan to a depth of one inch. Chill and cut into squares. Wrap in foil or waxed paper. Makes about 5 pounds. This will stay creamy for weeks.

Our Savior's Kvindherred Lutheran Church

Ice Cream Sugar Cookie Sandwiches

1 cup powdered sugar
1 cup white sugar
1 cup butter
1 cup vegetable oil
2 eggs
1 teaspoon vanilla flavoring

4 cups flour
1 teaspoon baking soda
1 teaspoon salt
1 teaspoon cream of tartar
Ice cream

Cream powdered sugar, white sugar, shortening, and vegetable oil; beat well. Add eggs and vanilla; beat until fluffy. Sift flour, baking soda, salt, and cream of tartar; add to creamed mixture. Roll into balls the size of walnuts and roll in granulated sugar. Place on ungreased cookie sheet and bake at 350° for 10 minutes.

Once cooled, place one dip of softened ice cream between cookies and slightly press together. Wrap in clear plastic and store in freezer. When serving, top with fudge sauce, whipped cream and a cherry.

Blue Willow's "Sweet Treasures"

Eskimo Pies, the popular ice cream treats, were invented in Onawa, Iowa, in 1920.

Fudge Puddles

½ cup butter or margarine,
   softened
½ cup creamy peanut butter
½ cup sugar
½ cup packed light brown
   sugar

1 egg
½ teaspoon vanilla extract
1¼ cups all-purpose flour
¾ teaspoon baking soda
½ teaspoon salt

In a mixing bowl cream butter, peanut butter, and sugars; add egg and vanilla. Stir together flour, baking soda, and salt. Add to creamed mixture. Mix well. Chill for one hour. Shape into 48 balls, 1 inch each. Place in lightly greased mini-muffin tins. Bake 14-16 minutes at 325° or until lightly browned. Remove from oven immediately; make "wells" in the center of each by lightly pressing with a melon baller. Cool in pans for 5 minutes then carefully remove to wire racks.

FUDGE FILLING:

1 cup (6 ounces) milk chocolate
   chips
1 cup (6 ounces) semi-sweet
   chocolate chips

1 (14-ounce) can sweetened
   condensed milk
1 teaspoon vanilla extract
Chopped peanuts

Melt chocolate chips in double boiler over simmering water. Stir in milk and vanilla. Mix well. Using a small pitcher or pastry bag, fill each shell with filling. Sprinkle with peanuts. Leftover filling can be stored in refrigerator and served warm over ice cream. Yield: 4 dozen.

Marcus, Iowa, Quasquicentennial Cookbook

Des Moines Fudge

3 cups sugar
1 envelope unflavored gelatin
1 cup milk
½ cup white corn syrup
3 squares unsweetened
  chocolate

1 cup butter or margarine
2 teaspoons vanilla
1 cup nuts

Use some of the butter to grease sides of heavy saucepan. Mix sugar and gelatin in pan. Add milk, corn syrup, chocolate, and butter. Cook over medium heat, stirring frequently until it reaches 238° on a candy thermometer. Pour into a large mixer bowl and cool for 15 minutes. Add vanilla and beat until thick. Add nuts and pour into buttered 9x9-inch pan. Cool well before cutting. This fudge keeps for 4-6 weeks in refrigerator.

The L.o.V.E Chocolate Cookbook

Merry Cranberry Christmas Fudge

1 (14-ounce) can sweetened
  condensed milk
3 cups semi-sweet chocolate
  chips (18 ounces)
¼ cup orange marmalade, long
  or big pieces of fruit chopped

1 teaspoon orange extract
¼ cup fresh cranberries, finely
  diced
¼ cup pecans, finely
  chopped

In a 4-cup glass measuring cup or microwave-safe bowl, combine milk and chocolate chips. Microwave 3 minutes or until chocolate is melted. Stir until smooth. Stir in remaining ingredients. Spoon into prepared paper cups. Cool. Makes 60-66 tiny cups.

The Amazing Little Cranberry Cookbook

Along the Grant Wood Scenic Byway, you'll recognize the things that inspired this Iowa painter: rolling hills, church spires, corn stalks, rounded haystacks. The "American Gothic" House of Grant Wood's famous painting is in Eldon.

Easter Nests

1/4 pound oleo
1/2 cup milk
2 cups sugar
6 tablespoons baking cocoa
1 teaspoon vanilla

1/2 cup peanut butter
2 1/2 cups quick oatmeal
1/2 cup coconut
1 bag jelly beans

Combine oleo, milk, sugar, and cocoa; bring to a boil. Boil hard for one minute. Remove from stove. Add remaining ingredients, except jelly beans; mix well. On waxed paper, drop by heaping tablespoons. Make an indention in center and immediately lay 3 colored jelly beans in the center. Let set on waxed paper until dry on the outside. Wrap individually with plastic wrap and store in an airtight container, or freeze until the Easter Bunny needs them. These make nice favors at each plate on the table for Easter dinner.

Woodbine Public Library

Chocolate and Peanut Butter Truffles

1 cup peanut butter chips
3/4 cup butter or margarine
1/2 cup cocoa powder

1 (14-ounce) can sweetened
   condensed milk
1 tablespoon vanilla extract

COATINGS:
Finely chopped nuts, or
   unsweetened cocoa, or
   graham cracker crumbs, or

confectioners' sugar, or
chocolate or candy sprinkles

In a heavy saucepan, over low heat, melt chips with butter. Stir in cocoa until smooth. Add milk and vanilla. Cook and stir until thickened and well blended, about 4 minutes. Remove from heat. Chill 2 hours or until firm enough to handle. Shape into 1-inch balls and roll in any of the above coatings. Chill until firm, about one hour. Store covered in refrigerator.

The L.o.V.E Chocolate Cookbook

Peanut Brittle

Easy and delicious!

1 cup sugar
1 cup raw peanuts

1 cup white syrup
1 teaspoon soda

Heat sugar and syrup until clear. Add raw peanuts and boil until it is amber in color (about like a penny). Remove from heat and add soda. Stir well (will be frothy). Pour into a well-buttered cookie sheet. Cool and break into pieces. Can add large flaked coconut if desired.

Country Cupboard Cookbook

Puffed Wheat Candy

A family tradition at Christmas; not sweet, but with distinctive flavor.

¹/₂ cup dark corn syrup
1 tablespoon molasses
1 teaspoon butter

1 tablespoon vinegar
¹/₄ teaspoon soda
4 cups Puffed Wheat cereal

Boil the first 4 ingredients to hard-boiled stage and add soda (will foam up). Pour over cereal. Put in buttered 8x8-inch pan. Cut in squares when cool.

Quasquicentennial / St. Olaf of Bode

Popcorn Balls

First grown commercially in 1888 by an Oldebolt farmer, popcorn is popular world-wide, thanks to Iowa exporters.

5 quarts of popped corn   **¹/₂ teaspoon salt**
1¹/₂ cups water   **1 teaspoon vinegar**
¹/₂ cup light corn syrup   **1 teaspoon vanilla**
2 cups sugar

Keep popcorn hot and crisp in a 300° oven. Butter sides of a saucepan. Combine remaining ingredients except the vanilla. Cook to hard ball stage, about 250°. Remove from heat. Add vanilla. Pour slowly over popcorn, stirring just enough to mix thoroughly. Butter hands and shape into balls. Makes 20-50 balls.

License to Cook Iowa Style

Pies and Desserts

The birthplace of Herbert Hoover. West Branch.

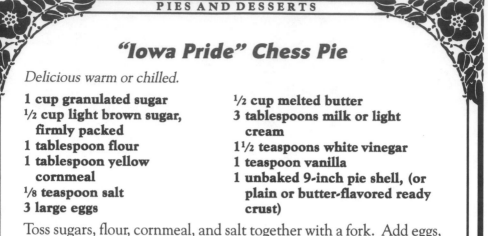

"Iowa Pride" Chess Pie

Delicious warm or chilled.

1 cup granulated sugar
½ cup light brown sugar, firmly packed
1 tablespoon flour
1 tablespoon yellow cornmeal
⅛ teaspoon salt
3 large eggs

½ cup melted butter
3 tablespoons milk or light cream
1½ teaspoons white vinegar
1 teaspoon vanilla
1 unbaked 9-inch pie shell, (or plain or butter-flavored ready crust)

Toss sugars, flour, cornmeal, and salt together with a fork. Add eggs, melted butter, milk or cream, vinegar, and vanilla. Beat mixture with electric beater until smooth. Pour into unbaked pie shell. Cover edges of crust with narrow strips of foil for first 25 minutes of baking to prevent overbrowning. Bake at 350° for 35-40 minutes or until a clean knife inserted in the center comes out clean. Can be frozen. Serves 6.

Recipes from Iowa with Love

Sour Cream Raisin Pie

1 cup sour cream
½ cup sugar
2 egg yolks (save whites)
1 tablespoon flour

1 teaspoon cinnamon
½ teaspoon cloves
1 cup raisins

Combine all ingredients and cook until thick. Pour into baked pie shell. Use egg whites for meringue.

MERINGUE:
2 egg whites
¼ teaspoon cream of tartar

¼ cup sugar

Whip egg whites and cream of tartar until frothy. Add sugar gradually and beat until stiff. Pile on hot pie filling. Bake at 400° for 8-10 minutes.

Lutheran Church Women Cookbook

Apple Pie with Sour Cream

2 tablespoons + ⅓ cup flour
¾ cup + ⅓ cup sugar
1¼ teaspoons cinnamon,
  divided
⅛ teaspoon salt
1 egg
½ teaspoon vanilla

1 cup sour cream
6 medium-sized apples, peeled,
  cored and sliced
1 (9-inch) pie shell, unbaked and
  chilled
¼ cup butter

Preheat oven to 400°. In a bowl, sift together 2 tablespoons flour, ¾ cup sugar, ¾ teaspoon cinnamon and salt. Stir in egg, vanilla, and sour cream. Fold in the apples and spoon mixture into pie shell. Bake 15 minutes, then reduce oven temperature to 350° and bake 30 minutes longer.

Meanwhile, combine the remaining flour, sugar, and cinnamon. With a pastry blender or fingertips, blend in the butter until mixture is crumbly. Increase the oven temperature to 400°. Sprinkle crumb mixture over the pie and bake 10 minutes longer.

German Recipes

Zucchini Pie

This pie tastes like Dutch apple pie.

4 cups zucchini, peeled
1½ teaspoons cream of
  tartar
Dash of salt
2 tablespoons flour
1 tablespoon lemon juice

Dash of nutmeg
1¼ cups sugar
1½ teaspoons cinnamon
1 teaspoon butter
1 (9-inch) unbaked pie shell

TOPPING:
1 stick margarine
½ cup sugar

1 cup flour

Peel zucchini. Cut lengthwise; scoop out seeds. Slice to resemble apple slices. Cook zucchini 10 minutes in small amount of water; drain. Mix cream of tartar, salt, flour, lemon juice, nutmeg, sugar, and cinnamon with zucchini. Pour into unbaked pie shell. Dot with butter. Make topping by mixing margarine, sugar, and flour and crumble over ingredients in pie shell. Bake at 375° for 45 minutes.

Fire Gals' Hot Pans Cookbook

Rhubarb Custard Pie

CRUST:

1 cup flour   1 tablespoon sugar
1/2 cup oleo

Mix until crumbly and push into pie plate. Bake at 350° until light
brown.

CUSTARD:

3 cups finely chopped   1 1/2 cups sugar
   rhubarb   1 1/2 tablespoons oleo
3 egg yolks   2 egg whites
2 tablespoons flour

Mix all ingredients, except egg whites, and cook until thick like custard. Pour into baked pie shell. Top with meringue made from egg
whites.

St. Paul's Woman's League 50th Anniversary Cook Book

Impossible Rhubarb Pie

2½ cups rhubarb, cut up
1 cup sugar
½ cup Bisquick
1 teaspoon cinnamon

¾ cup milk
2 eggs
2 tablespoons butter, melted
¼ teaspoon nutmeg

STREUSEL:
2 tablespoons firm butter
½ cup Bisquick

¼ cup brown sugar
¼ cup nuts, chopped

Arrange rhubarb in 9-inch pie plate. Mix remaining ingredients. Pour over top. Sprinkle evenly with Streusel topping. Bake at 375° for 40 minutes or until knife comes out clean.

Cookin' for Miracles

Rhubarb Crunch Pie

1 (9-inch) unbaked pie shell
3 cups fresh or frozen rhubarb, cut up
1 cup sugar
3 tablespoons flour

Dash of salt
⅔ cup flour
½ cup sugar
⅓ cup margarine, softened

Mix rhubarb, one cup sugar, 3 tablespoons flour, and salt; place in pie shell. Mix remaining flour and sugar with margarine. Sprinkle over the pie. Bake at 450° for 10 minutes, then at 350° for 40-50 minutes or until bubbly and browned.

Stirring Up Memories

Rhubarb Crisp

3½ cups rhubarb
1 cup sugar
3 tablespoons flour
1 cup brown sugar

1 cup oatmeal
1½ cups flour
1 cup oleo

Mix first 3 ingredients in 9x13-inch pan. Mix next 4 ingredients and crumble over top. Bake at 350° for 40 minutes. Can be doubled; just increase baking time.

The Great Iowa Home Cooking Expedition

Pink Lady Pie

CRUST:

1½ cups flour
¼ teaspoon salt
1½ tablespoons sugar

½ cup oil
2 tablespoons milk

Mix flour, salt, sugar, oil, and milk thoroughly. Press into 9-inch pie pan, making an edge or rim. Bake at 350° for 15-10 minutes. Set aside to cool.

FILLING:

2 cups diced rhubarb
1 cup sugar
1 (3-ounce) package strawberry gelatin

1 tablespoon lemon juice
2 cups whipped topping

Cook rhubarb and sugar slowly until tender. Add gelatin (dry). Stir gently until dissolved. Let cool. Add lemon juice. Cool to room temperature. Fold in whipped topping. Pour into cooled crust and refrigerate. This may be frozen. Top with additional whipped topping when served, if desired.

Country Cupboard Cookbook

Cream Puff Delight

1 cup water
1 stick butter
¼ teaspoon salt
1 cup flour
4 eggs
1 large box instant vanilla pudding

1 (8-ounce) package cream cheese
3 cups milk
Cool Whip
Hershey's Chocolate Syrup

Boil water; add butter and salt. Take off stove and add flour; stir until it forms a ball. Add eggs, one at a time, beating well after each. Spread out on cookie sheet. Bake at 350° for 25-30 minutes or until slightly brown; let cool. Mix package of vanilla pudding, cream cheese, and milk. Spread over crust. Spread Cool Whip over pudding mixture and drizzle chocolate syrup. Refrigerate.

The Berns Family Cookbook

French Apple Creme Pie

1 apple pie, baked
2 eggs, slightly beaten
1/2 cup sugar
1 tablespoon lemon juice

1 (3-ounce) package cream
   cheese, softened
1/2 cup sour cream

While pie is baking, combine eggs, sugar, and lemon juice and cook till thickened. Add cream cheese and sour cream, blending well. Take pie out of oven, cut a round hole out of top crust and pour cream sauce into it. This is guaranteed to get top raves.

Special Fare by Sisters II

Peach Cream Pie

4 sliced fresh peaches
1 (9-inch) unbaked pie shell
2/3 cup sugar
4 tablespoons flour

1/8 teaspoon salt
1/2 teaspoon mace
1 cup half-and-half

Arrange peaches in shell. Combine dry ingredients. Stir into cream. Pour over peaches. Bake at 400° for 45 minutes. Let cool. If it is not to be served for several hours and it is a hot summer day, it is wise to refrigerate this. However, it tastes best after cooling naturally. Serves 6-8.

Return Engagement

Walnut Pie

½ cup brown sugar, packed
2 tablespoons flour
1¼ cups light corn syrup
3 tablespoons butter
¼ teaspoon salt

3 eggs
1½ teaspoons vanilla
1 cup large pieces English
   walnuts
1 unbaked 9-inch pie shell

Mix brown sugar and flour in saucepan. Add corn syrup, butter and salt; warm over low heat just until butter is melted. Beat eggs with vanilla. Stir in sugar mixture. Turn into pie shell and sprinkle with walnuts. Bake below oven center at 375° for 40-45 minutes, or until filling is set in center. Cool before cutting.

Our Heritage

Pecan Tassies Cheese Pastry

1 (3-ounce) package cream
   cheese

½ cup butter or oleo
1 cup flour

Cream cheese and butter; add flour and blend. Shape into 2 dozen 1-inch balls. Place in a 1¾-inch tassie pan (very small muffin pans). Press dough against bottom and sides.

PECAN FILLING:
1 egg
¾ cup brown sugar
Dash of salt

1 teaspoon vanilla
1 teaspoon butter
⅔ cup pecans

Beat together until smooth, egg, sugar, salt, vanilla, and butter. Add pecans or you can put a few pecans in each cup. Bake at 325° for 25 minutes. Cool and remove.

Mom's Favorite Recipes

Peanut Butter Pie

1 (8-ounce) package cream
  cheese
½ cup sugar
½ cup creamy peanut butter
1 teaspoon vanilla
1 (8-ounce) carton whipping
  cream

1 (9-inch) graham cracker
  crust
1-2 tablespoons chopped salted
  peanuts (optional)

Combine cream cheese and sugar until smooth. Add peanut butter and vanilla. Beat well. Beat whipping cream to peaks. Fold into above. Add to crust. Sprinkle on peanuts. Chill 3 hours.

Generations of Good Cooking

Chocolate Chip Peanut Butter Pie

3 eggs, beaten
1 cup dark corn syrup
½ cup sugar
½ cup peanut butter

1 teaspoon vanilla
⅔ cup salted peanuts
1 cup chocolate chips
1 (9-inch) unbaked pie shell

Beat until smooth the eggs, dark corn syrup, sugar, peanut butter, and vanilla. Stir in peanuts. Sprinkle chocolate chips over the bottom of the pie shell and pour filling over chocolate chips. Bake at 400° for 15 minutes, then reduce heat to 350° and bake for another 30-35 minutes. Test outer edge for doneness. Cover with plastic wrap and refrigerate overnight.

Home Cooking with the Cummer Family

Government surveyors worked east to west, marking off uniform sections of land, planning the checkerboard of parcels that gives Iowa its orderly look.

Chocolate Mousse Pie

CRUST:

3 cups chocolate wafer crumbs (Oreos)   ½ cup (1 stick) unsalted butter, melted

Combine crumbs and butter. Press on bottom and completely up sides of 10-inch springform pan. Refrigerate 30 minutes (or chill in freezer).

FILLING:

1 pound semi-sweet chocolate

2 eggs

4 egg yolks

2 cups whipping cream

6 tablespoons powdered sugar

4 egg whites, room temperature

Soften chocolate in top of double boiler over simmering water. Let cool to lukewarm (95°). Add whole eggs and mix well. Add yolks and mix until thoroughly blended.

Whip cream with powdered sugar until soft peaks form. Beat egg whites until stiff, but not dry. Stir a little of the cream and whites into chocolate mixture to lighten. Fold in remaining cream and whites until completely incorporated. Turn into crust and chill at least 6 hours, or preferably overnight.

TOPPING:

2 cups whipping cream   Sugar

Whip remaining 2 cups cream with sugar to taste until quite stiff. Loosen crust on all sides using sharp knife; remove springform. Spread all but about ½ cup cream over top of mousse. Pipe remaining cream into rosettes in center of pie. Makes 10-12 servings.

I Love You

The picturesque city of Pella is architecturally like the Netherlands. The Dutch influence shows through in its food, festivities, and buildings. The annual Tulip Festival in May is a gorgeous and colorful sight for the eyes, a treat for the taste buds, and an enjoyable time to recapture Dutch traditions.

Prize Winning Grapefruit Pie

CREAM CHEESE MIXTURE:

4 ounces cream cheese,
 softened
1/3 cup powdered sugar

1 cup whipped topping
A few drops of red food
 coloring

Beat together cream cheese and powdered sugar. Then fold in whipped topping and food coloring.

GLAZE:

1 cup sugar
3 tablespoons cornstarch
Dash of salt
2 tablespoons dry strawberry
 gelatin
1 cup water

1/4 cup orange juice
1/4 cup grapefruit juice (drained
 from grapefruit)
1 tablespoon butter
Red food coloring

Mix together well the sugar, cornstarch, salt, and gelatin. Add water and juices. Bring to a boil, stirring constantly and boil one minute. Remove from fire and add butter and enough food coloring to make the desired color. Cool.

1 (8-inch) pie shell, baked
2-3 grapefruit, peeled,
 sectioned, drained well

1 envelope Dream Whip
1/2 cup milk
Red food coloring

Put cream cheese mixture in the bottom of a baked 8-inch pie shell. Add a layer of grapefruit sections. (Section and drain grapefruit the night before.) Cover grapefruit with half the cooled glaze. Add another layer of grapefruit and the rest of the glaze.

Beat Dream Whip with milk and a few drops of food coloring. Beat real stiff. Put on top of pie and trim as desired.

First Christian Church Centennial Cookbook

Fast Fruit Cocktail Cobbler

6 tablespoons Bisquick Reduced Fat Baking Mix
2 tablespoons Sugar Twin or
Sprinkle Sweet
⅓ cup Carnation Nonfat Dry
Milk Powder
1 cup (one 8-ounce can) fruit
cocktail, packed in fruit juice,
drained and ¼ cup juice
reserved

¼ teaspoon ground
cinnamon
2 tablespoons Cool Whip
Lite

Preheat oven to 350°. Spray 2 (1-cup) custard dishes with butter-
flavored cooking spray. In a medium bowl, combine baking mix,
Sugar Twin, and dry milk powder. Stir in reserved fruit juice. Add
drained fruit cocktail. Mix gently to combine. Evenly spoon mixture into prepared custard dishes. Evenly spoon cinnamon over top.
Place custard dishes on a baking sheet. Bake 20-25 minutes or until
top is lightly browned. Place custard dishes on a wire rack and allow
to cool. Top each with one tablespoon Cool Whip Lite. Serves 2.

Nutritional values per serving:
Healthy Exchanges:
1 bread, 1 fruit, ½ skim milk, 16 optional calories.
194 Cal; 2gm Fat; 6gm Prot; 38gm Carb; 318mg Sod; 1gm Fiber.
Diabetic: 1 starch, 1 fruit, ½ skim milk.

Dinner for Two

Apfel Küchelchen

(Apple Fritters)

½ cup flour	6 tablespoons milk
2 tablespoons sugar	2 eggs, separated
¼ teaspoon salt	4 apples, peeled and cored

Sift flour, sugar, and salt; add milk and egg yolks and beat well. Beat egg whites until stiff and fold into first mixture. Cut each apple into four rings and dip each ring into this batter, then fry in deep fat until nicely browned. Serve with the following sauce.

SAUCE:

2 cups milk	½ cup sugar
3 tablespoons flour	Pinch of salt
1 egg	

Scald 1½ cups milk. Blend flour with remaining milk and add rest of ingredients. Add to scalded milk and cook for 15 minutes in top of double boiler. Serve hot.

Amana Colony Recipes

Apple Turnovers

2½ cups flour	8-12 baking apples
1 cup oleo	¾ cup sugar
¾ teaspoon salt	½ teaspoon cinnamon
1 egg yolk	1 tablespoon flour
⅔ cup milk	2 tablespoons tapioca

Mix flour, oleo, and salt like you would a pie crust. Combine egg yolk and milk. Stir into flour mix. Take half of this dough and press into 10x15-inch baking sheet. Slice apples onto pastry. Combine sugar, cinnamon, flour, and tapioca. Sprinkle on the apples. Roll out remaining dough and lay on top, sealing edge as best you can. Beat egg white and brush on top of dough. Bake for 10 minutes at 425°. Then bake 20 minutes at 350°. Cool. Swirl a powdered sugar glaze over the top (1 cup powdered sugar and hot water, enough to make a glaze).

Saint Mary Catholic Church Cookbook

Pumpkin Chiffon Pie with Peanut Crust

CRUST:

1/2 cup (1 stick) butter
12/3 cups all-purpose flour
1/2 cup finely chopped peanuts
  or other nuts

Pinch of salt
3-4 tablespoons water

Preheat oven to 400°. With a pastry blender or two knives, cut the butter into the flour, nuts, and salt until mixture resembles coarse crumbs. Add water, one tablespoon at a time, tossing lightly with a fork. Gather dough into a ball. Roll dough out thinly and fit into a deep-dish 9-inch pie pan. Prick crust; bake in preheated oven until lightly browned, 10-12 minutes.

FILLING:

2 cups canned pumpkin
3 egg yolks
1/4 cup granulated sugar
1/2 cup milk
1/2 teaspoon salt
1 tablespoon cinnamon

1 package unflavored gelatin
1/4 cup cold water
3 egg whites
1/4 cup granulated sugar
1 pint whipping cream,
  whipped

Thoroughly whisk together pumpkin, egg yolks, sugar, milk, salt, and cinnamon in a saucepan. Cook over medium heat until thickened, about 10-15 minutes. Dissolve gelatin in cold water. Remove pumpkin mixture from heat and add the dissolved gelatin. Let cool. In a mixing bowl, beat egg whites, gradually adding sugar. Continue beating until stiff peaks form. Fold beaten egg whites into pumpkin mixture. Pour into cooled crust. Chill. Top with whipped cream before serving. Makes 1 (9-inch) pie.

A Cook's Tour of Iowa

Sugar-Free Lemon Chiffon Pie

1 cup diet Mountain Dew (or water)
¼ of a lemon (with skin and seeds), cut into chunks
1 (4-serving) package Jell-O sugar-free instant vanilla pudding mix
1 tub Crystal Light Lemonade Mix

⅔ cup nonfat dry milk powder
1½ cups plain fat-free yogurt
1 cup lite Cool Whip
1 pie crust

In a blender container, combine diet Mountain Dew and lemon chunks. Cover and process on blend for 60 seconds or until lemon pieces almost disappear. Set aside. In a large bowl, combine dry pudding mix, dry lemonade mix and dry milk powder. Add Mountain dew mixture and yogurt. Mix well with wire whisk. Blend in ¼ cup lite Cool Whip. Spread pudding mixture into pie crust. Refrigerate 5 minutes. Drop remaining lite Cool Whip by tablespoonsful to form 8 mounds. Refrigerate at least one hour.

T.W. and Anna Elliott Family Receipts

Lemon Cake Pie

This recipe is over 60 years old. It is good!

1 lemon, juice and grated rind
1¼ cups milk
1 cup sugar

2 heaping tablespoons flour
2 eggs, separated
1 tablespoon melted butter
1 (9-inch) pie crust, unbaked

Beat all ingredients (except 2 egg whites that have been beaten stiff) together; fold in beaten egg whites. Pour into pie crust, bake in slow (325°) oven for one hour or until done.

Oma's (Grandma's) Family Secrets

Betty's Lemon Pudding Pie

This pie won 1st prize at one of the 4th of July pie contests.

1¹/₂ cups sugar
1¹/₂ cups water
¹/₂ teaspoon salt
¹/₂ cup cornstarch
¹/₃ cup water
4 egg yolks, beaten

¹/₃ - ¹/₂ cup lemon juice
3 tablespoons butter
1 teaspoon lemon peel, grated
1 baked (9-inch) pie crust

Combine sugar, 1¹/₂ cups water, and salt in saucepan. Heat to boiling. Mix cornstarch and ¹/₃ cup water to make paste. Add to boiling mixture, stirring constantly. Cook until thick and clear. Remove from heat. Combine egg yolks and lemon juice. Add to mixture on stove; cook until bubbly. Remove from heat; stir in butter and lemon peel. Cool until lukewarm.

MERINGUE:

¹/₄ teaspoon salt
4 egg whites

¹/₂ cup sugar

Add salt to egg whites. Beat until frothy. Gradually add sugar until they become glossy and form peaks. Stir 2 rounded tablespoons of this meringue into the pie filling. Pour lemon filling in baked pie crust and cover with remaining meringue. Bake in 350° oven about 15 minutes. Cool at least one hour before cutting.

Colesburg Area Cookbook

Strawberry Glaze Pie

1 cup flour
¹/₂ cup butter
2 tablespoons powdered sugar
1 cup sugar

1¹/₂ cups water
2 tablespoons cornstarch
1 package strawberry Jell-O
Strawberries (approximately 2¹/₂ cups)

Preheat oven to 350°. Mix together the first 3 ingredients and press into pie pan. Bake at 350° for 10-15 minutes. Then place in saucepan sugar, water, and cornstarch. Cook this until clear. Add strawberry Jell-O and cool. Put strawberries into baked crust. Pour over the Jell-O mixture. Chill.

Favorite Recipes

Chocolate Meringue Pie

A memorable do-ahead dessert, especially for chocolate lovers!

CRUST:

2 egg whites
$^1/_8$ teaspoon salt
$^1/_8$ teaspoon cream of tartar

$^1/_2$ cup white sugar
$^1/_2$ cup pecans, chopped
$^1/_2$ teaspoon vanilla

Preheat oven to 300°. Lightly grease a 9- or 10-inch pie plate. In medium mixing bowl, beat egg whites until foamy. Add salt and cream of tartar. Beat until whites form peaks. Gradually add sugar, beating constantly. Continue to beat at high speed until mixture is glossy and stiff enough to stand straight up when beaters are lifted. Fold in nuts and vanilla. Spoon meringue into lightly greased pie pan, then spread with back of a spoon to cover bottom and sides, but not the rim; make the sides a little thicker than the bottom and about $^1/_2$ inch higher than the rim of the pan. Bake in slow oven for 55 minutes. Cool.

CHOCOLATE FILLING:

$^1/_4$ pound German sweet
   chocolate
3 tablespoons hot water

$^1/_2$ pint whipping cream (1
   cup)
1 teaspoon vanilla

In small saucepan over low heat, melt chocolate in hot water. Blend and cool. Whip cream and add vanilla. Fold chocolate into cream. Spoon into cooled pie shell. Refrigerate for several hours. At serving time garnish with a fluff of whipped cream, if desired. Makes 6-8 servings.

Singing in the Kitchen

Lemon Curd Tarts

An English recipe.

LEMON CURD FILLING:

Grated rind of 2 large
  lemons
1/2 cup lemon juice

2 cups sugar
1 cup butter or margarine
4 eggs, well beaten

Combine lemon rind, lemon juice, and sugar in top of double boiler. Add butter. Heat over boiling water, stirring, until butter is melted. Stir in eggs. Continue cooking, stirring constantly, until mixture is thick enough to pile slightly, about 15 minutes. Cool thoroughly.

TART SHELLS:

3 cups sifted flour
1 1/2 teaspoons salt

1 cup shortening
6 tablespoons cold water

Sift flour and salt; cut in shortening until size of large peas. Sprinkle water over mixture. Mix thoroughly until a smooth dough is formed. Roll out on floured surface to 1/8-inch thickness. Cut into 2 1/2-inch rounds; fit into 1 3/4-inch muffin pans. Prick. Bake at 450° for 10-20 minutes or until light golden brown. Spoon filling into shells. Yield: 4 dozen.

The Taste of the World

Jean's Cheshire Meringue

3 egg whites
1 cup sugar
1 teaspoon baking powder
16 Ritz crackers, crushed

1 ounce flaked almonds
2 ounces finely chopped
  walnuts
1 teaspoon vanilla

TOPPING:
1/2 pint sweet whipped cream   Grated sweet chocolate
  (fresh preferable)

Beat egg whites until stiff. Sieve sugar and baking powder; add to egg whites gradually. Beat again. Stir in crumbs, nuts, and vanilla. Put mixture in 2 pie pans and bake at 300° for 35-45 minutes, making sure it's dry all through. Cool meringues and put one on plate. Cover with whipped cream and sprinkle with chocolate. Place second meringue on top and cover all over with whipped cream. Sprinkle chocolate over all.

Madison County Cookbook

Peaches and Cream Cheesecake Pie

3/4 cup flour
1 (31/4-ounce) package regular
  vanilla pudding mix
1 teaspoon baking powder
1/8 teaspoon salt
1 egg, beaten
1/2 cup milk
3 tablespoons butter, softened

1 (29-ounce) can sliced peaches
  (reserve juice)
1 (8-ounce) package cream
  cheese, softened
1/2 cup plus 1 tablespoon
  granulated sugar
1/2 teaspoon cinnamon

Combine flour, pudding mix, baking powder, salt, egg, milk, and butter in large mixing bowl. Beat at high speed for 2 minutes. Pour into greased 10-inch deep dish pie plate. Drain peaches well, reserving the liquid. Arrange peach slices decoratively atop the batter. Combine cream cheese, sugar, and 3 tablespoons reserved peach juice in medium bowl. Beat with electric mixer at medium speed 2-3 minutes or until smooth. Carefully spread atop peaches to within one inch of edge of pie plate. Stir in one tablespoon sugar with 1/2 teaspoon ground cinnamon; sprinkle over cream cheese mixture. Bake in preheated 350° oven for 35-40 minutes, or until bottom and sides are golden brown. Cool. Serve warm or chilled. Makes 8-10 servings.

Generations of Good Cooking

Pina Colada Wedges

1 (8-ounce) package cream
  cheese, softened
1/3 cup sugar
2 tablespoons rum or 1/2
  teaspoon rum extract
3 1/2 cups thawed whipped
  topping

1 (8 1/4-ounce) can crushed
  pineapple in syrup
2 2/3 cups (7 ounces) coconut
  flakes

Beat cream cheese with sugar and rum until smooth. Fold in 2 cups
of the whipped topping, pineapple with syrup and 2 cups of the coconut. Spread in 8-inch round layer pan lined with plastic wrap.
Invert pan onto serving plate; remove pan and plastic wrap. Spread
with remaining whipped topping and sprinkle with remaining coconut.

Freeze until firm, about 2 hours. Cut into wedges. Garnish with
pineapple and cherries, if desired.

First Christian Church Centennial Cookbook

Chocolate Cream Cheese Dessert

1/2 cup margarine, softened
1 cup flour
1/2 cup pecans, finely
  chopped
1 (8-ounce) package cream
  cheese, softened

1 cup powdered sugar
1 1/2 cups Cool Whip
2 small packages chocolate
  instant pudding
3 cups milk

Blend margarine, flour, and pecans with a fork or pastry cutter. Pat
into a 9x13-inch pan and bake for 15 minutes at 350°. Cool. Mix
cream cheese, powdered sugar, and Cool Whip. Spread over cooled
crust. Mix pudding and milk until thick and smooth. Pour over
powdered sugar mixture. Top with a layer of Cool Whip and sprinkle
with a few finely-chopped pecans.

Variation: You may substitute other flavors of pudding in this recipe.

Woodbine Public Library

Butter Pecan Dessert

FIRST LAYER:

2 cups crushed pretzels   ¹/₄ cup sugar
¹/₂ stick melted oleo

Combine ingredients and press into the bottom of a 9x13-inch pan.
Freeze.

SECOND LAYER:

1 small container Cool Whip   1 (8-ounce) package cream
¹/₂ - 1 cup powdered sugar   cheese

Combine ingredients and spread over the first layer.

THIRD LAYER:

2 packages instant butter   3 cups milk
   pecan pudding

Prepare pudding, following directions. Spread a small amount of
Cool Whip on top. Refrigerate.

Centennial Cookbook

Easy Dessert

1 cup flour
1/2 cup brown sugar
1/2 cup margarine
1 cup coconut
1 (3-ounce) package almond
  slices

2 (3¼-ounce) packages instant
  pudding (chocolate, chocolate
  fudge or butterscotch)
2½ cups cold milk
1 (9-ounce) carton Cool
  Whip

Preheat oven to 350°. Mix together first 5 ingredients until crumbly. Put in cookie sheet. Bake 15 minutes at 350° or until golden brown. Stir often while baking. Let cool. Mix pudding and milk and let set. Add Cool Whip. Leave 1/2 baked mixture in bottom of pan (spread evenly). Spread on pudding and Cool Whip mixture. Sprinkle remaining crumbs on top. Refrigerate a few hours before serving.

Favorite Recipes

Coffee Tortoni

A light coffee-flavored dessert.

2 egg whites
1 tablespoon instant coffee
1/8 teaspoon salt
2 tablespoons sugar
1/2 pint whipping cream
1/4 cup sugar

1 tablespoon Kahlua or crème
  de cocoa
1/4 teaspoon almond extract
1/2 cup slivered almonds,
  toasted

Combine egg whites, coffee, and salt; beat till stiff. Add sugar gradually. Whip cream until it is almost stiff. Continue beating slowly while adding remaining ingredients, except for almonds. Fold whipped cream mixture into the egg whites. Gently fold in the almonds. Spoon into parfait or sherbet glasses and freeze 2 or 3 hours. Serves 4.

Recipes from Iowa with Love

The Des Moines Botanical Center is home to the world's largest collection of exotic plants which are encased in a 150-foot diameter dome.

Bridge Dessert

1 package lemon Jell-O
1 cup boiling water
1/2 cup sugar
1/8 teaspoon salt
Juice and rind of 1 lemon
1 can evaporated milk,
   chilled

1 pint peaches, sweetened,
   drained and mashed
2 1/2 cups vanilla wafer
   crumbs
Cream

Dissolve Jell-O in boiling water; add sugar, salt, lemon juice, and rind. When congealed slightly, beat milk until stiff and whip Jell-O mixture into it; add mashed peaches. Spread half of the crumbs in 9x13-inch pan, pour Jell-O mixture over it, top with remaining crumbs and chill 3 hours. Serve with cream.

A Taste of Grace

Mrs. Eisenhower's Frosted Mint Delight

Mamie Doud Eisenhower was born in 1896 in Boone, Iowa. She was the wife of President Dwight D. Eisenhower.

3/4 cup pure mint-flavored
   apple jelly
2 (1-pound) cans crushed
   pineapple, undrained
   (reserve 1 cup juice)

1 package unflavored gelatin
1 pint whipping cream
2 teaspoons confectioners'
   sugar

Melt the jelly and mix the crushed pineapple into it. Dissolve the gelatin in one cup of the juice from the pineapple. Mix the gelatin mixture into the jelly mixture and heat to dissolve. Cool until partially set. Whip the cream, sweeten it with the sugar, and fold it into the mixture. Put into the freezer until firm. Do not freeze solid. Serves 10-12.

License to Cook Iowa Style

Lisa's Strawberry Dessert

This tastes like strawberry cream pie.

CRUST:

1 cup flour
1 stick margarine, softened

⅓ cup powdered sugar

Mix ingredients together; put in a 9x13-inch pan. Bake at 350° for 15 minutes.

FILLING:

1 (8-ounce) package cream
cheese, softened
1 (8-ounce) carton Cool
Whip

1 cup powdered sugar

Mix filling together. Spread over cooled crust. Refrigerate until firm.

TOPPING:

2 cups water
1½ cups sugar
⅓ cup white corn syrup
4 tablespoons cornstarch

1 (3-ounce) box strawberry
Jell-O
1 quart fresh strawberries,
sliced

Mix the 2 cups water, sugar, corn syrup, and cornstarch together in a saucepan. Bring to a boil. This will become thick and shiny. Remove from heat. Add Jell-O; stir well. Let this cool. Add sliced strawberries. Spoon carefully over filling layer. Refrigerate until firm.

Titonka Centennial Cookbook

Strawberry Pretzel Dessert

1½ cups pretzels, crushed
½ cup sugar
½ cup margarine, melted
1 (8-ounce) package cream
  cheese, softened
1 cup powdered sugar

1 (9-ounce) carton Cool Whip
2 (3-ounce) packages
  strawberry gelatin
2 cups boiling water
2 (10-ounce) packages frozen
  strawberries, partially thawed

Mix pretzels, sugar, and margarine together. Pat into a 9x13-inch pan. Bake at 350° for 10 minutes. Cool. Mix cream cheese, powdered sugar, and Cool Whip together and spread over cooled pretzel crust. Cool. Dissolve gelatin in boiling water. Add both packages strawberries. Let mixture partially set, then spread over cooled ingredients. Refrigerate a few hours or overnight.

The Nading Family Cookbook

Marzi Pan Strawberries

1 cup sweetened condensed
  milk
1 pound coconut, ground
2 tablespoons sugar
¼ pound ground blanched
  almonds

1 teaspoon vanilla
2 (3-ounce) packages
  strawberry Jell-O, divided

Mix all but ½ package Jell-O thoroughly. Shape into strawberries. Roll in remaining ½ package Jell-O. Decorate with green frosting leaf. Allow to remain on cookie sheet overnight to dry. These freeze well.

Note: Can use other Jell-O flavors; orange is good.

Quasquicentennial / St. Olaf of Bode

Sioux City, on the Missouri River, puts us "on the shoreline of the prairie," where legendary explorers Lewis and Clark left their mark.

Mississippi Mud Dessert

1 cup flour
1 stick oleo
½ cup chopped nuts
1 (8-ounce) package cream
cheese
1 cup powdered sugar

1 (8-ounce) carton Cool
Whip
2 small packages instant
chocolate pudding
3 cups milk

Mix the flour, oleo, and nuts as for pie crust. Spread in 9x13-inch pan and bake at 350° for 20 minutes; cool. Cream together cream cheese, powdered sugar, 1 cup Cool Whip. Spread on crust (hard to spread). Put chocolate pudding and milk in mixer bowl; beat with mixer until thick. Spread over cream cheese layer. Top with remaining Cool whip and sprinkle with nuts, if desired. Refrigerate. Can make a day ahead. Also can use butterscotch pudding.

Thompson Family Cookbook

Chocolate Trifle

1 (18½-ounce) package
chocolate fudge cake mix
1 (6-ounce) package instant
chocolate pudding mix
½ cup strong coffee

1 (12-ounce) frozen whipped
topping
6 (1.4-ounce) chocolate covered
toffee bars, crushed

Bake cake according to package directions. Cool. Prepare pudding according to package directions and set aside. Crumble cake, reserving ½ cup. Place half the remaining cake crumbs in the bottom of a 4½- or 5-quart trifle bowl or decorative glass bowl. Layer with half of the coffee, half of the pudding, half of the whipped topping and half of the crushed candy bars. Repeat the layers of cake, coffee, pudding and whipped topping. Combine remaining cake crumbs and crushed candy bars. Sprinkle over top and refrigerate 4-5 hours before serving. Makes 8-10 servings.

The L.o.V.E Chocolate Cookbook

Chocolate Angel Food Cake Dessert

1 (6-ounce) package chocolate chips or 8 ounces sweet chocolate
2 tablespoons water
1 tablespoon sugar
4 egg yolks, well-beaten
4 egg whites, beaten
1 cup cream, whipped
Angel food cake

Melt chocolate chips or sweet chocolate in double boiler. Then add water and sugar and well-beaten egg yolks gradually. Beat thoroughly, then cool. Now fold in well-beaten egg whites and whipped cream. Break angel food cake in 13x9-inch buttered pan. Put a layer of cake and layer of chocolate mixture. Repeat layers. Let chill for 12-24 hours.

The Walnut Centennial Cookbook

Cream Puff Dessert

1 stick margarine
1 cup water
1 cup flour
4 eggs

Boil margarine in one cup water. Add flour and beat hard until it forms a ball. Add eggs one at a time. Spread in 9x13-inch pan that has been sprayed with Pam. Bake at 400° for 30 minutes. Cool.

FILLING:

2 (3-ounce) packages instant vanilla pudding
3 cups milk
1 (8-ounce) package cream cheese
1 (8-ounce) carton Cool Whip
Hershey's Syrup

Blend pudding with milk and soften cream cheese. Let stand for 15 minutes. Spread over cooled crust. Top with Cool Whip. Drizzle small amount of Hershey's syrup over Cool Whip. Refrigerate.

Our Savior's Kvindherred Lutheran Church

The "Little Brown Church" of the hymn, "The Church in the Wildwood" is in Nashua. It is a popular wedding site. There is a wedding reunion held at the church each August.

Windbeutel
(Cream Puffs)

2 cups water	3 cups flour
½ pound butter	8 eggs

Bring water and butter to boil; add flour, all at one time and boil for one minute. Cool slightly, then add eggs, one at a time and beat thoroughly. Drop by tablespoons onto greased baking sheet and bake for 15 minutes in 425° oven, then decrease heat to 350° and bake for 30 minutes longer or until well browned. When cool, cut into one side and fill with the following filling.

FILLING:

4 cups milk	2 eggs
5 tablespoons cornstarch	1 teaspoon butter
1 cup sugar	1 teaspoon vanilla

Heat milk in a heavy saucepan or skillet. Mix cornstarch, sugar, and eggs together. After milk is heated, mix one cup of heated milk into sugar and egg mixture and then add it to milk in pan. Stir until it thickens. Remove from heat and add butter and vanilla. When cool, fill into cream puffs.

German Heritage Recipes Cookbook

Quick Skillet Custard

Makes perfect custard!

2 large or 3 small eggs, slightly beaten	1 teaspoon vanilla
¼ teaspoon salt	1½ cups milk
⅓ cup sugar	Nutmeg

Mix all ingredients except nutmeg. Pour into custard cups. Sprinkle with nutmeg. Place cups in a skillet. Pour hot tap water in around the cups as high as possible. Bring water to a full boil. Turn off heat. Cover skillet and let stand 10 minutes, or until knife inserted into the custard comes out clean. Remove cups from the water and chill.

Country Lady Nibbling and Scribbling

Caramel Dumplings

½ cup sugar	Pinch of salt
1 tablespoon oleo	½ cup milk
1 cup flour	½ teaspoon vanilla
3 teaspoons baking powder	

Cream sugar and oleo. Combine flour, baking powder, and salt in separate bowl. Combine milk and vanilla. Add flour mixture and milk mixture alternately to sugar. Add more flour to make a stiff batter. Drop by tablespoon into boiling syrup. Cover and boil until dumplings are done. Or bake in oven at 375° for 20 minutes or until done. Serve plain or top with ice cream.

SYRUP:

1½ cups sugar	1 tablespoon oleo
2 cups boiling water	

Melt 1 cup sugar slowly in a 10-inch frying pan until light brown. Add boiling water; stir until dissolved. Add ½ cup sugar and oleo. Bring to a boil.

Appanoose County Cookbook

Whiskey Bread Pudding

This otherwise "homey" bread pudding is deliciously enhanced by a warm Whiskey Sauce.

BREAD PUDDING:

3 cups skim milk
¾ cup granulated sugar
½ cup egg substitute
1½ tablespoons vanilla

1 tablespoon pear baby food
4 cups cubed fat-free firm white
  or French bread
½ cup raisins

Preheat oven to 350° Combine milk, granulated sugar, egg substitute, vanilla, and pear baby food in a large mixing bowl and blend well. Add bread cubes and raisins and blend well. Pour bread pudding into an 8 x 11½ x 2-inch baking dish that has been coated with vegetable spray. Bake for one hour.

WHISKEY SAUCE:

¼ cup pear baby food
2 tablespoons light
  margarine

1 cup powdered sugar
¼ cup egg substitute
¼ cup whiskey

Twenty minutes before bread pudding is done, combine pear baby food, margarine, and powdered sugar in a small heavy saucepan over moderate heat and stir until the mixture is smooth and hot. Remove saucepan from heat and add ¼ cup egg substitute and whiskey and quickly blend with a whisk until smooth. Spoon a generous amount of warm sauce over each serving of hot bread pudding. Makes 16 servings.

Nutritional analysis per serving: 133 Cal; 6% Cal from Fat; 3g Prot; 27g Carbo; 1g Fat; 0g Fiber; 75mg Sod; 1mg Chol.

101 Great Lowfat Desserts

Originally in Iowa City, the capital of Iowa is now in Des Moines.

Pioneer Bread Pudding

2 cups stale but not dry bread cubes
2 cups milk
3 tablespoons butter

¼ cup sugar
2 eggs
Dash salt
¼ teaspoon vanilla

Place bread cubes in a one-quart buttered baking dish. Scald the milk with the butter and sugar. Beat eggs slightly, add the salt, then stir in the warm milk and vanilla. Pour over the bread cubes. Set the baking dish in a pan containing warm water up to the level of the pudding and bake about one hour at 350°, or until a knife comes out clean when inserted in center of pudding. Makes 4-6 servings. Serve warm with plain cream, currant jelly, or Lemon Pudding Sauce.

LEMON PUDDING SAUCE:

½ cup sugar
1 tablespoon cornstarch
1 cup boiling water
2 tablespoons butter

1 tablespoon grated lemon rind
3 tablespoons lemon juice
⅛ teaspoon salt

Combine sugar and cornstarch; add boiling water slowly and stir until dissolved. Cook slowly, stirring constantly, until thickened and clear. Remove from heat and add remaining ingredients. Serve warm.

Neighboring on the Air

Schokolade Brot Pudding
(Chocolate Bread Pudding)

1 tablespoon butter
1 square unsweetened chocolate
2 cups milk, scalded

1 cup bread crumbs
2 eggs, separated
½ cup sugar

Melt butter and chocolate in scalded milk and pour over bread crumbs. Beat egg yolks, blend in sugar and add to crumb mixture. Fold in stiffly beaten egg whites, pour into greased casserole and bake in 350° oven until set (about 40 minutes).

Amana Colony Recipes

Rice Mold with Butterscotch Sauce

1 cup rice	1 teaspoon vanilla
1¹/₂ quarts milk	2 packages gelatine
¹/₂ teaspoon salt	¹/₃ cup cold water
2 cups sugar	1 pint heavy whipping cream,
4 eggs, beaten	whipped

Cook rice in milk in a double boiler until tender. Add salt, sugar, beaten eggs, and vanilla; return to stove and cook until thick, then add unflavored gelatine which has been soaking in cold water. Let cool. Add whipped cream and put in 10x14-inch glass pan; chill thoroughly.

BUTTERSCOTCH SAUCE:

³/₄ cup oleo	2 cups brown sugar
¹/₂ cup evaporated milk	2 beaten eggs

Cook in double boiler until thick. Serve warm over chilled rice mold.

Our Heritage

Swedish Rice Pudding

³/₄ cup long-grain rice	1 teaspoon almond extract
5 cups milk	6 egg whites
6 eggs, beaten	¹/₂ cup sugar
³/₄ cup sugar	1 (14¹/₂-ounce) jar
2 teaspoons vanilla	lingonberries

Cook rice according to package directions; do not cool. In a large mixing bowl, combine milk, eggs, ¾ cup sugar, vanilla, and almond extract. Stir in hot rice. Pour into a 9x13x2-inch baking dish. Bake in a 350° oven for 20 minutes. Reduce oven temperature to 300° and bake one hour. Meanwhile, beat egg whites until soft peaks form (tips curl). Gradually add ½ cup sugar and beat until stiff peaks form. Carefully spread over rice pudding. Bake in 350° oven for 10-15 minutes or until golden. Serve warm or cooled with lingonberries. Refrigerate leftovers. Serves 12-15.

Community Centennial Cookbook

Mrs. Young's Frozen Fruit Cups

1 quart buttermilk
2 cups sugar
1 teaspoon vanilla
Food coloring (if desired)

1 (20-ounce) can fruit cocktail, drained
1 (20-ounce) can crushed pineapple, drained

Combine buttermilk, sugar, and vanilla. Stir to dissolve sugar. Add food coloring if you wish. Add drained fruits. Put in serving-size paper or plastic cups and freeze. You can add other kinds of fruit as you like. Remove from freezer one hour before serving to partially thaw. It needs to be partially frozen to be best.

Special Recipes from our Hearts

Oreo Dessert

1 (16-ounce) package Oreo cookies
1/3 cup margarine, melted
1 gallon of vanilla ice cream

Drizzle chocolate syrup topping
1 carton Cool Whip
Drizzle butterscotch topping

Crush Oreo cookies; take out one cup and add margarine to remaining crumbs. Press into a 9x13-inch pan. Add vanilla ice cream; top with chocolate syrup topping, Cool Whip, and butterscotch topping. Sprinkle with reserved crumbs on top and place in freezer.

Teresa's Heavenly Cakes and Treasures

Caramel Ice Cream Dessert

1 stick butter, melted
2 cups graham cracker crumbs
1 1/2 cups brown sugar

1 cup chopped pecans
1 cup caramel topping
1/2 gallon ice cream, softened

Mix melted butter, graham cracker crumbs and brown sugar. Reserve 1/4 of the mixture. Press the remaining crumb mixture in the bottom of a 9x13-inch pan. Bake at 350° for 15 minutes. Let cool. Layer nuts on top of baked crumbs, then caramel topping, then softened ice cream. Top with reserved crumb mixture. Freeze before serving.

SEP Junior Women's Club 25th Anniversary Cookbook

Homemade Chocolate Grape Nut Ice Cream

5 eggs	2 capsful lemon flavoring
3 cups sugar	2 pints Coffee Rich
2 capsful vanilla flavoring	1 can evaporated milk
1/2 cup cocoa (melt with a little hot water)	Milk (to fill container)
	3/4 - 1 cup Grape Nuts

Blend together eggs and sugar. Add rest of ingredients, except Grape Nuts, and pour into ice cream freezer. Then fill to top of paddle with milk. Add Grape Nuts and stir with paddle.

The Orient Volunteer Fire Department Cookbook

Ice Cream

4 eggs, beaten until light	2 1/2 tablespoons vanilla
2 heaping cups sugar	1 package instant vanilla pudding
1 teaspoon salt	
2 cups cream	Milk to fill can

Mix together first 6 ingredients well and put into ice cream freezer. Fill can with whole milk, allowing 2 inches from top of can. Churn freezer according to directions.

The Berns Family Cookbook

Sweetened Condensed Milk

1 cup + 2 tablespoons powdered milk	1/2 cup warm water
	3/4 cup sugar

Dissolve powdered milk in water in top of double boiler. Add sugar; cook 17 minutes, stirring at all times.

Appanoose County Cookbook

Blueberry Sauce

4 cups blueberries
2 cups water
1 cup sugar

1 tablespoon lemon juice
2 tablespoons cornstarch

Boil first 4 ingredients for 5 minutes. Dissolve cornstarch in 1/2 cup water, then add to boiling berries; boil 2-3 minutes. Serve over waffles, pancakes, rice pudding, or ice cream.

Oma's (Grandma's) Family Secrets

Hot Fudge Sauce

1/2 cup butter
1 cup chocolate chips
2 cups powdered sugar

1 (12-ounce) can evaporated milk

Bring to boil over medium heat, stirring constantly. Cook and stir for 8-10 minutes more. Let cool and pour over your favorite ice cream or dessert.

Madison County Cookbook

Cranberry-Lemon Ice

3 cups fresh or frozen
   cranberries
1 cup granulated sugar

2 cups water
1/4 cup lemon juice

In a 1-quart saucepan, bring sugar, water, and cranberries to a boil over high heat. Reduce heat to medium high. Cook 15 minutes. Sieve into small bowl. Cool 10 minutes, stirring occasionally. Stir in lemon juice. Pour mixture into freezing tray. Freeze several hours or until firm. Remove from freezer. Cut into chunks into a medium mixing bowl. Beat at medium speed of mixer until slushy. Pour into a deep pan. Freeze again until firm. Makes 6 individual 1/4-cup servings.

The Amazing Little Cranberry Cookbook

Snake Alley, perhaps Burlington's most famous landmark, is called by *Ripley's Believe It or Not*, the "Crookedest Street in the World." A real test for your driving or bicycling skills, it consists of five half-curves and two quarter-curves and drops 58 feet over a distance of 275 feet.

Catalog of Contributing Cookbooks

Snake Alley is called "The Crookedist Street in the World" by Ripley's Believe It or Not. Burlington.

CATALOG of CONTRITUTING COOKBOOKS

All recipes in this book have been submitted from the cookbooks shown on the following pages. Individuals who wish to obtain a copy of a particular book can do so by sending a check or money order to the address listed. Prices are subject to change. Please note the postage and handling charges that may be required. State residents add tax only when requested. Retailers are invited to call or write to same address for wholesale information. Some of these contributing cookbooks may have gone out of print since the original publication of this book. Quail Ridge Press is proud to preserve America's food heritage by keeping many of their recipes in print.

ALTA UNITED METHODIST CHURCH COOKBOOK

Susannah Wesley Circle
5508 30th Avenue
Alta, IA 51022   712-284-1332

The *Alta United Methodist Church Cookbook* contains over 1000 recipes collected from our congregation and friends. The 395-page, 3-ring, hard cover book has recipes for everyone, young and old, as well as simple recipes and recipes for the chef in your family.

$ 10.00   Retail price
$ 3.00   Postage and handling
Make check payable to Susannah Wesley Circle

AMANA COLONY RECIPES

Ladies Auxiliary of the Homestead Welfare Club
P.O. Box 36
Homestead, IA 52236   319-622-3099

Amana Colony Recipes is a 120-page paperbound book containing over 150 family-size recipes of foods prepared in the former communal kitchens of the seven Amana Villages. It includes sketches of kitchen scenes and utensils, chapter introductions pertaining to Amana customs and a brief history of the Amana Society.

$ 6.50   Retail price
$ 1.75   Postage and handling
Make check payable to Homestead Welfare Club

THE AMAZING LITTLE CRANBERRY COOKBOOK

by Regi Donaldson
P. O. Box 31056
Des Moines, IA 50310   515-276-6263

A traditional cranberry pudding sparked the author's love for cranberries, and over the years, she discovered their amazing versatility. Thirty-one recipes and notes use cranberries for vegetable dip, cider, meat glaze, fudge, fruit-leather roses, and even note cards. Cranberries aren't grown in Iowa, they're only made better here!

$ 9.95   Retail price
Applicable tax for Iowa residents
$ 2.00   Postage and handling
Make check payable to Regi Donaldson

THE AMERICAN GOTHIC COOKBOOK

Penfield Press
215 Brown Street
Iowa City, IA 52245-5842   800-728-9998

Recipes come from the artist, the models who posed for American Gothic, and people who knew them, including famous colleagues and neighbors. 160 pages, 3 x 5. Includes reproductions of paintings and drawings by Grant Wood.

$ 6.95   Retail price (Postpaid) 2/$12, 3/$18 / ISBN 1-57216-004-7
Make check payable to Penfield Press

APPANOOSE COUNTY COOKBOOK

Appanoose County Historical Museum
Centerville, IA 52544

Celebrating Appanoose County's 150th anniversary with over 900 recipes collected from good cooks throughout the county. The divider pages give historical facts about towns and places in the county. A popular cookbook in the area and sure to please cooks everywhere. Currently out of print.

APPLAUSE, APPLAUSE

Attn: Roberta Coleman
223 E. Linn Street
Coggon, IA 52218   319-435-2112

Featuring a cast of 1267 recipes by Standing Ovation Cooks from Coggon, across Iowa and beyond. The cookbook is organized into 11 acts, along with Intermission and Encore sections. Low-fat recipes are identified. Proceeds support Old Opera House renovations. Perfect as a gift, or for cooks and collectors alike. 511 pages.

$ 14.00   Retail price
$ 2.00   Postage and handling
Make check payable to Coggon Opera House Cookbook

ARMSTRONG CENTENNIAL COOKBOOK

Armstrong Heritage Museum
Box 374
Armstrong, IA 50514   712-864-3350

Compiled for the Armstrong Centennial Celebration of 1993, this 302-page, 3-ring binder cookbook contains over 800 recipes from 256 cooks. In this small Northwest Iowa community, serving food or "coffee and" is a tradition at every gathering, small or large.

$ 10.00   Retail price
$ 1.95   Postage and handling
Make check payable to Armstrong Heritage Museum

BERNS FAMILY COOKBOOK

c/o Betty Howe
367 Ellingson Bridge Drive
Waukon, IA 52172

The Berns Family Cookbook is a collection of over 600 favorite recipes from all 110 members, and a blend of German, Dutch, Irish and Norwegian foods. It has a laminated cover, colorful dividers, wire binding and over 200 pages. Contains helpful hints, anecdotes we grew up with, and ancestral heritage. Currently out of print.

BLUE WILLOW'S "SWEET TREASURES"

by C. J. Gustafson
CT of IA., Inc.
Box 356 Hwy 169
Harcourt, IA 50544   515-354-5295

Our book was designed as a memory for celebrating the 20th anniversary of our shoppe, the Blue Willow Tea Room. It includes recipes used for dessert tray for our "High Tea." Every recipe is a well-used favorite.

$ 12.95   Retail price
$ 4.00   Postage and handling
Make check payable to Country Treasures

CELEBRATING IOWA

First United Methodist Church UMW
214 East Jefferson Street
Iowa City, IA 52245

The first United Church women have collected favorite recipes from members and friends to make up this outstanding recipe collection. The book is bound in a convenient hard cover loose-leaf format. Divider pages are of treasured pictures from the church's history. 258 pages. 664 recipes.

$ 12.50   Retail price
$ 3.50   Postage and handling
Make check payable to United Methodist Women

CENTENNIAL COOKBOOK

Arispe Centennial Cookbook Committee
Arispe Development Corporation
Arispe, IA 50831   515-346-2239

The Centennial Cookbook was one of the fundraising projects while getting ready for the Arispe Centennial in 1987. The book is a 3-ring binder of 330 pages with over 1000 tried and tested recipes. The recipes are from heritage and family favorites to more modern ones. It features 14 sections with a different photo of our town at the beginning of each section.

$ 10.00   Retail price
$ 4.00   Postage and handling
Make check payable to Arispe Development Corp.

CHERISHED CZECH RECIPES

Penfield Press
215 Brown Street
Iowa City, IA 52245-5842   800-728-9998

Filled with favorite Czech recipes, maxims and mottos, this little book is a delightful collection. 143 pages, 3 x 5. From Dumplings and Noodles, Kolaches and Fillings, to "Old World" Christmas Recipes.

$ 6.95   Retail price (Postpaid) 2/$12, 3/$18 / ISBN 0-941016-46-3
Make check payable to Penfield Press

COLESBURG AREA COOKBOOK

Sesquicentennial Committee
Colesburg, IA 52035

Our cookbook contains, within 230 pages, 600 recipes provided by local residents. We feel we've received the very best recipes from our area. The book contains tried and tested recipes featuring a good variety of down-home-recipes. Ingredients are available at your local small-town grocery store. Currently out of print.

COMMUNITY CENTENNIAL COOKBOOK

RR 1 Box 39
Harcourt, IA 50544

In celebration of 100-year centennial, the Harcourt residents assembled a collection of 1368 hearty and delicious recipes which have long been part of the farming community. Its 552 pages cover a variety including recipes of the Scandinavian heritage. A big book; one every cook will enjoy. Currently out of print.

COOK OF THE WEEK COOKBOOK

Humboldt Independent Newspaper
Humboldt, IA 50548-0157

Each week the Humboldt Independent features a different "Cook of the Week" in the newspaper. Favorite recipes from the weekly Cooks of the Week are featured in the cookbook. We have taken favorites from each of our cooks from 1988 through 1992. The cookbook contains nearly 800 recipes and has 260 pages. Our first edition was published in 1988 featuring 780 recipes. Currently out of print.

A COOK'S TOUR OF IOWA

University of Iowa Press
c/o Chicago Distribution Center
11030 S. Langley Avenue
Chicago, IL 60628   800-621-2736

Putting to rest the myth that Iowa's cuisine is boring, Puckett reveals the distinctly delicious foodways of the Hawkeye State. "A rarity among cookbooks," say Jane and Michael Stern. 310 pages, 52 photos, paperback.

$ 16.95   Retail price
Applicable tax for Iowa residents
$ 3.50   Postage and handling
Make check payable to University of Iowa Press
ISBN 0-87745-289-X

COOKIN' FOR MIRACLES

310 Community Credit Union
475 NW Hoffman Lane
Des Moines, IA 50313

Cookin' For Miracles has 376 pages and over 800 favorite recipes from our employees and members of the credit union. All proceeds will be donated to the Children's Miracle Network (CMN), a foundation for children with all types of afflictions and diseases. We enjoyed putting the cookbook together and hope you enjoy all the recipes. Currently out of print.

COOKIN' FOR THE CREW

Spangler Chapel and Friends Church
c/o Terri Denkman
1265 North Isett
Moscow, IA 52760   319-732-3372

A collection of over 1000 recipes from the Midwest. Favorite recipes from farm wives, career women, men and children. This cookbook offers something for everyone; including low cholesterol, diabetic, quick time-saving and wild game. Most every recipe, you already have the ingredients in the cupboard.

$ 10.00   Retail price
$ 2.50   Postage and handling
Make check payable to Circle of Faith

COOKING HEALTHY WITH A MAN IN MIND

by JoAnna M. Lund
Healthy Exchanges
P.O. Box 80
DeWitt, IA 52742   800-766-8961

More than 200 lip-smacking, man-sized, soul-satisfying soups, stews, main dishes, and lots of desserts that just happen to be low in fat, sugar, calories and cholesterol.

$ 21.00   Retail price includes postage and handling
Make check payable to Healthy Exchanges
ISBN 0-399-14265-7

COUNTRY CUPBOARD COOKBOOK

Panora Church of the Brethern Women
c/o Eileen Ellis
6900 Starview Point
Panora, IA 50216   515-755-2486

The Panora Church of the Brethern Women has compiled a collection of over 700 recipes of food for the body and spirit on 346 pages. Interspersed between the pages and 14 chapters are inspirational verses and scriptures.

$ 9.00   Retail price (3 for $25.00)
$ 2.00   Postage and handling each
Make check payable to PCOB Women

COUNTRY LADY, NIBBLING AND SCRIBBLING

by Alice Howard
Country Lady Productions
811 Main
Elgin, IA 52141   319-426-5266

Country dwellers will recognize themselves with pleasure, and "citified" readers will get in touch with a vanishing view of America in this book of stories that takes one through the years up to the present. Each story is accompanied by one or more tested recipes. 116 pages, 76 recipes.

$ 10.95   Retail price
Applicable tax for Iowa residents
$ 1.50   Postage and handling
Make check payable to Alice Howard
ISBN 0-944266-22-3

DANDY DUTCH RECIPES

Penfield Press
215 Brown Street
Iowa City, IA 52245-1358   800-728-9998

"Honger is de beste saus" (Hunger is the best sauce), and also "When the stomach is full, the heart is glad" are Dutch proverbs that set the tone for this dandy little cookbook (3 x 5, 160 pages). These classic Dutch recipes were compiled by Mina Baker-Roelofs and Carol Van Klompenburg.

$ 6.95   Retail price, postpaid. (2/$12; 3/$18) / ISBN 0941016-84-6
Make check payable to Penfield Press

THE DES MOINES REGISTER COOKBOOK

University of Iowa Press
c/o Chicago Distribution Center
11030 S. Langley Avenue
Chicago, IL 60628   800-621-2736

Hundreds of favorite recipes from the experts at the Des Moines Register, Iowa's acclaimed statewide newspaper. Columnist Donald Kaul says, "Anyone who can't cook a good, hearty meal out of this book belongs in the Home for the Culinarily Challenged." 308 pages, 47 drawings, paperback.

$ 17.95   Retail price
Applicable tax for Iowa residents
$ 3.50   Postage and handling plus .50 for each additional book
Make check payable to University of Iowa Press
ISBN 0-87745-515-5

THE DIABETIC'S HEALTHY EXCHANGES COOKBOOK

by JoAnna M. Lund
Healthy Exchanges
P. O. Box 124
DeWitt, IA 52742   800-766-8961

Real food for people living in the real world with diabetes. 150 quick and delicious recipes for every day and special occasions.

$ 15.00   Retail price includes postage and handling
Make check payable to Healthy Exchanges
ISBN 0-399-52235-2

DINNER FOR TWO

by JoAnna M. Lund
Healthy Exchanges
P. O. Box 124
DeWitt, IA 52742   800-766-8961

This is a 64-page cookbook with recipes created with only two servings; everything from soups to desserts.

$ 6.50   Retail price includes postage and handling
Make check payable to Healthy Exchanges

DUTCH TOUCHES

Penfield Press
215 Brown Street
Iowa City, IA 52245-1358   800-728-9998

Dutch Touches is a revised and expanded version of two previous publications, Delightfully Dutch and Dutch Treats. Besides its wonderful authentic Dutch recipes, the book features Dutch heritage and history, windmill lore, wooden shoe comfort, Dutch art, tulip festivals, and tells much about the Dutch settlements in America. Paperback. 176 pages.

$ 12.95   Retail price (Postpaid) $14.95 / ISBN 1-57216-024-1
Make check payable to Penfield Press

ENJOY

by Martha Harrison
Toledo, IA 52342

Recipes dating back to World War II obtained from my grandmother, my mother, my aunt, others who touched my life; some of these written on regular recipe cards, some jotted down on scraps of paper and some torn out of newspapers/magazines. Now, all put together under one cover: Enjoy. Currently out of print.

FAVORITE RECIPES

Holy Trinity Parish
Protivin, IA 52163

Protivin Senior Citizens gathered favorite recipes from members of our parish and community for our cookbook. It consists of twelve separate sections of recipes. It contains 606 recipes and 236 pages. Also includes kitchen math with metric and substitutions and 416 household hints. Currently out of print.

FIRE GALS' HOT PANS COOKBOOK

Garrison Emergency Service Auxiliary
c/o Nancy Hendricks
P.O. box 146
Garrison, IA 52229   319-477-8525

We hope that this small-town cookbook has created a collection of palate pleasing recipes that your family and guests will enjoy. It has everything from cookies to wild game. There are over 800 recipes and more than 350 pages.

$ 10.00   Retail price
$ 2.00   Postage and handling
Make check payable to G.E.S.A.

FIRST CHRISTIAN CHURCH CENTENNIAL COOKBOOK

Christian Women's Fellowship
318 North Adams
Mason City, IA 50401   515-423-3519

This will be a cookbook that you use perhaps more than any other. Time-tested recipes from a century of our church's cooks were included. Our women's fellowship collected 555 recipes on 184 pages, including some from even as far back as the early 1900s.

$ 3.00   Retail price
$ 1.50   Postage and handling
Make check payable to First Christian Church

FONTANELLE GOOD SAMARITAN CENTER COOKBOOK

Fontanelle Good Samaritan Center
Fontanelle, IA 50846

Contains 370 pages, approximately 1000 recipes for good food made with ingredients that you probably have on hand. Recipes are indexed for easy location. Hard, 3-ring binder cover with break-away easel. Dividers have cooking tips printed on them. Recipes contributed by residents, staff, and family members. Currently out of print.

FROM THE COZY KITCHENS OF LONG GROVE

Long Grove Civic League
P. O. Box 210
Long Grove, IA 52756

We are proud to present this 350-page cookbook with over 750 of our favorite recipes. The Civic League is dedicated to restoring the historic community center, once a 2-room schoolhouse built in the 1860's, and now home to various civic groups. Proceeds from this cookbook contribute to the renovation of this facility.

$ 12.00 Retail price
$ 3.00 Postage and handling
Make check payable to Long Grove Civic League

GENERATIONS OF GOOD COOKING

St. Mary's Parish
Box 80
Oxford, IA 52322

Generations of Good Cooking is recipes of families and friends of St. Mary's Parish. Some of these recipes have been in families for generations. 482 pages, 14 sections.

$ 12.00 Retail price
$ 2.00 Postage and handling
Make check payable to Altar Rosary Society

GERMAN HERITAGE RECIPES COOKBOOK

American/Schleswig-Holstein Heritage Society
P. O. Box 313
Davenport, IA 52805-0313

Over 600 recipes on 352 pages from German cooks, many "from memory" with various terms for measurements. Two favorite recipes were given a separate chapter (Futtjen and Hans) with varying names and ingredients prepared by as many cooks, yet all with similar taste or flavor.

$ 10.00 Retail price
$ 3.00 Postage and handling
Make check payable to ASHHS-Recipes

GERMAN RECIPES: OLD WORLD SPECIALTIES AND PHOTOGRAPHY FROM THE AMANA COLONIES

215 Brown Street
Iowa City, IA 52245-1358   800-728-9998

One of the state's major tourist attractions, the seven historic villages that make up the Amanas were settled by German-speaking members of the Community of True Inspiration seeking religious freedom in the 19th century. Over 100 recipes, including ones for traditional shower of wedding cakes and other customs. Rare, historic photographs.

$ 8.95 Retail price
Make check payable to Penfield Press
ISBN 1-57216-007-1

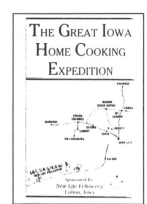

THE GREAT IOWA HOME COOKING EXPEDITION

New Life Fellowship
230 East Market Street
Lisbon, IA 52253   319-455-5000

This 418-page cookbook of over 800 recipes is a gathering of family recipes handed down from generation to generation with a variety of tastes and styles in cooking. There are thirteen sections that include an index, wild game, pages to list favorite recipes and helpful hints and suggestions.

$ 12.00   Retail price
$ 2.00   Postage and handling
Make check payable to New Life Fellowship

HOME COOKING WITH THE CUMMER FAMILY

11800 Deer Valley Trail
Dubuque, IA 52001

Home Cooking with the Cummer Family consists of 160 pages of favorite recipes turned in by Cummer family members. There are over 500 recipes— all of which have been tried by at least one of the almost 300 decendents of Louis and Barb Cummer. Currently out of print.

I LOVE YOU

by Sondra Smith
1411 Sheridan Avenue
Iowa City, IA 52240

To celebrate the college graduations of her three daughters, Sondra Smith created this unique collection of recipes from her family and 20 year catering career. Spiced with children's art and family stories, Sondra's book provides over 125 recipes, from pot stickers to potato pancakes. A warm and inventive family cookbook.

$ 10.00   Retail price
Applicable tax for Iowa residents
$ 2.00   Postage and handling
Make check payable to Sondra Smith

IOWA GRANGES: CELEBRATING 125 YEARS OF COOKING

Iowa State Grange
129 Cherry Hill Road NW
Cedar Rapids, IA 52405

Iowa Granges: Celebrating 125 Years of Cooking contains 498 pages with over 1200 recipes. In celebration of the 125th anniversary of the Iowa State Grange, Grange members share favorite recipes from their rural Iowa kitchens. Everything from casseroles to pies.

$ 10.00   Retail price
$ 3.50   Postage and handling
Make check payable to Iowa State Grange

THE L.O.V.E. CHOCOLATE COOKBOOK

by Jean Van Elsen Haney
P. O. Box 1561
Waterloo, IA 50704

Chocolate, "food of the gods"! 700 chocolate recipes, easy to gourmet, for "chocoholics" or chocolate connoisseurs. Contains 13 categories including lower-fat and sugar-free sections, plus facts about chocolate, fat lowering techniques for your favorite chocolate recipes and a household hints section.

$ 21.95   Retail price
Applicable tax for Iowa residents
    3.00   Postage and handling
Make check payable to Jean Haney

LEHIGH PUBLIC LIBRARY COOKBOOK

Lehigh Public Library
241 Elm Street
Lehigh, IA 50557   515-359-2967

This 264 page spiral-bound cookbook contains more than 650 recipes from local residents. Several Italian recipes are included. There is also a section containing diabetic recipes. A limited number of 3-ring notebook editions are available for $9.35.

$ 3.00   Retail price
    2.00   Postage and handling
Make check payable to Lehigh Public Library

LICENSE TO COOK IOWA STYLE

Penfield Press
215 Brown Street
Iowa City, IA 52245-5842   800-728-9998

Iowa celebrated its sesquicentennial in 1996, and this little cookbook celebrates its typical recipes that have spanned these 150 years. Also full of interesting facts. Recipe card size at only 3 x 5, it makes a neat little stocking stuffer.

$ 6.95 Retail price, postpaid (2/$12; 3/$18) / ISBN 1-57216-055-1
Applicable tax for Iowa residents
Make check payable to Penfield Press

THE LOWFAT GRILL

by Donna Rodnitzky
Prima Publishing   916-789-7000
3000 Lava Ridge Court   Fax 916-789-7001
Roseville, CA 95661   Email sales@primapublishing.com

The Lowfat Grill shows you how to choose leaner cuts of meat, exchange heavy sauces for light and savory complements, and use professional techniques to enjoy the distinctive smoky flavor of grilling in more healthful ways. You will find 200 ideas for delicious and mouth-watering grilled food and exceptional accompaniments. (318 pages).

$ 18.00   Retail price
$ 4.00   Postage and handling
Make check payable to Prima Publishing
ISBN 0-7615-0265-3

LUTHERAN CHURCH WOMEN COOKBOOK

Lutheran Church Women of Missouri Valley
724 N. 8th Street
Missouri Valley, IA 51555   712-642-2483 or 642-4327

Lutheran Church Women Cookbook contains favorite recipes compiled by the ladies of First Lutheran Church, Missouri Valley. Some were taken from the favorites of their earlier cookbook. Over 545 recipes, hardcover, 219 pages.

$ 5.95   Retail price
$ 2.45   Postage and handling
Make check payable to Lutheran Church Women

THE MACHINE SHED FARM STYLE COOKING

The Machine Shed
111 West 76th Street
Davenport, IA 52806   319-391-2427

A collection of recipes from our own restaurants and from our customers. 262 pages; 6 sections; over 450 recipes.

$ 12.95   Retail price
Applicable tax for Iowa residents
     2.50   Postage and handling
Make check payable to The Machine Shed

MADISON COUNTY COOKBOOK

St. Joseph Catholic Church
607 West Green Street
Winterset, IA 50273 515-462-1083   515-462-1083

This book offers a unique look at a small community where the simple values of faith, friends and family have not been forgotten. Over 500 recipes are featured in this 512-page book. Interspersed with anecdotes, stories and traditions, old fashioned down-home country recipes—many from scratch—make this a cook's delight!

$ 19.00   Retail price
$ 2.95   Postage and handling
Make check payable to St. Joseph Catholic Church
ISBN 0-9644705-0-0

MARCUS, IOWA QUASQUICENTENNIAL COOKBOOK 1871-1996

QQC Cookbook Committee
Marcus, IA 51035

This cookbook was assembled by a committee of 29 women but includes recipes from the whole community and former residents. The 480-page book contains over 2000 recipes plus a Helpful Hints section. Marcus is a rural community of 1200 in northwest Iowa. Currently out of print.

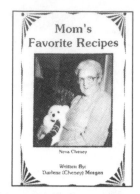

MOM'S FAVORITE RECIPES

by Darlene (Cheney) Morgan
4501 SE 3rd Court
Des Moines, IA 50315   515-287-6632

Here is a grand cookbook with all Neva Cheney's collected recipes. It contains over 500 recipes of just pure down-home cooking.

$ 14.00   Retail price
Make check payable to Darlene Morgan

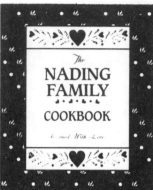

THE NADING FAMILY COOKBOOK:
SEASONED WITH LOVE

c/o Mildred Fear
P. O. Box 132
Aurora, IA 50607

This 544-recipe, 184-page *Nading Cookbook* is dedicated to helping defray hospital costs for Nicki Nading. She has undergone a very lengthy hospital stay due to an illness she contracted six years ago. She has suffered ongoing complications since then and we hope this cookbook gives her support. Currently out of print.

NEIGHBORING ON THE AIR: COOKING WITH
THE KMA RADIO HOMEMAKERS

University of Iowa Press
c/o Chicago Distribution Center
11030 S. Langley Avenue
Chicago, IL 60628   800-621-2736

In 1925 KMA Radio—960 from Shenandoah, Iowa, began broadcasting daily programs by lively, personable women who became known as the KMA Radio Homemakers. Here are the voices, recipes, and endearing companionship of these radio homemakers. 349 pages, 118 photos, paperback.

$ 16.95   Retail price
Applicable tax for Iowa residents
$ 3.50   Postage and handling plus .50 for each additional book
Make check payable to University of Iowa Press
ISBN 0-87745-316-0

NEW BEGINNINGS

First Congregational United Church of Christ
DeWitt, IA 52742

New Beginnings is a self-standing, washable vinyl cookbook with 256 pages. There are nine categories including recipes from the past, this and that, and game recipes. This book includes recipes from 1888 through the present. Currently out of print.

NEW TASTES OF IOWA

by Peg Hein/Kathryn Designs
2215 A Westlake Drive
Austin, TX 78746   512-328-5042

A collection of lighter, leaner recipes for the way most Iowan's cook today. Good Iowa cooks combine the abundance of the Iowa harvest with their own knowledge of what tastes good in 116 pages of recipes from good cooks all over Iowa.

$ 13.00   Retail price
$ 2.25   Postage and handling
Make check payable to Kathryn Designs
ISBN 0-9613881-2-0

OMA'S (GRANDMA'S) FAMILY SECRETS: GENERATIONS OF AMANA COOKING

by Linda F. Selzer
4319 V. Street
Homestead, IA 52236

Linda Selzer, a lifelong resident of a historic German settlement, the Amana Colonies, has blended a collection of old-world and new recipes. *Oma's (Grandma's) Family Secrets* is a foundation of happy kitchens and happy homes that have pleased her family and guests for generations. This handwritten cookbook has over 200 recipes and is a must for collectors.

$ 12.00   Retail price
Applicable tax for Iowa residents
$ 2.50   Postage and handling
Make check payable to Helen Selzer

101 GREAT LOWFAT DESSERTS

by Donna Rodnitzky
Prima Publishing
Roseville, CA 95661

101 Great Lowfat Desserts contains 285 pages of deliciously decadent lowfat dessert recipes for elegant tortes, rich layer cakes, irresistible cookies, and sweet breads—all having the same taste, texture, and appearance found in traditional desserts, but without the butter or fat. Currently out of print.

125TH ANNIVERSARY CELEBRATION COOK BOOK

Congregational Women's Fellowship
316 6th Street N
Forest City, IA 50446

This book consists of 87 pages of recipes plus pages for notes and recipes; it also has informational dividers. There are approximately 246 recipes, including breads, main dishes, desserts and salads.

$ 5.00   Retail price
$ 2.50   Postage and handling
Make check payable to Congregational Women's Fellowship

125 YEARS—WALKING IN FAITH
Women's Fellowship, First Congregational Church
Spencer, IA 51301

The First Congregational Church's Quasquacentennial's cookbook, *125 Years—Walking In Faith* is a masterpiece of 695 mouth-watering recipes. The collection is contained in a vinyl 3-ring snapback easel binder with tab dividers. There are 300 pages of many unique and valuable recipes along with many of the familiar favorites. Currently out of print.

ORIENT VOLUNTEER FIRE DEPARTMENT COOKBOOK
Orient Volunteer Fire Department
P. O. Box 125
Orient, IA 50858   515-337-5403

The Orient Volunteer Fire Department Cookbook has 319 pages containing 800 of our favorite recipes that are quick, easy as well as delicious. We've also included throughout the cookbook past historical facts of the department. We feel our cookbook reflects the wonderful down-home cooking of rural Southwest Iowa.

$ 10.00   Retail price
$ 2.00   Postage and handling
Make check payable to Orient Volunteer Fire Department

OUR HERITAGE: RECIPES FROM KITCHENS PAST AND PRESENT
by Gayla Voss
58673 110th Avenue
Fonda, IA 50540

A collection of recipes from the Heartland. Beautiful, spiral bound, 290 pages, over 800 recipes. Recipes from the past, homemade soap, canned beef and chicken, desserts Grandma made to recipes from the modern busy cook. Every recipe is a tried and proven family favorite that bursts with flavor. Enjoy recipes from the heartland that boasts of the best cooks.

$ 10.00   Retail price
Applicable tax for Iowa residents
$ 3.50   Postage and handling
Make check payable to Gayla Voss

OUR SAVIOR'S KVINDHERRED COOKBOOK
Our Savior's Lutheran Church
Attn: Jason Bousselot
2671 165th Avenue
Calamus, IA 52729   319-246-2723

Our Savior's Kvindherred Cookbook contains recipes from members of our church, founded in 1861 by Norwegian immigrants. Scandinavian heritage recipes and family favorites are found within its 207 pages. Hard cover, spiral bound and tabbed dividers make our cookbook convenient to use. Proceeds given to Kvindherred Momerial Pipe Organ Fund.

$ 10.00   Retail price
$ 2.00   Postage and handling
Make check payable to Our Savior's Organ Fund

QUASQUICENTENNIAL / ST. OLAF OF BODE COOKBOOK

St. Olaf Lutheran Church
P. O. Box 2
Bode, IA 50519   515-379-1772

Not everyone is Norwegian, but all celebrate with recipes and heritage of 125 years. This, our 5th cookbook, features history and details of our 70th Annual Lutefisk Supper. Original Scandinavian designs, 15 categories, large print, 800 old/new recipes and fun info. Good reading! Good eating! Mange-tuk! (Many thanks)!

$ 8.00   Retail price
$ 2.25   Postage and handling
Make check payable to St. Olaf Lutheran Church

RECIPES FROM IOWA WITH LOVE

by Peg Hein and Kathryn Cramer
Branches/Strawberry Point, Inc.
16163 Fillmore Avenue Southeast
Prior Lake, MN 55372   800-999-5858

A delicious collection of favorite recipes from fine cooks throughout Iowa combined with highlights of history, places and people that make the state unique. Features recipes for easy to prepare family meals and relaxed entertaining plus unusual and memorable dishes for those special occasions. Includes original illustrations and a comprehensive index.

$ 13.95   Retail price
Applicable tax for Minnesota residents
$ 1.50   Postage and handling
Make check payable to Strawberry Point, Inc.
ISBN 0-913703-01-X

RETURN ENGAGEMENT

Volunteers for Symphony
Quad City Symphony Orchestra
P. O. Box 1144
Davenport, IA 52805   319-322-0931

The soufflé, hallmark of accomplished cooking, serves as the focal point for the cover of our book. Created by request for those who expect recipes that are dependable, multiple tested, and of exceptional quality, this 300 page cookbook offers the traditional best and family favorites.

$ 13.95   Retail price
$ 4.00   Postage and handling
Make check payable to Volunteers for Symphony
ISBN 0-9621733-0-4

SAINT MARY CATHOLIC CHURCH COOKBOOK

St. Mary's School
P. O. Box 100
Guttenberg, IA 52052   319-252-1577

Our personalized cookbook features recipes from members of our church. It has a vinyl 3-ring binder and has an easel binder so it stands up on your counter. It has 10 different categories with mylar tabs and features over 900 favorite recipes. 352 pages.

$ 12.00   Retail price
$ 3.00   Postage and handling
Make check payable to St. Mary Home School

SEP JUNIOR WOMEN'S CLUB 25TH ANNIVERSARY COOKBOOK

c/o Debb DeBoef
P. O. Box 338
Mitchellville, IA 50169   515-967-5812

This three-ring notebook with easel back, so that it is free-standing while using, includes 400 recipes with 168 pages. Labeled tab dividers, index, and helpful hints.

$ 12.50   Retail price
$ 3.00   Postage and handling
Make check payable to Southeast Polk Junior Women's Club

SHARING OUR BEST

The Old Homestead
920 2nd Street NW
Waukon, IA 52172-1004   319-568-4188

The recipes included in this cookbook were graciously given by consignors, workers and quilters of the Waukon area. We thank them for their sharing. Waukon is located in northeast Iowa, about 20 miles from the mighty Mississippi River.

$ 7.00   Retail price
Applicable tax for Iowa residents
$ 1.50   Postage and handling
Make check payable to Joyce Bakke

SHARING TRADITIONS FROM PEOPLE YOU KNOW

The American Cancer Society/Iowa Division
8364 Hickman Road Suite D
Des Moines, IA 50325   800-688-0147

Almost 400 delicious recipes from American Cancer Society volunteers and staff from across Iowa are included in this 12-chapter, 240-page cookbook. Noted artist P. Buckley Moss, herself a breast cancer survivor, donated thirteen of her images for the cover and chapter divider pages.

$ 15.00   Retail price
$ 2.50   Postage and handling
Make check payable to The American Cancer Society

SINGING IN THE KITCHEN

by Mavis Punt
1915 Third Avenue SE
Sioux Center, IA 51250   712-722-2305

You will be *Singing in the Kitchen* with this Victorian motif cookbook of over 450 tested recipes that run the gamut from simple to elegant; plus tips throughout to assist you. Comments accompany each recipe and the instructions are detailed. A must for collectors. 311 pages printed on cream stock.

$ 14.95   Retail price
$ 2.00   Postage and handling
Make check payable to Mavis Punt

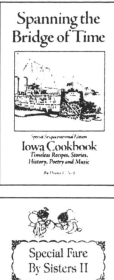

SPANNING THE BRIDGE OF TIME

by Diana L. Neff
806 2nd Street
Princeton, IA 52768-9752   800-390-2923

Spanning the Bridge of Time is a 546-page Iowa Special Sesquicentennial Edition Cookbook containing 700 timeless recipes; many ethnic, some 100 years old. Iowa tourist attractions, with histories, serve as the 14 dividers. Stories, poetry, anecdotes, and special features of music and hand-written recipes personalize this unique, entertaining, and exciting cookbook!

$ 21.95   Retail price
Applicable tax for Iowa residents
$ 3.00   Postage and handling
Make check payable to Diana's Creations
ISBN 1-57216-073-X

SPECIAL FARE BY SISTERS II

Ione Burham and Joyce Chorpening
Box 1179
Laurie, MO 65038   573-374-0110

Special Fare by Sisters II, an all-occasion, hardback cookbook, is a compilation of over 400 recipes that can be prepared in advance, have eye appeal, and a "home-cooked" flavor. From appetizers to desserts, simple fare to gourmet, the novice or experienced cook will find preparation for entertaining made easier.

$ 13.95   Retail price
Applicable tax for Iowa residents
$ 3.00   Postage and handling
Make check payable to Ione S. Burham

SPECIAL RECIPES FROM OUR HEARTS

The United Methodist Church of DeWitt
c/o JoAnn Harrington
2816 234rh Street
DeWitt, IA 52742-9100   319-659-3172

Our special cookbook contains 190 pages of 408 tried and true recipes in the usual categories plus a large section of "Special Diet" recipes. We hope you enjoy these recipes and feel the love that has gone into *Special Recipes from Our Hearts* as it flows from the pages.

$ 8.50   Retail price
Applicable tax for Iowa residents
$ 2.00   Postage and handling
Make check payable to United Methodist Women

SPITFIRE ANNIVERSARY COOKBOOK

Quimby Spitfire Ladies Auxiliary
Box 11
Quimby, IA 51049-0011   712-445-2674

The Spitfire Anniversary Cookbook was printed in 1996; it is the Fireman's 75th Anniversary and the Spitfire's 15th Anniversary. The cookbook has 234 pages of recipes, approximately 700 recipes.

$ 5.00   Retail price
$ 2.00   Postage and handling
Make check payable to Quimby Spitfire's

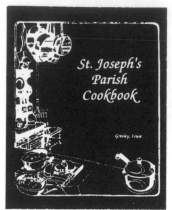

ST. JOSEPH'S PARISH COOKBOOK

St. Joseph's Altar and Rosary
208 East Second Street
Greeley, IA 52050

St. Joseph's Cookbook has over 300 pages of uncomplicated recipes. An unusual feature in that it includes the first cookbook they published in 1952. Combined there are over 450 recipes, household and cooking hints. The cover is unique because it has a stand-up feature for easier viewing.

$ 10.00   Retail price
$ 3.00   Postage and handling
Make check payable to St. Joseph's Altar and Rosary

ST. PAUL'S WOMAN'S LEAGUE
50TH ANNIVERSARY COOK BOOK

915 27th Street
Marion, IA 52302   319-377-4687

This cookbook includes over 275 recipes on 114 pages. It also has 25 pages of helpful hints. The book was compiled from recipes submitted by the entire congregation of St. Paul's to share in the celebration of the 50th anniversary in the Lutheran Women's Missionary League.

$ 5.00   Retail price
$ 1.50   Postage and handling
Make check payable to St. Paul's Women's League

STIRRING UP MEMORIES

Platte Center Presbyterian Church
Creston, IA 50801

A collection of favorite recipes submitted by farm families that have ties to the historic, 125-year-old Platte Center Presbyterian Church in Union County. This easy-to-read cookbook has 1000 recipes (some with the cook's personal comments), a separate heritage section, church history and complete index. Currently out of print.

T.W. AND ANNA ELLIOTT FAMILY RECEIPTS

601 Bishop Avenue
La Porte City, IA 50651-1551   319-342-3285

The *T.W. and Anna Elliott Family Receipts* was published in Iowa in the year of Iowa's Sesquicentennial (1996), and incorporates six generations' personalized recipes and domestic tips, Black Hawk and Benton County heartland history from 1882 and family history from 1823 with family photos. The book contains 338 pages with over 1,000 recipes.

$ 12.00   Retail price
Applicable tax for Iowa residents
$ 3.00   Postage and handling
Make check payable to Elliott Family Receipts

A TASTE OF GRACE

Grace Lutheran Women
P. O. Box 156
DeWitt, IA 52742   319-659-9153

A 354-page cookbook with sections on breads, casseroles, desserts, etc; also, special needs, kid's recipes, microwave recipes and more. Title page for each section features unique recipes, prayers or special thoughts.

$ 10.00   Retail price
$ 2.00   Postage and handling
Make check payable to Grace Lutheran Church Cookbook

A TASTE OF THE WORLD

Central College Auxiliary
Central College
812 University
Pella, IA 50219   515-628-7035

Our cookbook has a Holland-Dutch Section, large International section with menu suggestions plus exciting recipes from all over the U.S.A. Delft plate graces the cover with Pella landmark sketches for dividers. The book has healthy recipes, historic favorites, essay on Dutch cooking, plus Jaarsma's Dutch Letter recipe, and 332 pages with over 650 recipes.

$ 10.00   Retail price
$ 2.50   Postage and handling
Make check payable to Central College Auxiliary

TERESA'S HEAVENLY CAKES AND TREASURERS

by Teresa Ann Martin
Walnut, IA 51577-3001

The most unique cookbook ever printed. A talented homemaker, wedding consultant shares generations of mouth-watering Iowa recipes. Wedding ideas, wedding cake pictures, household hints, flower arranging and family stories are in this 184-page book with over 1140 recipes. You will love it. Currently out of print.

THOMPSON FAMILY COOKBOOK

by Janice Winter
4207 160 Avenue
Lakota, IA 50451   515-886-2534

My mom was a very good cook. She obviously got a lot of practice considering all the cooking she had to do for my dad and we twelve children. Lauren and Goldie Thompson farmed all their married life—almost 60 years. I have written down these recipes in memory of my mom and dad.

$ 6.00   Retail price
$ 2.00   Postage and handling
Make check payable to Janice Winter

TITONKA CENTENNIAL COOKBOOK

Titonka Centennial Committee
Box 124
Titonka, IA 50480   515-928-2308

Titonka will celebrate its centennial in 1998 and to start the party early, there's a Titonka Centennial Cookbook which has 1200 recipes. It also has unique vinyl easel-style cover which opens to make its own stand and features plastic page savers as well.

$ 12.00   Retail price
$ 3.00   Postage and handling
Make check payable to Titonka Centennial Cookbook

TITONKA
CENTENNIAL
COOKBOOK

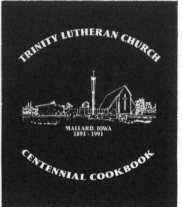

TRINITY LUTHERAN CHURCH CENTENNIAL COOKBOOK

Trinity LWML/Mary Clausen
43402 200th Avenue
Havelock, IA 50546-7541   712-776-2340

Trinity's cookbook is a 3-ring, vinyl-covered collection of favorite recipes. The category dividers contain useful and interesting information. A special feature of this cookbook is that it also contains the church cookbook from 1957 under the title of "Good Old Days."

$ 10.00   Retail price
$ 3.50   Postage and handling
Make check payable to Trinity LWML

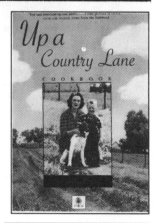

UP A COUNTRY LANE COOKBOOK

University of Iowa Press
c/o Chicago Distribution Center
11030 S. Langley Avenue
Chicago, IL 60628   800-621-2736

Evelyn Birkby, longtime newspaper and radio personality, has chosen the best recipes from her column and interspersed them with a wealth of stories of rural life in the 1940s and 1950s; she has created a book that encompasses a lost time. 276 pages, 63 photos, hardback.

$ 22.95   Retail price
Applicable tax for Iowa residents
$ 3.50   Postage and handling plus .50 for each additional book
Make check payable to University of Iowa Press
ISBN 0-87745-420-5

Recipes from the
Swedish Heritage Society
Swedesburg, Iowa

VÄLKOMMEN TILL SWEDESBURG

Swedish Heritage Society
107 Hwy 218
Swedesburg, IA 52652-0074   319-254-2317

This collection includes favorite dishes from Iowa farm kitchens, traditional Swedish foods like ostkaka and rye bread, and background notes on Swedish customs. This cookbook from Swedesburg, a small farming community proud of its Swedish heritage, includes a brief history of its Scandinavian founders and recipes from yesterday and today.

$ 8.00   Retail price
$ 3.00   Postage and handling
Make check payable to Swedish American Museum

VISITATION PARISH COOKBOOK

St. Rita's Circle of Visitation Parish
c/o Therese Halbach
Box 235
Stacyville, IA 50476   515-737-2112

A spiral bound collection of 900 plus favorite recipes from a parish of over 200 families. It includes a large selection of recipes using Iowa corn-fed beef and pork along with fruit and vegetable favorites.

$ 8.00 Retail price
Applicable tax for Iowa residents
$ 2.00 Postage and handling
Make check payable to St. Rita's Circle

WALNUT CENTENNIAL COOK BOOK

Walnut American Legion Auxiliary
c/o Audrey Carroll
Avoca, IA 51521-3203   712-784-3923

Many categories of recipes are by several area past and present residents of Walnut. This book was originally done for the 1971 Centennial and has sold well and been reprinted ever since. Enjoy.

$ 15.00 Retail price including tax and postage
Make check payable to Audrey Carroll

WILDLIFE HARVEST GAME COOKBOOK

Game Cookbook; Wildlife Harvest Publications, Inc.
P. O. Box 96
Goose Lake, IA 52750   319-259-4000

Over 200 pages and 335 recipes for preparing sumptuous game dinners. Favorite recipes of North America's Hunting Preserves, Game Farms, and Gourmet Chefs. The book includes recipes for pheasant, duck, goose, quail, partridge, wild turkey, venison, fish, and many other miscellaneous treats.

$ 17.95 Retail price
Applicable tax for Iowa residents
$ 3.00 Postage and handling
Make check payable to Wildlife Harvest Publications, Inc.
ISBN 0-929902-00-9

WOODBINE PUBLIC LIBRARY COMMUNITY COOKBOOK

Woodbine Public Library
58 5th Street
Woodbine, IA 51579   712-647-2750

This cookbook has 412 pages with some history of the town of Woodbine. This project will help the building fund for the Woodbine Public Library. All proceeds go to the library for the building fund.

$ 12.00 Retail price
$ 3.00 Postage and handling
Make check payable to Woodbine Public Library

THE LITTLE TOWN WITH A ♥

Community Cookbook
1st. Edition 1987

X_____ COMMUNITY COOKBOOK

Exline Committee
c/o Joy Golden
P.O. Box 156
Exline, IA 52555   515-658-2637

This book contains 223 pages of yummy recipes from appetizers through desserts. It also provides hints, charts, poems, amusing comments and sketches. It was originally compiled to help finance a community center for Exline, a town of less than 200 people, known as "the little town with a big heart."

$ 6.00   Retail price
$ 1.30   Postage and handling
Make check payable to Exline Recreation Fund

READLYN — "857 friendly people and one old grump"

COOKBOOK
By Families and Friends Of
Zion Lutheran Church
Readlyn, Iowa

ZION LUTHERAN CHURCH COOKBOOK

Zion Lutheran Church
Readlyn, IA 50668

Our cookbook was published as a fundraiser for our 75th anniversary of our church. The book includes 1223 recipes in 451 pages. Over 3800 copies have been sold. Currently out of print.

Index

Boone & Scenic Valley Railroad. Boone.

INDEX

A

All-At-Once Spaghetti 107
Almond Cookies 207
Almost Pizza 104
American Gothic Cheese Loaf 26
Angel Food Cake 171
Apfel Küchelchen 227
Apple:
    Apfel Küchelchen 227
    Applesauce Cake 164
    Cabbage and Apple Slaw with Walnuts 69
    Carrot-Apple Cake 165
    Cider Syrup 44
    Cranberry Pancake Puff 43
    Diabetic Applesauce Cookies 203
    Edna's Fresh Apple Cake 163
    French Apple Creme Pie 221
    Fresh Apple Bars 188
    Goodie 165
    Party Apple Salad 64
    Pie Bars 188
    Pie with Sour Cream 217
    Pumpkin Apple Streusel Muffins 38
    Snicker Apple Salad 64
    Spinach Salad with Bacon and Apple 59
    Turnovers 227
Ardith's Rolls 31
Asparagus in the Dutch Way 89
Aunt Darlene's Black Bottom Cupcakes 175

B

Baked Chicken Breast 123
Baked Chicken Salad 74
Baked Fish and Vegetables 100
Baked German Potato Salad 57
Baked Stuffed Tomatoes 88
Baked Zucchini 92
Baking Powder Biscuits 35
Banana Marshmallow Cake 167
Barbecued Beef Sandwiches 143
Barbecued Brisket 143
Barbecued Hamburger Crispies 151
BBQ Ribs 143
Beef:
    All-At-Once Spaghetti 107
    Almost Pizza 104
    Barbecued Beef Sandwiches 143
    Barbecued Brisket 143
    Barbecued Hamburger Crispies 151
    Best Meat in Iowa 144
    Birds' Nests 152
    Bohemian Beef Dinner 160
    Cavatelli 110
    Cavatini 110
    Cheese Spaghetti 106
    Cowboy Goulash 103
    Cranberry Meat Balls 155
    Czech Goulash 159
    Enchilada Casserole 113
    Four-Hour Stew 156
    Glazed Country Steak 145
    Grant Wood's Cabbage Rolls 160
    Ground Nut Stew 156
    Hash with Corn Muffin Mix 157
    Italian Beef Pot Roast 145
    Italian "Carne Pane" 149
    Make Ahead Lasagna 105
    Manhattan Meatballs 153
    Maytag Steak Au Poivre 147
    Meat Balls 154
    Memorial Day Roast 144
    Mexican Lasagna 105
    Mince Meat 158
    Nana's Swiss Steak 146
    Pasghetti Pizza 104
    Pepper Steak 146
    Pizza Burgers 154
    Roast 144
    Salisbury Steak 148
    Sizzling Steak Fajitas 148
    Spaghetti Bake 106
    Spaghetti Pie 107
    Steak Stroganoff 150
    Stew 157
    Stir-Fry 147
    Stroganoff 150
    Stromboli 151
    Stuffed French Bread 26
    Stuffed Hamburger 152
    Swedish Meatballs 153
Beets, Deluxe 96

Berry Delicious Bread 31
Best Ever Banana Bread 30
Best Meat in Iowa 144
Better Than Sex Cake 180
Betty's Lemon Pudding Pie 230
Birds' Nests 152
Biscuits:
  Baking Powder Biscuits 35
  Cheese-Garlic Biscuits 35
  Italian Biscuit Ring 34
Blue Cheese—Artichoke Salad 59
Blueberry Sauce 249
Bohemian Beef Dinner 160
Bohemian Chewy Bars 190
Bread:
  American Gothic Cheese Loaf 26
  Ardith's Rolls 31
  Baking Powder Biscuits 35
  Berry Delicious Bread 31
  Best Ever Banana Bread 30
  Cheese Bread 27
  Cheese-Garlic Biscuits 35
  Chive and Black Pepper Corn Bread 36
  Christmas Morning Sticky Rolls 32
  Cocoa Banana Muffins 39
  Corn Fritters 37
  Deb's Maple Bread Ring 28
  English Muffins 36
  Garlic Bubble Bread 27
  Georgia's Apple Coffee Cake 40
  Italian Biscuit Ring 34
  Kringles 40
  Lemon Poppy Seed Bread 29
  Overnight Bread or Rolls 33
  Overnight Butterhorn Rolls 33
  Overnight Sweet Rolls with Cream 29
  Peach Pudding Coffee Cake 41
  Pineapple Muffins 39
  Pizza Crust Dough 37
  Poppy Seed Bread 29
  Pumpkin Apple Streusel Muffins 38
  Raised Doughnuts 43
  Refrigerator Rolls 34
  Sticky Maple Bacon Rolls 32
  Strawberry Banana Bread 30
  Stuffed French Bread 26
  Stuffed French Bread Strata 44
  Super-Easy Ham and Cheese Muffins 37
Breakfast:
  Apple-Cranberry Pancake Puff 43
  Elegant Brunch Eggs 44
  German Apple Pancakes 42
  Iowa Corn Pancakes 42
  Pigs-in-a-Blanket 46
  Pizza 45
  Swedish Pancakes 41
Bridge Dessert 237
Broccoli:
  and Cauliflower Salad 60
  and Rice 91
  Hot Dish 116
  Salad 60
  Soufflé, Spinach or 91
  Vegetable Sauté, Chicken 124
Brown Beans with Bacon 94
Brown Jug Soup 51
Brownies:
  Cream Cheese 198
  Dump 198
  Pen Pal 195
  Zucchini 199
Butter Brickle Bars 196
Butter Pecan Dessert 235

C

Cabbage and Apple Slaw with Walnuts 69
Cabbage and Noodle Casserole, Ham, 103
Cabbage Rolls, Grant Wood's 160
Cabbage, Spiced Red 90
Cakes:
  Angel Food Cake 171
  Apple Goodie 165
  Applesauce Cake 164
  Aunt Darlene's Black Bottom Cupcakes 175
  Banana Marshmallow Cake 167
  Better Than Sex Cake 180
  Carrot-Apple Cake 165
  Cheese Cake 185
  Cherry Chocolate Cake 177
  Corn Cake 170
  Double Chocolate Cupcakes 176
  Edna's Fresh Apple Cake 163
  French Chocolate Cake 179
  Grant Wood's Strawberry Shortcake 179
  Home Style Dutch Crullers 183
  Hot Fudge Pudding Cake 178
  Hot Milk Cake 162
  Iowa Dirt Cake 186
  Lemon Pudding Cake 172
  Mandarin Orange Cake 166
  Marshmallow Chocolate Fudge Cake 177
  Myrtle's Famous Banana Cake 168

Orange Push-Up Cheesecake 184
Pigout Cake 180
Pistachio Cake 171
Polynesian Cake 166
Poppy Seed Cake 170
Pumpkin Jellyroll 174
Punch Bowl Cake 182
Quick Lemon Cheesecake 185
Radio Cake 178
Rhubarb Cake 168
Snowballs 183
Sour Cream Lemon Pound Cake 174
Special Lemon Cake 172
Strawberry Fluff 182
Sunshine Lemon Cake 173
Tomato Soup Cake 169
Tropical Delight 181
Turtle Cheesecake 186
Watergate Cake 181
Candy:
Chocolate and Peanut Butter Truffles 212
Des Moines Fudge 211
Easter Nests 212
Fudge 209
Merry Cranberry Christmas Fudge 211
Peanut Brittle 213
Popcorn Balls 214
Puffed Wheat Candy 213
Canned Cream Soup Substitute 52
Cantonese Celery 90
Caramel Dumplings 243
Caramel Ice Cream Dessert 247
Caramel-Filled Chocolate Cookies 201
Card Club Chicken Salad 73
Carrots:
Apple Cake 165
Casserole 86
Dill 86
in Dill Butter 86
Marinated 87
Sandwich Filling 87
Vegetable Loaf 94
Cashew Cookies 204
Cavatelli 110
Cavatelli and Three Cheeses 111
Cavatini 110
Celery, Cantonese 90
Chaud Eriod 71
Cheese:
American Gothic Cheese Loaf 26
Cake 185
Cavatelli and Three Cheeses 111

Cheese Bread 27
Cheese-Garlic Biscuits 35
Cheesy Potatoes and Ham 117
Corn Cheese Casserole 79
Garlic Biscuits 35
Holland Cheese Chicken Rolls 122
Orange Push-Up Cheesecake 184
Quick Lemon Cheesecake 185
Sauce for Potatoes 83
Sour Cream and Cheddar Supreme
Pot 84
Spaghetti 106
Turtle Cheesecake 186
Cheesy BBQ Potato Bake 82
Cheesy Ham-Potato Soup 50
Cheesy Potatoes and Ham 117
Cherry Chocolate Cake 177
Chess Pie, "Iowa Pride" 216
Chicken:
a la King 125
and Wild Rice Casserole 115
Baked Chicken Breast 123
Baked Chicken Salad 74
Broccoli Vegetable Sauté 124
Card Club Chicken Salad 73
Casserole 126, 127
Cordon Bleu 124
Crispy Sesame Chicken 123
Dijon 121
Enchiladas 125
Essex 127
French Onion Chicken Bake 120
Fresh Herb Grilled Chicken 122
Fruited Chicken Salad 75
Garden Club Salad 73
Holland Cheese Chicken Rolls 122
Hot Chicken Salad 129
Kay's Chicken Salad 75
Lemon Asparagus Chicken 123
L'Orange 122
Margery's Chicken 'n' Niffles 128
Moroccan Chicken and Wild Rice Salad 72
Oven-Fried Chicken with Honey Butter
Sauce 121
Salad 72
Salad In-A-Ring 74
Scalloped Chicken 120
Tea Room Chicken 126
Chili, Stormy Weather 54
Chive and Black Pepper Corn Bread 36
Chocolate:
and Peanut Butter Truffles 212

Angel Food Cake Dessert 241
Better Than Sex Cake 180
Caramel-Filled Chocolate Cookies 201
Cherry Chocolate Cake 177
Chip Peanut Butter Pie 223
Chip Pudding Cookies 202
Chocolate Meringue Pie 231
Cream Cheese Dessert 234
Double Chocolate Cupcakes 176
Double-Chocolate Sugar Cookies 200
Festive Fudge Filled Bars 192
French Chocolate Cake 179
Fudge 209
Fudge Puddles 210
Homemade Chocolate Grape Nut Ice
    Cream 248
Hot Fudge Pudding Cake 178
Hot Fudge Sauce 249
Marshmallow Chocolate Fudge Cake 177
Mousse Pie 224
Never Fail Chocolate Frosting 198
Pen Pal Brownies 195
Radio Cake 178
Schokolade Brot Pudding 245
Scotchies 208
Snicker Bars 195
Trifle 240
Christmas Morning Sticky Rolls 32
Cinnamon Bars 193
Cocoa Banana Muffins 39
Coffee Cake, Georgia's Apple 40
Coffee Cake, Peach Pudding 41
Coffee Tortoni 236
Company Potatoes 80
Congealed Spinach Salad 65
Cookie Brittle 208
Cookies:
    Almond Cookies 207
    Apple Pie Bars 188
    Bohemian Chewy Bars 190
    Butter Brickle Bars 196
    Caramel-Filled Chocolate Cookies 201
    Cashew Cookies 204
    Chocolate Chip Pudding Cookies 202
    Cinnamon Bars 193
    Cookie Brittle 208
    Cream Cheese Brownies 198
    Delta Bars 194
    Diabetic Applesauce Cookies 203
    Double-Chocolate Sugar Cookies 200
    Dump Brownies 198
    Dutch Handkerchiefs 207

Dutch Letters 206
Festive Fudge Filled Bars 192
Fresh Apple Bars 188
Fudge Puddles 210
Ice Cream Sugar Cookie Sandwiches 209
Krakalinger 205
Ladyfingers 208
Lemon Squares 200
Mix 201
Mom's Pineapple Drop Cookies 203
Moon Bars 193
Mound Bars 192
Nuss Plätzchen 197
Orange Slice Cookies 204
Paddington's Peanut Logs 197
Pen Pal Brownies 195
Pride of Iowa Cookies 207
Pumpkin Bars 189
Salted Nut Roll Bars 196
Scotchies 208
S'Mores 199
Snicker Bars 195
Sour Cream Bars 190
Triple Good Raisin Bars 194
Unbaked Peanut Butter Cookies 202
World's Best Cookie Bars 191
Yummy Cherry Bars 189
Zucchini Brownies 199
Corn:
    and Oyster Casserole 102
    Cake 170
    Cheese Casserole 79
    Cowboy Goulash 103
    Easy Corn on the Cob 78
    Fritters 37
    Iowa Corn Pancakes 42
    Noodle Casserole 112
    Skillet Sweet 78
    Soup 52
Corn Bread, Chive and Black Pepper 36
Cowboy Goulash 103
Cranberries:
    Apple-Cranberry Pancake Puff 43
    Cranberry Meat Balls 155
    Cranberry Salad 64
    Cranberry-Lemon Ice 250
    Merry Cranberry Christmas Fudge 211
Cream Cheese Brownies 198
Cream Frosting 163
Cream Puff Delight 220
Cream Puff Dessert 241
Creamed Onions 90

Crispy Sesame Chicken 123
Crock-Pot Dressing 130
Crunchy Top Sweet Potato Soufflé 84
Cucumber Dill Pasta Salad 70
Cupcakes, Aunt Darlene's Black Bottom 175
Czech Goulash 159

D

Danish Dumplings 156
Deb's Maple Bread Ring 28
Delta Bars 194
Deluxe Beets 96
Depression Potato Soup 50
Des Moines Fudge 211
Desserts:
    Blueberry Sauce 249
    Bridge Dessert 237
    Butter Pecan Dessert 235
    Caramel Dumplings 243
    Caramel Ice Cream Dessert 247
    Chocolate Angel Food Cake Dessert 241
    Chocolate Cream Cheese Dessert 234
    Chocolate Trifle 240
    Coffee Tortoni 236
    Cranberry-Lemon Ice 250
    Cream Puff Delight 220
    Cream Puff Dessert 241
    Easy Dessert 236
    Homemade Chocolate Grape Nut Ice
        Cream 248
    Hot Fudge Sauce 249
    Ice Cream 248
    Lisa's Strawberry Dessert 238
    Marzi Pan Strawberries 239
    Mississippi Mud Dessert 240
    Mrs. Young's Frozen Fruit Cups 247
    Oreo Dessert 247
    Pioneer Bread Pudding 245
    Pretzel Salad or Dessert 66
    Quick Skillet Custard 242
    Rice Mold with Butterscotch Sauce 246
    Schokolade Brot Pudding 245
    Strawberry Pretzel Dessert 239
    Swedish Rice Pudding 246
    Sweetened Condensed Milk 248
    Whiskey Bread Pudding 244
    Windbeutel 242
Diabetic Applesauce Cookies 203
Dill Carrots 86
Do Ahead Mashed Potatoes 79
Double Chocolate Cupcakes 176

Double-Chocolate Sugar Cookies 200
Doughnuts, Raised 43
Dressing, Crock-Pot 130
Dressing, West Special 76
Dump Brownies 198
Dumplings, Danish 156
Dutch Handkerchiefs 207
Dutch Letters 206
Dutch Lettuce 58

E

Easter Nests 212
Easy Brown Rice 114
Easy Corn on the Cob 78
Easy Dessert 236
Easy Potatoes 80
Easy Twice-Baked Potatoes 80
Edna's Fresh Apple Cake 163
Eggs, Elegant Brunch 44
Elegant Brunch Eggs 44
Enchilada Casserole 113
Endive, Amsterdam Style 96
English Muffins 36

F

Farmhouse Potatoes 'n' Ham 118
Fast Fruit Cocktail Cobbler 226
Festive Fudge Filled Bars 192
Fettuccine Alfredo 109
Four-Hour Stew 156
French Apple Creme Pie 221
French Bread Strata, Stuffed 44
French Chocolate Cake 179
French Dressing 76
French Onion Chicken Bake 120
Fresh Apple Bars 188
Fresh Herb Grilled Chicken 122
Frosting:
    Cream 163
    Never Fail Chocolate 198
    Peanut Butter 162
Frozen Tomato Sauce 97
Fruit Filled Apricot Ring Salad 66
Fruited Chicken Salad 75
Fruited Roast Pork 140
Fudge 209
Fudge Puddles 210

G

Garden Club Salad 73

Garlic Bubble Bread 27
Georgia's Apple Coffee Cake 40
German Apple Pancakes 42
Glazed Country Steak 145
Glazed Turkey Breast 130
Gourmet Cream of Zucchini Soup 51
Grant Wood's Cabbage Rolls 160
Grant Wood's Strawberry Shortcake 179
Greek Shrimp Salad 71
Green Peppers, Stuffed 88
Ground Nut Stew 156
Grouse or Partridge, Stuffed 132

H

Ham Balls 142
Ham, Cabbage and Noodle Casserole 103
Ham Casserole 108
Hamburger, Stuffed 152
Harvest Barbecued Pork Roast 140
Hash Brown Chicken Casserole 116
He-Man Spanish Rice 114
Hearty Potato Sauerkraut Soup 49
Holiday Salad and Dressing 68
Holland Cheese Chicken Rolls 122
Home Style Dutch Crullers 183
Homemade Chocolate Grape Nut Ice Cream
    248
Homemade Potato Soup 49
Honey Dressing 76
Hot Chicken Salad 129
Hot Dishes:
    Broccoli Hot Dish 116
    Cheesy Potatoes and Ham 117
    Chicken and Wild Rice Casserole 115
    Chicken Casserole 126, 127
    Corn and Oyster Casserole 102
    Easy Brown Rice 114
    Enchilada Casserole 113
    Farmhouse Potatoes 'n' Ham 118
    Ham, Cabbage and Noodle Casserole 103
    Ham Casserole 108
    Hash Brown Chicken Casserole 116
    He-Man Spanish Rice 114
    Reuben Potato Casserole 117
    Rice, Corn, Celery Casserole 113
    Shrimp-Rice Marguerite 115
    Tuna Noodle Casserole 101
Hot Fudge Pudding Cake 178
Hot Fudge Sauce 249
Hot Ham Buns 142
Hot Milk Cake 162
Hot Vegetable Medley 95

I

Ice Cream 248
Ice Cream Sugar Cookie Sandwiches 209
Impossible Rhubarb Pie 219
Indonesian Pork Tenderloin 139
Iowa Chops 134
Iowa Corn Pancakes 42
Iowa Dirt Cake 186
"Iowa Pride" Chess Pie 216
Iowa's Grilled Turkey Tenderloin 129
Italian Beef Pot Roast 145
Italian Biscuit Ring 34
Italian "Carne Pane" 149

J

Jean's Cheshire Meringue 233
Joe's Onion Soup 48
Joseph's Coat 62

K

Kay's Chicken Salad 75
Krakalinger 205
Kringles 40

L

Ladyfingers 208
Lasagna, Make Ahead 105
Lasagna, Mexican 105
Lemon:
    Asparagus Chicken 123
    Betty's Lemon Pudding Pie 230
    Cake Pie 229
    Curd Tarts 232
    Dill Potatoes 81
    Poppy Seed Bread 29
    Pudding Cake 172
    Quick Lemon Cheesecake 185
    Sour Cream Lemon Pound Cake 174
    Special Lemon Cake 172
    Squares 200
    Sugar-Free Lemon Chiffon Pie 229
    Sunshine Lemon Cake 173
Lena's End of the Garden Relish 98
Lisa's Strawberry Dessert 238

M

Mac 'n' Cheese, Skillet Tomato 112
Macaroni Salad Dressing 70
Make Ahead Lasagna 105
Mandarin Orange Cake 166

Mandarin Salad 63
Manhattan Meatballs 153
Margery's Chicken 'n' Niffles 128
Marinade, Soy-Garlic 158
Marinated Carrots 87
Marinated Green Beans 62
Marinated Tomatoes 61
Marshmallow Chocolate Fudge Cake 177
Marv's Seafood Pasta 108
Mary Ellen Wall's Stuffed Iowa Chops 135
Marzi Pan Strawberries 239
Maytag Steak Au Poivre 147
Meat Balls 154
Memorial Day Roast 144
Merry Cranberry Christmas Fudge 211
Mexican Lasagna 105
Mild Tomato Aspic Salad 63
Millie's Noodles 110
Mince Meat 158
Mississippi Mud Dessert 240
Mom's Pineapple Drop Cookies 203
Mom's Potato Salad 56
Moon Bars 193
Moroccan Chicken and Wild Rice Salad 72
Mound Bars 192
Mrs. Young's Frozen Fruit Cups 247
Muffins:
    Cocoa Banana 39
    English 36
    Pineapple 39
    Pumpkin Apple Streusel 38
    Super-Easy Ham and Cheese 37
Mushrooms Florentine 89
Myrtle's Famous Banana Cake 168

N

Nana's Swiss Steak 146
Never Fail Chocolate Frosting 198
Nuss Plätzchen 197

O

Onion Pie 88
Onion Soup, Joe's 48
Onions, Creamed 90
Orange Delight Quick Salad 67
Orange Push-Up Cheesecake 184
Orange Slice Cookies 204
Oreo Dessert 247
Oven-Fried Chicken with Honey Butter Sauce
    121
Oven-Fried Potatoes 81

Overnight Bread or Rolls 33
Overnight Butterhorn Rolls 33
Overnight Sweet Rolls with Cream 29
Oyster Casserole, Corn and 102
Oyster Soup 53
Oysters, Quail Stuffed with 131

P

Paddington's Peanut Logs 197
Pancakes:
    Apple-Cranberry Pancake Puff 43
    German Apple 42
    Iowa Corn 42
    Swedish 41
Partridge, Stuffed Grouse or 132
Party Apple Salad 64
Pasghetti Pizza 104
Pasta:
    All-At-Once Spaghetti 107
    Cavatelli 110
    Cavatelli and Three Cheeses 111
    Cavatini 110
    Cheese Spaghetti 106
    Corn Noodle Casserole 112
    Cowboy Goulash 103
    Cucumber Dill Pasta Salad 70
    Fettuccine Alfredo 109
    Ham, Cabbage and Noodle Casserole 103
    Macaroni Salad Dressing 70
    Make Ahead Lasagna 105
    Marv's Seafood Pasta 108
    Millie's Noodles 110
    Pasghetti Pizza 104
    Skillet Tomato Mac 'n' Cheese 112
    Spaghetti Bake 106
    Spaghetti Pie 107
    Super Salad 70
    Tuna Noodle Casserole 101
    Vegetable Pasta Pie 109
Peach Cream Pie 221
Peach Pudding Coffee Cake 41
Peaches and Cream Cheesecake Pie 233
Peanut Brittle 213
Peanut Butter Frosting 162
Peanut Butter Pie 223
Pecan Tassies Cheese Pastry 222
Pen Pal Brownies 195
Pepper Steak 146
Pickled Beets (Süsz-Sauere Roterüben) 96
Pickles, Sweet Watermelon 75
Pies:
    Apfel Küchelchen 227

Apple Pie with Sour Cream 217
Apple Turnovers 227
Betty's Lemon Pudding Pie 230
Chocolate Chip Peanut Butter Pie 223
Chocolate Meringue Pie 231
Chocolate Mousse Pie 224
Fast Fruit Cocktail Cobbler 226
French Apple Creme Pie 221
Impossible Rhubarb Pie 219
"Iowa Pride" Chess Pie 216
Jean's Cheshire Meringue 233
Lemon Cake Pie 229
Lemon Curd Tarts 232
Peach Cream Pie 221
Peaches and Cream Cheesecake Pie 233
Peanut Butter Pie 223
Pecan Tassies Cheese Pastry 222
Pina Colada Wedges 234
Pink Lady Pie 220
Prize Winning Grapefruit Pie 225
Pumpkin Chiffon Pie with Peanut Crust 228
Rhubarb Crisp 219
Rhubarb Crunch Pie 219
Rhubarb Custard Pie 218
Sour Cream Raisin Pie 216
Sugar-Free Lemon Chiffon Pie 229
Walnut Pie 222
Zucchini Pie 217
Pigout Cake 180
Pigs-in-a-Blanket 46
Pina Colada Wedges 234
Pineapple Muffins 39
Pink Champagne Salad 68
Pink Lady Pie 220
Pioneer Bread Pudding 245
Pistachio Cake 171
Pizza Burgers 154
Pizza Crust Dough 37
Polynesian Cake 166
Poorman's Lobster 101
Popcorn Balls 214
Poppy Seed Bread 29
Poppy Seed Cake 170
Pork:
   BBQ Ribs 143
   Cheesy Ham-Potato Soup 50
   Cheesy Potatoes and Ham 117
   Chop Casserole 140
   Chop Corn Bake 137
   Chop 'n' Potato Bake 137
   Chops a' la McKee 136

Chops with Dressing 136
Farmhouse Potatoes 'n' Ham 118
Fruited Roast Pork 140
Ham Balls 142
Ham, Cabbage and Noodle Casserole 103
Ham Casserole 108
Harvest Barbecued Pork Roast 140
Hot Ham Buns 142
Indonesian Pork Tenderloin 139
Iowa Chops 134
Loin Roulade 139
Loin with Fruited Stuffing 138
Mary Ellen Wall's Stuffed Iowa Chops 135
Pigs-in-a-Blanket 46
Stuffed Glazed Chops 135
Stuffed Pork Loin 138
Sweet Ham Loaf 141
Zucchini Pork Dish 141
Potatoes:
   Almost Pizza 104
   Baked German Potato Salad 57
   Brown Jug Soup 51
   Cheese Sauce for Potatoes 83
   Cheesy BBQ Potato Bake 82
   Cheesy Ham Potato Soup 50
   Cheesy Potatoes and Ham 117
   Company 80
   Crunchy Top Sweet Potato Soufflé 84
   Depression Potato Soup 50
   Do Ahead Mashed Potatoes 79
   Easy 80
   Easy Twice-Baked Potatoes 80
   Farmhouse Potatoes 'n' Ham 118
   Hash Brown Chicken Casserole 116
   Hearty Potato Sauerkraut Soup 49
   Homemade Potato Soup 49
   Lemon Dill 81
   Mom's Potato Salad 56
   Oven-Fried 81
   Pie 83
   Pork Chop 'n' Potato Bake 137
   Quick Scalloped 83
   Reuben Potato Casserole 117
   Salad 56
   Sour Cream and Cheddar Supreme 84
   Sweet Potato and Cashew Bake 85
   Vegetable Loaf 94
   Yvonne's Berry-Yam Bake 85
Poultry:
   Baked Chicken Breast 123

Baked Chicken Salad 74
Card Club Chicken Salad 73
Chicken a la King 125
Chicken and Wild Rice Casserole 115
Chicken Broccoli Vegetable Sauté 124
Chicken Casserole 127
Chicken Cordon Bleu 124
Chicken Dijon 121
Chicken Enchiladas 125
Chicken Essex 127
Chicken L'Orange 122
Chicken Salad 72
Chicken Salad In-A-Ring 74
Crispy Sesame Chicken 123
Crock-Pot Dressing 130
French Onion Chicken Bake 120
Fresh Herb Grilled Chicken 122
Fruited Chicken Salad 75
Garden Club Salad 73
Glazed Turkey Breast 130
Hash Brown Chicken Casserole 116
Holland Cheese Chicken Rolls 122
Hot Chicken Salad 129
Iowa's Grilled Turkey Tenderloin 129
Kay's Chicken Salad 75
Lemon Asparagus Chicken 123
Margery's Chicken 'n' Niffles 128
Oven-Fried Chicken with Honey Butter
   Sauce 121
Quail Stuffed with Oysters 131
Scalloped Chicken 120
Stuffed Grouse or Partridge 132
Tea Room Chicken 126
Turkey and Spinach Burgers 131
Pretzel Salad or Dessert 66
Pride of Iowa Cookies 207
Prize Winning Grapefruit Pie 225
Pudding:
   Pioneer Bread 245
   Pudding, Schokolade Brot 245
   Pudding, Swedish Rice 246
   Pudding, Whiskey Bread 244
Puffed Wheat Candy 213
Pumpkin:
   Apple Streusel Muffins 38
   Bars 189
   Chiffon Pie with Peanut Crust 228
   Jellyroll 174
Punch Bowl Cake 182

Q

Quail Stuffed with Oysters 131

Quick Lemon Cheesecake 185
Quick Scalloped Potatoes 83
Quick Skillet Custard 242

R

Radio Cake 178
Raised Doughnuts 43
Ramen Salad 69
Refrigerator Rolls 34
Reuben Potato Casserole 117
Rhubarb:
   Cake 168
   Crisp 219
   Crunch Pie 219
   Custard Pie 218
   Impossible Rhubarb Pie 219
   Pink Lady Pie 220
   Swirl Salad 65
Rice:
   Broccoli and 91
   Casserole, Chicken and Wild 115
   Corn, Celery Casserole 113
   Easy Brown 114
   He-Man Spanish 114
   Marguerite, Shrimp- 115
   Mold with Butterscotch Sauce 246
Riviera Salad 60
Rolls:
   Ardith's Rolls 31
   Christmas Morning Sticky Rolls 32
   Overnight Bread or Rolls 33
   Overnight Butterhorn Rolls 33
   Overnight Sweet Rolls with Cream 29
   Refrigerator Rolls 34
   Sticky Maple Bacon Rolls 32

S

Salad:
   Baked Chicken Salad 74
   Baked German Potato Salad 57
   Blue Cheese—Artichoke Salad 59
   Broccoli and Cauliflower Salad 60
   Broccoli Salad 60
   Cabbage and Apple Slaw with Walnuts 69
   Card Club Chicken Salad 73
   Chaud Eriod 71
   Chicken Salad 72
   Chicken Salad In-A-Ring 74
   Congealed Spinach Salad 65
   Cranberry Salad 64
   Cucumber Dill Pasta Salad 70
   Dutch Lettuce 58

French Dressing 76
Fruit Filled Apricot Ring Salad 66
Fruited Chicken Salad 75
Garden Club Salad 73
Greek Shrimp Salad 71
Holiday Salad and Dressing 68
Honey Dressing 76
Joseph's Coat 62
Kay's Chicken Salad 75
Macaroni Salad Dressing 70
Mandarin Salad 63
Marinated Green Beans 62
Marinated Tomatoes 61
Mild Tomato Aspic Salad 63
Mom's Potato Salad 56
Moroccan Chicken and Wild Rice Salad 72
Orange Delight Quick Salad 67
Party Apple Salad 64
Pink Champagne Salad 68
Potato Salad 56
Pretzel Salad or Dessert 66
Ramen Salad 69
Rhubarb Swirl Salad 65
Riviera Salad 60
Shrim 71
Snicker Apple Salad 64
Spinach Salad, Congealed 65
Spinach Salad with Bacon and Apple 59
Super Salad 70
Tomato Salad with Onion and Peppers
    61
Tuna Salad Supreme 71
Tutti Fruiti Salad 67
Yum-Yum Salad 65
Salisbury Steak 148
Salted Nut Roll Bars 196
Sandy's Spicy Shrimp 100
Sauce, Blueberry 249
Sauce, Hot Fudge 249
Scalloped Chicken 120
Schokolade Brot Pudding 245
Scotchies 208
Seafood:
    Baked Fish and Vegetables 100
    Corn and Oyster Casserole 102
    Marv's Seafood Pasta 108
    Poorman's Lobster 101
    Sandy's Spicy Shrimp 100
    Shrimp-Rice Marguerite 115
    Shrimp Salad, Greek 71
    Tuna Burgers 102
    Tuna Noodle Casserole 101
Shrimp Salad, Greek 71

Shrimp, Sandy's Spicy 100
Shrimp-Rice Marguerite 115
Sizzling Steak Fajitas 148
Skillet Sweet Corn 78
Skillet Tomato Mac 'n' Cheese 112
Slaw with Walnuts, Cabbage and Apple 69
S'Mores 199
Snicker Apple Salad 64
Snicker Bars 195
Snowballs 183
Soup:
    Brown Jug Soup 51
    Canned Cream Soup Substitute 52
    Cheesy Ham-Potato Soup 50
    Corn Soup 52
    Depression Potato Soup 50
    Gourmet Cream of Zucchini Soup 51
    Hearty Potato Sauerkraut Soup 49
    Homemade Potato Soup 49
    Joe's Onion Soup 48
    Oyster Soup 53
    Stormy Weather Chili 54
    Triple-Flavored Wild Rice Soup 53
    Velvety Almond Cream Soup 53
    Wild Rice Soup, Triple-Flavored 53
    Zucchini, Gourmet Cream of 51
Sour Cream and Cheddar Supreme Potatoes
    84
Sour Cream Bars 190
Sour Cream Lemon Pound Cake 174
Sour Cream Raisin Pie 216
Soy-Garlic Marinade 158
Spaghetti Bake 106
Spaghetti Pie 107
Special Lemon Cake 172
Spiced Red Cabbage 90
Spinach or Broccoli Soufflé 91
Spinach Salad with Bacon and Apple 59
Steak Stroganoff 150
Stew:
    Beef 157
    Four-Hour 156
    Ground Nut 156
    Venison 159
Sticky Maple Bacon Rolls 32
Stir-Fry 147
Stormy Weather Chili 54
Strawberry:
    Banana Bread 30
    Fluff 182
    Pretzel Dessert 239
    Shortcake, Grant Wood's 179
Stuffed French Bread 26

Stuffed French Bread Strata 44
Stuffed Glazed Chops 135
Stuffed Green Peppers 88
Stuffed Grouse or Partridge 132
Stuffed Hamburger 152
Stuffed Pork Loin 138
Sugar-Free Lemon Chiffon Pie 229
Sunshine Lemon Cake 173
Super Salad 70
Super-Easy Ham and Cheese Muffins 37
Süsz-Sauere Roterüben (Pickled Beets) 96
Swedish Meatballs 153
Swedish Pancakes 41
Swedish Rice Pudding 246
Sweet Ham Loaf 141
Sweet Potato and Cashew Bake 85
Sweet Potato Soufflé, Crunchy Top 84
Sweet Watermelon Pickles 75
Sweetened Condensed Milk 248
Swiss Vegetable Medley 95

T

Tea Room Chicken 126
Tomatoes:
    Baked Stuffed 88
    Chutney 97
    Salad with Onion and Peppers 61
    Sauce, Frozen 97
    Soup Cake 169
    Vegetable Pie 87
Triple Good Raisin Bars 194
Triple-Flavored Wild Rice Soup 53
Tropical Delight 181
Tuna Burgers 102
Tuna Noodle Casserole 101
Tuna Salad Supreme 71
Turkey and Spinach Burgers 131
Turkey Breast, Glazed 130
Turkey Tenderloin, Iowa's Grilled 129

Turtle Cheesecake 186
Tutti Fruiti Salad 67

U

Unbaked Peanut Butter Cookies 202

V

Vegetable:
    Loaf 94
    Medley, Hot 95
    Medley, Swiss 95
    Pasta Pie 109
Vegetables, Baked Fish and 100
Velvety Almond Cream Soup 53
Venison Stew 159

W

Walnut Pie 222
Watergate Cake 181
West Special Dressing 76
Whiskey Bread Pudding 244
Windbeutel 242
World's Best Cookie Bars 191

Y

Yum-Yum Salad 65
Yummy Cherry Bars 189
Yvonne's Berry-Yam Bake 85

Z

Zucchini:
    Bake 93
    Baked 92
    Brownies 199
    Casserole 93
    Pie 217
    Pork Dish 141

Preserving America's Food Heritage

BEST OF THE BEST STATE COOKBOOK SERIES

Cookbooks listed below have been completed as of December 31, 2000.

Best of the Best from
ALABAMA
288 pages, $16.95

Best of the Best from
ARIZONA
288 pages, $16.95

Best of the Best from
ARKANSAS
288 pages, $16.95

Best of the Best from
CALIFORNIA
384 pages, $16.95

Best of the Best from
COLORADO
288 pages, $16.95

Best of the Best from
FLORIDA
288 pages, $16.95

Best of the Best from
GEORGIA
336 pages, $16.95

Best of the Best from the
GREAT PLAINS
288 pages, $16.95

Best of the Best from
ILLINOIS
288 pages, $16.95

Best of the Best from
INDIANA
288 pages, $16.95

Best of the Best from
IOWA
288 pages, $16.95

Best of the Best from
KENTUCKY
288 pages, $16.95

Best of the Best from
LOUISIANA
288 pages, $16.95

Best of the Best from
LOUISIANA II
288 pages, $16.95

Best of the Best from
MICHIGAN
288 pages, $16.95

Best of the Best from
MINNESOTA
288 pages, $16.95

Best of the Best from
MISSISSIPPI
288 pages, $16.95

Best of the Best from
MISSOURI
304 pages, $16.95

Best of the Best from
NEW ENGLAND
368 pages, $16.95

Best of the Best from
NEW MEXICO
288 pages, $16.95

Best of the Best from
NORTH CAROLINA
288 pages, $16.95

Best of the Best from
OHIO
352 pages, $16.95

Best of the Best from
OKLAHOMA
288 pages, $16.95

Best of the Best from
PENNSYLVANIA
320 pages, $16.95

Best of the Best from
SOUTH CAROLINA
288 pages, $16.95

Best of the Best from
TENNESSEE
288 pages, $16.95

Best of the Best from
TEXAS
352 pages, $16.95

Best of the Best from
TEXAS II
352 pages, $16.95

Best of the Best from
VIRGINIA
320 pages, $16.95

Best of the Best from
WISCONSIN
288 pages, $16.95

Note: All cookbooks
are ringbound except
California, which is
paperbound.

Special discount offers available!

(See previous page for details.)

To order by credit card, call toll-free **1-800-343-1583** or send check or money order to:
QUAIL RIDGE PRESS • P. O. Box 123 • Brandon, MS 39043
Visit our website at **www.quailridge.com** to order online!

Order form

Send completed form and payment to:
QUAIL RIDGE PRESS • P. O. Box 123 • Brandon, MS 39043

❏ Check enclosed

Charge to: ❏ Visa ❏ MasterCard
❏ Discover ❏ American Express

Card #_____

Expiration Date _____

Signature _____

Name _____

Address _____

City/State/Zip_____

Phone # _____

Qty.	Title of Book (State)	Total

Subtotal _____

7% Tax for MS residents _____

Postage ($3.00 any number of books) **+ 3.00**

Total _____